POWER IN
THE WORKPLACE

SUNY Series in the Sociology of Work
Richard H. Hall, Editor

POWER IN THE WORKPLACE

The Politics of Production at AT&T

STEVEN PETER VALLAS

State University
of New York
Press

Published by
State University of New York Press, Albany

© 1993   State University of New York

For information, address State University of New York
Press, State University Plaza, Albany, NY 12246

Production by Susan Geraghty
Marketing by Fran Keneston

Library of Congress Cataloging-in-Publication Data

Vallas, Steven P. (Steven Peter), 1951–
    Power in the workplace : the politics of production at AT&T /
Steven Peter Vallas.
        p.   cm. — (SUNY series in the sociology of work)
    Includes bibliographical references and index.
    ISBN 0–7914–1273–3 (acid-free) : $49.50. — ISBN 0–7914–1274–1
(pbk. : acid-free) : $16.95
        1. American Telephone and Telegraph Company—Employees.
2. Telecommunication—United States—Employees—Case studies.
3. Industrial relations—United States—Case studies.   4. Industrial
sociology—United States—Case studies.   5. Organizational behavior-
-United States—Case studies.   I. Title.   II. Series.
HD8039.T24U68   1993
331.7'613846'0973—dc20
                                                        91–42558
                                                          CIP

10 9 8 7 6 5 4 3 2 1

To
the Mulveys, Sushkos,
and Pereyras
of this society—
and the next.

CONTENTS

ABBREVIATIONS

ASCCs	Automated Switching Control Centers
AWT	Average Working Time
CATs	Craft Access Terminals
CIMAP	Circuit Installation and Maintainance Administration Package
CO	Central Office
CWA	Communications Workers of America
DOT	Dictionary of Occupational Titles
ESS	Electronic Switching Systems
IBEW	International Brotherhood of Electrical Workers
ILM	Internal Labor Market
IMC	Installation and Maintenance Center
LAC	Loop Assignment Center
LDMC	Loop Data Maintenance Center
MLT	Mechanized Loop Testing Equipment
NFTW	National Federation of Telephone Workers
NC	Numerical Control equipment
QWL	Quality of Work Life
RSAs	Repair Service Attendants

Preface

Although it is easy to trace the decline of American labor to the Reagan assault on the Professional Air Traffic Controllers' Organization (PATCO), the ordeal of the U.S. workers' movement began when Ronald Reagan was still in Hollywood. For in spite of the rise of industrial unionism in the late 1930s and the temporary upsurge in labor struggle during World War II, American workers have been fighting a losing, defensive battle throughout the entire second half of this century. With the emergence of economic austerity in the middle 1970s, American corporations lost little time in exploiting labor's weaknesses, and successfully imposed a growing list of concessions on their workers, easily winning 'givebacks' that had taken workers generations to attain. Remarkably, American workers have been unable to muster any sustained response to this employers' offensive, mounting but a few sporadic and often desperate struggles (for example, at Hormel, Greyhound and the New York *Daily News*). This turn of events has led many to conclude that labor's heroic youth has long since given way to a tragic middle age or even death. How has all this come to pass?

Theorists have cited any number of economic, political, and social reasons to explain labor's bleak fate. Some theorists have stressed the restructuring of the economy. In this view the 'hyper-mobility of capital' threatens workers with plant shutdowns and places them at the mercy of competitive forces, while the old manufacturing industries that nourished the workers' movement have given way to newer ones whose class composition is inherently ambiguous. Others point toward the disjunction between economics and politics in the United States. Lacking a political party, U.S. trade union leaders have adopted a narrow form of 'contract unionism' that transforms industrial conflict into an empty, institutionalized ritual which takes managerial prerogatives for granted. Still others cite the sharp racial and ethnic divisions that splinter the American proletariat, promoting internecine tensions rather than solidarity. These and other factors have been discussed by many writers and surely contribute to the weakness of the American workers' movement.[1] This book adopts a different line of analysis, however, rooted mainly in the social organization of production itself.

In this respect my study grows out of a wider effort among labor historians, industrial sociologists and others who have studied the systems of labor control that have evolved within specific branches and periods in the development of industrial capitalism. Two assumptions have informed this developing tradition: First, that among the most fundamental (but hardly the sole) influences shaping the distribution of power among different classes are the social relations of production that surround people during the course of their working days. Second, that the existence of class hierarchy and inequality cannot be viewed as necessary facts of economic life—rather, they are social constructs that cry out to be explained. My study has embraced both of these assumptions, and sets out to understand the evolving character of labor control within a particular branch of the capitalist economy.

Versed in the theoretical debates that consumed students of labor and social class, by the late 1970s I sought to trade abstract generalizations for a more fine-grained view of concrete social processes. Several serendipitous events lent shape to my research, prompting me to focus on developments underway in the telecommunications industry. These events included a short stint as an organizer with the Communications Workers of America (CWA), AFL-CIO; informal contacts with people employed in Bell operating companies; as well as an intellectual challenge from an older colleague to "take technology seriously." So impelled, in 1984 I requested support from the CWA's District I for a study of the working conditions, broadly conceived, in the telecommunications industry. Numerous delays, tangents, and two children later, this book is the result.

The study of work organizations has been in a state of creative disarray for some time now, with little consensus about the field's fundamental unit of analysis. In this study I am concerned mainly with the links between the firm and the wider class structure within a single industry. The study therefore harbors many of the limitations that inhere within case studies. Yet it seems fair to note that developments in this branch of production are of particular interest for theories of the labor process. As argued below, the industry combines many (if not all) of those features that theorists have stressed in seeking to understand labor control within the modern bureaucratic-capitalist firm. Mindful of this fact, many theorists have explicitly invoked the case of AT&T to develop and illustrate their models of work and authority.[2] Hence, a case study—but one that hopes to achieve particular 'efficiency,' shedding an especially sharp light on the social relations of production within the most advanced quarters of monopoly capitalism.

The study that CWA officials first commissioned bears little resemblance to the final product. The original research design was a cross-sectional survey based on a stratified random sample of twenty-nine telephone work locations located throughout the states of New Jersey and New York. The survey succeeded in representing virtually all union-eligible occupations at Bell operating companies (mainly operators, clerks, craftworkers, and business office employees) and provided a rich set of data on shifts in workplace technology and work content, levels of alienation, and attitudes toward management, among many other such dimensions. Yet the more I learned about the industry, the more I felt compelled to draw upon other, qualitative sources of data. Open-ended interviews led to a second, more focused survey of workers in a single local union, and then to retrospective interviews designed to unearth shifts in the work experience. This in turn led me to develop a more fully historical focus on the politics of production in the communications industry, using both archival sources (AT&T Archives and newspaper reports) as well as existing historical accounts. Following my sociological muse, then, I was led to develop a multi-method study of production politics in the Bell system.

At varying times my research angered both managers and labor union officials, providing some initial evidence that I was in fact asking the right questions. I often drew inspiration from the workers I studied, who showed remarkable commitment to their jobs even under inhospitable conditions. I hope they can recognize themselves in the mirror I have fashioned, however critical it might seem at times.

My intellectual debts are too enormous to cite, yet let me try. District I of the CWA was indispensable in arranging and supporting the surveys. In different ways, Mark Chernoff, Carmine

Turgghi, Bob Master, and other members of the district staff were extremely helpful guides. I am especially grateful for the support I received from Locals 1104 and 1122 (Don Hoak and especially Bobby Lilja) and to the officers and stewards who keep these locals strong. Within the sociological community, I am particularly indebted to the Russell Sage Foundation, which provided much-needed material and intellectual support. I was fortunate to enjoy the counsel of William Kornblum, Kai Erikson, Robert Merton, and Charles Tilly who read various portions of the manuscript, and the collegial inspiration and advice of Cynthia Fuchs Epstein (whose own book on this industry will appear shortly). Kenneth Spenner, Dick Hall, Howard Kimeldorf, William Form, and Philip Kraft offered insightful comments and suggestions on various parts of the study. Bill Calabro was a helpful accomplice at the outset of the study. His participation was instrumental in getting the research off the ground. I should like to thank Mr. Raymond Williams and Dr. Sheldon Hochheiser of AT&T for their cooperation and to gratefully acknowledge the AT&T Archives for permission to use historical materials from their collection. A number of Bell managers deserve thanks, but discretion prevents me from printing their names.

Early versions of the manuscript have appeared in the following publications: "White Collar Proletarians? The Structure of Clerical Work and Levels of Class Consciousness," *The Sociological Quarterly* 28, 4 (1987):523–540; "New Technology, Job Content and Worker Alienation: A Test of Two Rival Perspectives," *Work and Occupations* 15, 2 (May 1988):148–179; "Workers, Firms and the Dominant Ideology: Hegemony and Consciousness in the Monopoly Core," *The Sociological Quarterly* 32, 1 (1991):61–83.

CHAPTER 1

Introduction

The building was located just behind the tracks of the Long Island Rail Road. I had passed by this work location dozens of times without knowing what it was. Behind the wheel of the truck I rode in was my guide for the day, a bearded, barrel-chested Irishman who was a chief steward for the CWA when he wasn't laying cable for New York Telephone. We rode in his truck between repair sites and he showed me the ropes.

It was barely seven A.M. and I was hardly awake, but he was raring to go. We parked his truck in the company lot and went into the garage where telephone craftworkers started their working days, 'shooting troubles' in the system's grid of cable. We leaned on the company's trucks, drinking coffee while two dozen workers awaited their trouble tickets for the day. It was a rowdy but congenial bunch. One man showed up wearing a Bart Simpson mask, prompting his co-workers to remark that he was looking much better than usual. Another man served as the good-natured butt of jokes, most of which involved his ability to sleep anywhere at any time. A cigar box filled with dollars made the rounds—the pool for the workers' game of Lucky Buck. The union had arranged for my guide and I to trail a craftsmen on the job, beginning a crash course on telephone work. We got our trouble tickets, climbed into the truck and slowly drove off, my teacher lecturing on the ways of the working man while I studiously made notes.

By this time I had grown familiar with the leaders of this local union and the word had apparently spread that I was someone who could be trusted. Thus my guide was not shy about revealing the least flattering sides of the telephone workers' subculture. The workers' habits were a serious concern among both union and company officials, it developed, at least partly because splicers and other craftworkers sometimes like to congregate at eating and drinking establishments during the course of the working day. Said my guide: "You can get away with a lot on this job if you want to." He was unabashedly proud of that fact—proud that craftworkers had maintained substantial residues of control over their own labor, sometimes working feverishly to put a cable back into service before returning to their garage, yet retaining their ability to rest when the situation allowed. One man recalled enjoying the coming of warm weather by visiting the region's beaches and "watching the bathing suits" after an exhausting stint of work underground.

This day's tour was in fact quite hot, but there was little time out for fun. The splicer's job, I would learn, remains among the most arduous and dangerous of the industry's crafts. After shooting troubles in the hot sun for most of the day, attaching cable insulation with an acetylene torch and rewiring connection boxes by hand, one splicer climbed down from his pole, caught his breath for a moment, and said with evident sarcasm, "Oh yeah, it's all automated now. None of that manual labor anymore." In fact, my guide was under medication for severe back pain from a fall he suffered some time ago. He only hoped to put in his time and enjoy his retirement in good health. Many of his co-workers had not enjoyed such good luck.

Rarely asked to share their views and experiences, these workers eagerly lead me down the organizational corridors that link them to their managers, helping me sketch the changing face of managerial power in the monopoly capitalist firm. Through such forays as this, through surveys of the industry's workforce, and historical analysis of its structure over time, I have addressed a set of questions that focus squarely on the nature of work and authority under modern capitalism. What social mechanisms enable management to harness workers' productive capacities, while maintaining workers' subordinate position within the firm? When technologies lay hold of craft and clerical work, how are the prevailing levels and forms of working knowledge affected? Have American workers come to view managerial authority as an unalterable fact of working life, as so many theorists have claimed? And precisely how has the present institutional pattern of authority evolved out of the ties that bound workers to their employers in prior decades?

Issues such as these have been much debated among industrial sociologists, but as yet little or no consensus has emerged.[1] Some theorists of work and authority advocate a de-skilling perspective toward work processes, which views the fate of skilled, autonomous work in largely tragic terms. In this view, companies invoke new and ever-more sophisticated technologies at least partly to reduce their dependence on their employees. The end result uproots workers' skills and deepens management control over virtually all aspects of the work process. Other theorists depart from this tragic view, arguing that information technologies impel work organizations down a far more flexible, "post-hierarchical" path. The notion here is that information technologies increasingly overturn the traditional ethos of obedience that accompanied industrial capitalism, substituting a new division of labor founded on responsibility, commitment, and social integration. Still other theorists disavow the prevailing tendency to emphasize the organization of workers' tasks and the technology of work, focusing instead on the broader social fabric of work relations that takes root within the modern firm. Put simply, this third perspective argues that ideology, not technology, provides the key to understanding the nature of labor control within the modern corporation. One goal of this book is to adjudicate between these rival perspectives on work and managerial power, to identify their respective virtues and limitations, and in so doing to make possible a fuller, more adequate understanding of the system of class relations that has unfolded at the point of production itself.

Previous efforts along these lines have moved in one of two directions. The first has involved the use of national data on changes in skill requirements in the overall economy, seeking to establish the nature of trends in the structure of work. Often, research in this mode has made use of aggregate data—for example, the *Dictionary of Occupational Titles (DOT)* compiled by the Department of Labor—to analyze changes in the complexity of work.[2] This type of research carries with it real advantages: it allows us to draw generalizations at the macrosocial level of analysis—where most of our theories are couched—and to do so with great precision. For this reason aggregate research has been especially influential in defining the course of the discussion. Yet less often acknowledged are the costs implied in this research strategy.

Reliance on formally derived measures of occupational complexity often blinds us to the *in*formal processes at work that may underlie or even contradict data on occupational conditions. Although aggregate studies which use the *DOT* contain a rich set of measures that bear on occupational complexity, they are less generous in their treatment of other, equally critical dimensions of work—especially changing forms or degrees of control. For these reasons the use of aggregate data often introduces a yawning gap not only between between theory and research, but also between the researcher and the concrete work settings he or she seeks to understand.[3]

A second research strategy has relied on varying types of case study designs. Some research in this vein has tried to maintain the quantitative rigor of aggregate research while using a more delimited and therefore more nuanced approach. Often researchers have designed inter-industry studies of the work organizations located within an area or region (Hull, Friedman, and Rogers 1982; Kalleberg and Leicht 1986). Other studies have constructed national samples of firms in a given industry (Kelley 1990). Still other case studies have adopted a qualitative approach, seeking to unearth the texture of work relations within particular firms, organizations, or occupations over time (for example, Kraft 1977; Cockburn 1983; Wilkinson 1983; Halle 1984; Noble 1984; Zuboff 1988, and many others). Although the latter studies can seldom make broad generalizations about workplace trends more broadly, their attention to the fine grain of workplace relations has equipped them to make a disproportionate contribution to sociological debate and analysis.[4]

One particularly useful research strategy has sought to combine the richness of the case study design with the generalizeability of aggregate research: studies which focus on a critical case or strategic research site.[5] Particularly among researchers interested in the link between advanced technologies and skill requirements, it has been common practice to explore the nature of continuous-process industries—most notably petrochemical firms—which are assumed to provide a privileged view of the trajectory of workplace automation writ large.[6] In retrospect, however, this fascination with continuous-process industries seems unfortunate. To begin with, it is by no means clear why continuous-process work is inherently more 'advanced' than other branches of production. Do the tubes, pipes, and vats needed to cook fluids and gases necessarily reflect a more fully developed technology than is used in other production contexts? Moreover, the peculiarities involved in chemical work seem so great as to imperil the application of the findings to other manufacturing contexts, let alone to other sectors of the economy more broadly. Most important, case studies of chemical work tell us little about the more knowledge-intensive branches of the capitalist economy, which assume a growing importance apace with technological change and about which so much remains to be learned.

These considerations underlie the research developed in this book, a case study of the telecommunications industry. Long the privileged domain of AT&T, this branch of production has historically been in the vanguard of American management's efforts to forge systems of labor control.[7] The industry's conditions of employment (its automated work process, provisions for upward mobility, and relatively high wages) epitomize those ingredients that scholars have stressed as making up the bureaucratic-capitalist firm. Moreover, the industry is broadly reflective of the burgeoning 'information' industries, which figure so prominently everywhere except in the research literature. Particularly in light of the infusion of competitive forces into this industry (a process that began well before the breakup), research on this terrain can tell us a great deal about the changing character of managerial power within the monopoly capitalist firm.

Ironically, the very features that make this industry revealing acted to impede the conduct of research. The study began at precisely the moment when the Modified Final Judgment broke the Bell system apart, imposing an unprecedented economic restructuring that rendered obsolete ordinary methods of coping with uncertainty. Both management and the industry's major union (CWA) struggled to gain leverage as the first round of post-divestiture negotiations approached. This fact, coupled with my prior association with the CWA, magnified the difficulties involved in doing jointly sponsored research, and ruled out the involvement of top management. Although it later proved possible to enlist the support of many middle-level managers, who provided access for ethnographic research, top management's distrust of the project impeded the full application of qualitative methods to this research terrain.

At the same time, the trust and cooperation I enjoyed with union leaders opened doors that were at least as valuable as those that management had closed. With sponsorship from the District I staff, I gained the trust of union officials and stewards at fourteen local unions in both New Jersey and New York. With help from local union officers and stewards, I designed a cross-sectional survey that explored the links among new technologies, the organization of the labor process, and workers' attitudes toward both their jobs and their employers. Eventually, two such surveys were administered—the first a 'regional' survey including more than eight hundred workers and the second a more intensive study of 175 workers in a single local—bearing on the situations and experience of communications workers in all the industry's major occupations.

Sociologists of work have increasingly turned toward historical analysis in an effort to understand patterns of authority and resistance. Mindful of the limits of cross-sectional surveys alone, I was led to move in two further directions at once: (1) to conduct a 'micro-historical' analysis using retrospective interviews to piece together the unfolding of production relations within a single Bell operating company (New York Telephone), and (2) to develop a more broadly historical analysis of labor control systems at AT&T during the early part of this century. Working backward and at these two levels, then, the study has sought to understand the emergence and transformation of labor control systems within the Bell system during the twentieth century.

The book begins at the theoretical level. Chapter 2 critically reviews the current debate over managerial power and labor control within the advanced capitalist firm. My aim is to outline the three rival images of work mentioned above—theories of deskilling, upgrading (or enskilling), and managerial hegemony—extracting from them themes and empirical claims can be judged against the social relations that have actually unfolded in this branch of production.

The substantive analysis begins in Chapter 3, where I explore the mechanisms Bell management historically invoked in the effort to control its workers. As the chapter shows, scientific management techniques were abundantly present within AT&T's telephone exchanges beginning as early as the middle 1890s. Yet the significance and the outcome of Taylorism as a means of labor control are far less abundantly clear. Put simply, Chapter 3 suggests that Taylorism by and large failed to arrest (indeed, actually promoted) the rise of labor struggle and organization of Bell employees. This corner of labor history is not well known: tales of syndicalist battles and sit-down strikes have attracted far more attention than the struggles of pedestrian workers laboring at switchboards, central offices, and telephone poles.[8] Yet the course of labor struggle in this industry is revealing, not only because of the vibrant growth of trade unionism among women operators (who built the largest woman-controlled union in the history of the American workers' movement),[9] but also because of the conspicuous silence of these same workers during the turbulent decade of the 1930s. Chapter three explains this trajectory by tracing the emergence and persistence of a formidable system of industrial paternalism throughout AT&T.

The historical roots of this system reach back to feminization of the Bell work force in the 1880s, which gradually led management to adopt a set of 'special responsibilities' toward its workers, beginning with the provision of dormitories for night workers in the 1890s, and generally infusing a familial character into the nation's telephone exchanges. These offices were in fact designed to replicate the workers' homes (or, at least, management's conception of them), with sitting parlors, dining rooms, and other such amenities. Once management adopted the AT&T Benefit Plan (an early version of welfare capitalism) and then a latticework of company unions, the elements of a powerful system of paternalistic authority were in place, allowing the company to stem the tide of workers' resistance for decades. The course of these developments lends support to the arguments of Michael Burawoy (especially Burawoy 1985), for the company's exercise of control over its workers emanated not from the labor process (Taylorism or machines) but from the wider political apparatuses of the firm.

By the end of World War II, however, the effectiveness of Bell paternalism had almost completely decayed. Exploring the forces that underlay the transformation of managerial paternalism brings into focus certain weaknesses implied in Burawoy's theory of production politics. Most important, his theory fails to note the workings of the internal contradictions that can unfold within managerial regimes. For the collapse of Bell paternalism was not merely the product of wider political and economic forces imposed on production politics from without. In addition, there were important *endogenous* sources of change, as Bell paternalism itself provided workers with precisely those resources they needed to challenge managerial control. Paternalism manifested unanticipated consequences, then, as it evolved down paths that management could neither foresee nor control.

By World War II the rise of industrial unionism within the Bell system brought the era of paternalism to a close, forcing the company to devise new means of controlling labor even in the context of labor organization. What means of control emerged, and with what effects? To address this question, the analysis focuses on developments affecting workplace *technology* (explored in Chapter 4) and managerial *ideology* (the focus of Chapter 5).

During the immediate postwar years, skilled craftworkers made up an increasingly prominent occupational category within the industry's work force as the spread of machine-based switching systems required increasing numbers of skilled workers to maintain the new equipment. As Chapter 4 reveals, customary work arrangements left these workers considerable discretion in the conduct of their jobs, achieving a temporary pattern of mutual accomodation between the company and its craftworkers. As economic competition began to emerge (a process that began decades before the final divestiture), AT&T management was forced to restructure its internal operations. Beginning in the late 1960s and early 1970s, the company instituted a sweeping campaign of restructuring that uprooted informal, customary work relations and disrupted the temporary equilibrium that existed between capital and labor. Prominently featured in this process of change was a wide array of microelectronic systems—including "stored program" switching equipment, microprocessor-based systems that automated the work of testing and system diagnosis, and highly integrated database technologies—the overall effect of which brought the provision of telephone service ever closer to a continuous-process form of production, with control rooms monitoring the functioning of remote installations. The key questions addressed in Chapter 4 are whether this shift has enabled management to uproot workers' skills and degrade their work situations, or instead opened up a path that leads beyond hierarchical structures and toward new, more flexible forms of work organization.

Put bluntly, the answer is that neither model adequately captures the transformation of the industry's work processes. To be sure, skilled manual work has often come under frontal attack, much as de-skilling theorists contend. This process has been especially pronounced among skilled manual workers engaged in diagnostic work (the Test Deskmen), where programmable machines have incorporated the knowledge that craftworkers had taken decades to amass. This instance conforms to the experience of machinists faced with Computerized Numerical Control (CNC) systems, as has been widely studied. Other craft jobs too have suffered. Yet my analysis suggests that a different, more subtle dynamic has occurred than the de-skilling paradigm predicts.

In important respects, new technologies have indeed pried loose craftworkers' control over the labor process, as new information technologies have displaced workers who occupied strategic locations within the labor process. Yet such changes have by no means issued in a simple or uniform process of de-skilling; nor have they resulted in the homogenization of workers' tasks. Even under conditions where managers have had both the motive and the opportunity to uproot craftworkers' skills, management has been unable to abolish the need for skilled crafts. Rather than simply eliminating workers' skills, new technologies have often tended to replenish them, redistributing skilled functions among new claimants within the firm. The overall result has been to reproduce or perpetuate skilled work as an occupational category, even as the nature and importance of skill has been transformed in certain far-reaching ways.

A different process has gripped routine office workers. As is especially clear in Bell departments devoted to maintenance or plant functions, clerical workers have traditionally occupied subordinate positions, laboring in support of skilled craftworkers. Clerks, a predominantly female group, have assisted craftworkers by fielding incoming reports of trouble, filing data on service histories, and retrieving data relevant to the work of installation and repair. Workers performing these relatively unskilled functions have found their jobs especially vulnerable to the de-skilling process, as Bell firms have shifted toward larger and ever more tightly controlled office settings in which VDTs have served not only as data entry devices but also as powerful levers of control. The evidence suggests, then, that automation has not in fact promoted the homogenization of work, but has maintained (and perhaps even reinforced) the older dualism between craft and clerical employees. Viewed historically, this suggests that new technologies have been assimilated into the existing division of labor, reproducing the inequalities that predated the introduction of the new information systems.

Analysis of technological change, however, is only one element of the larger analysis of labor control. Before drawing any firm conclusions regarding contemporary authority relations in this branch of production, the analysis explores the degree to which wider organizational processes have established a pattern of *normative* or *ideological* controls, quite independent of the structure of workers' tasks. In varying ways, precisely this claim underlies the work of many recent theorists of workplace authority who have variously formulated what can be termed the "hegemony" thesis. This perspective, represented in the writings of Burawoy, Richard Edwards, Claus Offe, Andrew Friedman, and several others, insists that the politics of production under advanced capitalism increasingly resembles the politics of state democracy: mechanisms of consensus formation serve to integrate divergent classes into the system, inviting subordinate groups to take for granted the underlying "rules of the game." Whether due to the spread of an ideology of industrial citizenship or to informal mechanisms of adaptation to inequality, managerial hegemony induces workers to consent to the status quo and even to implicitly collude in their own exploitation. Chapter 5 explores the adequacy of this 'hegemonic' model in depicting the substance of worker consciousness and its susceptibility to managerial control.

Bell firms are an especially appropriate site on which to address this theme, for the industry has been host to many of the conditions on which hegemony theory rests. Workplace reform efforts have been well represented here, as the Quality of Work Life process has been encouraged by both management and the union. A system of internal labor markets—an institutionalized set of rules governing the distribution of workers into positions—

is also apparent here. Finally, the economic restructuring of the industry has posed an external threat to these workers' well-being, conforming to conditions that hegemony theorists believe should encourage workers to close ranks behind their employer. Has this occurred? Has the work organization generated a 'consensual' form of discourse that invites workers to identify more with the firm than with the members of their own social class?

The evidence presented in Chapter 5 casts serious doubt on the validity of hegemony theory as a portrayal of production politics, for management's ideological dominance over its workers seems far less effective than this model allows. Although one finds evidence of workers and occupational groups who *do* consent to managers' power over their labor or otherwise manifest managerial inclinations, the majority of these workers harbor an *oppositional* consciousness. They consider themselves members of the working class, they perceive the company in dichotomous terms, and they are not shy about walking the picket line to defend their hard-won gains.[10] Moreover, few workers subscribe to ideological portrayals of new technology as merely the avatar of 'progress.' Although there are distinct variations in the character of workers' consciousness, these workers do not lack the ideological resources they need to press their needs to the fore. How then is labor control achieved?

As Chapter 6 concludes, a new managerial regime has begun to emerge, based partly on the growing power of digital technologies. At work here has been a process that has *severed the tie* between technical skill and control over the labor process. As information technologies have been applied to the most central, directive nodes of production, human labor has been repositioned, shifted to an increasingly auxiliary role within the labor process. Even workers whose tasks remain relatively complex find that they have purchase on a narrower proportion of the labor process than ever before. In short, an 'algorithmic' set of controls has begun to unfold that enables information technologies to regulate the labor process more fully than ever before (Appelbaum and Albin, 1989). Indeed, it becomes increasingly problematic to speak of the automated firm's operations as a "labor" process at all.

The implications of these developments for theories of work are manifold. First, they suggest that the existing dichotomy between the labor process (the organization of work methods)

and the political apparatuses of production (the authority relations through which management exerts control) has begun to
collapse. As programmable machines acquire the ability to regulate the internal operations of the firm—to control the flow of
work between different departments, to monitor the functioning
of remote installations, to adjust the system's functioning when
faults occur, and to assign tasks to human workers when the need
arises—the technology of work has absorbed the functions of
control that had previously been external to it.

Further, the study begins to point toward the need for much
greater care in the interpretation of workplace change with respect
to the separate dimensions of work content. Thus, theorists have
often used the terms 'skill' and 'control' as if they were inter-
changeable or as if the former dimension were invariably linked to
the latter. That linkage may have been true in older manufacturing
industries where the mastery of one's tools conferred power of the
labor process. But in contexts where the object of production is
information and in which programmable machines occupy
increasingly central positions with the firm's operations, the performance of complex, specialized operations no longer gives workers purchase over production. The specter that haunts labor, then,
is not an electronic version of the familiar factory system, but
rather *the consignment of human labor to ever more peripheral
locations within a digitally regulated production process whose
functioning has grown largely independent of the worker's skills.*

This nascent system of algorithmic controls is not self-sufficient. Vital to its growth and persistence are decidedly *non*-tech-
nological structures that theories of labor control seldom
acknowledge. One is a set of political and legal influences that
places pivotal groups of technical employees beyond the pale of
trade unionism. Second and even more important is a system of
collective bargaining that has tended to institutionalize managerial prerogatives. Caught within an institutional web of legal
obligations, the major union in this industry has implicitly sanc-
tioned the rise of a new regime, as if the restoration of managerial
power might not return to take its revenge. Thus, if the trade
union leadership now confronts a more subtle and powerful form
of labor regulation than this century has known, it faces an oppo-
nent it has implicitly brought into being.

Much has been written about the emergence of flexible and egalitarian forms of work organization in high-tech industries. The bulk of this literature has been directed toward managerial officials in the hope that they might lead their firms beyond the rigid hierarchies of industrial capitalism. Yet this study suggests that top management has little inherent interest in taking such a step. Information technologies appear to provide management with precisely those controls they seek in order to ensure the achievement of their objectives. Indeed, the algorithmic controls that have emerged seem to dwarf the old regime of paternalism both in power and sophistication. The sources of change in this nascent regime, then, must come from below—from workers and lower-level union leaders. The clock is ticking, both for communications workers and their counterparts in other information industries.

CHAPTER 2

Work, Power, and
the Monopoly Corporation

Classical social theory placed labor at the very center of its concerns. For Marx, of course, a society's mode of production revealed its "innermost secret, the hidden basis of the entire social structure."[1] While disavowing so materialist a perspective, Max Weber nonetheless viewed work as the engine of the rationalization process, driving formally rational action into all departments of modern life. However divergent were these theorists' views, both implicitly agreed that neither the origins nor the fate of industrial capitalism could be understood apart from the structure and the experience of work.

If classical approaches toward work are notable for their historical sweep and bold macrostructural vision, contemporary analysis of work as an institution has been most impressive for its lack of these very traits. Rather than seeking to lay bare the division of labor, sociological analysis of work has instead fallen victim to the very process it would study, generating a fragmented array of professional specializations that lack any conception of the wider totality. Moreover, the various parts of the field have fastened on different units of analysis—with some scholars engaged in the sociology of industries, others the study of occupations, and still others the study of either organizations or markets—yielding little agreement on the relative merits of each point of departure and even less understanding of how work structures interrelate. Thus balkanized, the sociology of work in the United States has sustained notably little effort to theorize the nature of work or to think through the place it holds in the wider society.[2]

When theoretical paradigms on work have been put forward, these have stemmed from human relations and functionalist perspectives, variants on the 'order' perspective that views labor struggle as an aberrant or even irrational phenomenon. As a result, for most of this century American approaches toward work have taken for granted what most needs to be explained—the achievement and persistence of managerial control (Crozier 1964, and Burawoy 1979, Ch. 1 and 2).[3]

Much of this has changed in recent years. While the resurgence of industrial conflict during the 1960s and early 1970s proved more ephemeral than anyone assumed, it left its mark on intellectual efforts to understand the nature of work. In its wake there has emerged a 'new labor history' that stresses the formative capacities of workers, whose struggles actively shape the industrial order to which they belong (E. P. Thompson, 1963; Montgomery 1979, 1987; Brody 1980; Wilentz 1984). It has engendered novel approaches toward the anthropology of work, which stress the symbolic aspects of labor and which open up informal relations and shop-floor culture as themes to be explored. Finally, the resurgence of the women's movement has given rise to equally important shifts in thinking as sociologists of work have focused on the phenomena of sex segregation and gender inequality. In so doing they have begun to recast the fundamental assumptions that inform the field.

Earlier generations of industrial sociologists often viewed technologies with an uncritical eye, seeing them as socially neutral phenomena. Increasingly, however, scholars have sought to understand the ways in which social and ideological factors might actively enter into and shape particular tools and machines.[4] Typically, students of industry "conceived of rules as if they developed and operated without the intervention of interested groups...which have different degrees of power" (Gouldner 1954:27). Yet this outlook too has given way, as scholars have grown more aware of the processes of conflict, control, and resistance within work organizations.[5] Haltingly and in varying ways, the concepts of inequality, dominance, and ideology have come to occupy center stage as sociologists of work have brought *power* back into the analysis. This book seeks to empirically adjudicate between several prevailing theories of work and authority, to identify their limitations, and to shed light on the contemporary face of labor control within the monopoly capitalist firm.

In this chapter I pay close attention to three influential models of work and power that have surfaced in recent years. The first of these stems from neo-Marxist analyses of capitalist production and sees work as increasingly alienated or de-skilled. Most systematically developed by Braverman (1974) and his followers, this view contends that modern work processes have been subject to a relentless process of homogenization and simplification, beginning with the rise of scientific management and developing to full maturity only in more recent times.[6] This perspective builds on a long tradition within Marxist theory, from the *Manifesto* to the Second International, which held that capitalism would proletarianize the middle strata of capitalist society, enlarging the material base of support for qualitative social change.[7] At a time when advanced technologies have been introduced into virtually every branch of the capitalist economy, de-skilling theory has found renewed application, emboldening proponents who claim that programmable automation tends to cheapen skilled work, to simplify it and thereby subject workers to greater managerial control.

In partial opposition to the de-skilling perspective there has developed a second theory of work and power whose advocates seek to substantially revise the classical Marxist heritage. Theorists in this second vein have sought to articulate models of the *multiplicity* of labor control systems which have historically emerged in different periods and branches of the capitalist economy. Thus this second school implicitly seeks to enrich or transcend both Marxist and Weberian theories of workplace authority. For theorists in this vein, Taylorism is by no means the 'normal' form of labor control under capitalism. Indeed, what is most decisive is the coexistence of *non*-Taylorist forms of labor control—especially those that rest on the social production of consent to the status quo.

Theorists in this second genre have developed a number of different conceptions with which to understand the contemporary formation of worker consent. Thus, we have Andrew Friedman's "responsible autonomy," Richard Edwards' "bureaucratic control," Claus Offe's "achievement principle," Michael Burawoy's "hegemonic organization of work," and other, parallel formulations.[8] Despite internal differences within this second school, its adherents view the achievement of managerial control as largely due to organizational processes that enable monopoly capitalist firms to establish and maintain their ideological hegemony over their employees. In this view, the advanced capitalist workplace is an arena in which not technology but ideology secures and perpetuates the worker's subordination.[9]

If the second, 'hegemonic' image of work and power introduces major revisions into the classical Marxist conceptual apparatus, the third image goes even further and seeks to 'historicize' Marxist analysis itself. This view holds that the Marxist critique of wage labor was appropriate merely to a specific stage in the development of industrial capitalism and that subsequent developments in the nature of work have rendered that critique increasingly obsolete. The argument found its first influential expression in Robert Blauner's *Alienation and Freedom* (1964), which took Marx's theory of alienation as its point of departure. Blauner and his followers acknowledged that the rise of industrialism had aggravated the problem of worker discontent and bred an increasing estrangement of labor, but they concluded that further evolution of the work process tended to reduce the prevalence of machine-paced labor and the alienation it produced. The end result was prefigured in the most advanced branches of the capitalist economy, where firms have moved beyond the ethos of obedience on which industrial capitalism relied. Taking up the same theme, later theorists contend that flexible, egalitarian forms of authority relations begin to take root in automated firms and that, as the economy begins to shift toward "post-capitalist" and "post-hierarchical" models of work relations, there develops a qualitative break with rigid, centralized work structures (Hirschhorn 1984; Piore and Sabel 1984; Zuboff 1988; and Adler 1988).

My study begins by critically examining and juxtaposing these three rival images of work and power, setting the stage for the empirical analysis below.

THE EMISERATION OF LABOR?

By the middle of the twentieth century, most sociologists of work had embraced a conception of industrial society that was notably silent on issues of class, inequality, or domination. The conventional wisdom (indirectly derived from functionalist theory) was that the economic expansion of the postwar period had largely resolved the contradictions of capitalist society, so improving material conditions in the West as to integrate the working class into the structure of capitalist society. This was in fact the central claim of *embourgeoisement* theory: in a context marked by the spread of suburbanization, mass media, and rising standards of consumption, it was widely assumed that the working class had adopted middle-class values and ways of life, consigning instances of worker discontent and mobilization to the ever more distant past. As Jessie Barnard's formulation put it: "The proletariat has not absorbed the middle class but rather the other way around" (in Goldthorpe et al., 1969:9).[10]

Criticism of *embourgeoisement* theory was fueled by the resurgence of the workers' movement during the 1960s, which began to challenge the conventional wisdom about the Western working classes. Although workers in the United States had few institutional ties to student movements and no autonomous political organization—characteristics that set them apart from French and Italian workers—expressions of worker discontent among American workers grew too common to ignore, leading even a federally appointed commission to view the American workplace with some alarm.[11] Advanced capitalism had, it seemed, rediscovered the labor question.

In this context, the most persuasive analysis of work that appeared was that of Harry Braverman, whose *Labor and Monopoly Capital* provided the theoretical orientation for many historical and sociological studies of labor, technology, and work organization.[12] As did Marx, Braverman used as his point of departure the distinction between labor and labor power. Employers purchase units of labor power—productive *capacities*—but then must translate them into finished commodities that embody profit. However, insofar as workers are separated from the object of their labor and set to work for purposes that are quite alien to them, they typically lack any interest in complying with their employers' directives and seek only to minimize their own exploitation as a group. Since the spur of competition forces each firm to increase its rate of exploitation, employers must find ways of breaking down their workers' resistance in order to extract as much surplus value as they can. Precisely how management secures the profits it needs while limiting workers' capacity to resist has been at the center of the labor process debate.

Analysts after Marx traditionally defined class in terms of "relation to the means of production," a phrase that was usually defined in terms of property ownership. From this standpoint, the separation of the workers from the means of production was assumed to be complete when the great mass of a nation's workers were forced to sell their labor power for a wage.[13] In sharp contrast to this traditional view, Braverman developed a richer, more penetrating approach that moved beyond formal property ownership to consider the dynamics of control within the capitalist process of production. In Braverman's view, workers retained a special "relation to the means of production" even *after* capitalists had concentrated the bulk of a nation's property in their own hands. This special relationship, in Braverman's view, stemmed from the workers' *de facto* possession of skill and technical expertise.[14]

Braverman believed that when workers remained in possession of production knowledge, they could exert leverage over their employers, setting appreciable limits on the exploitation of their own labor. "Workers who retain their grip on the actual processes of labor," Braverman wrote, "will thwart efforts to realize the full potential inherent in their labor power" (1974:100). Therefore, the development of the capitalist mode of production required that such obstacles be uprooted and that employers eliminate their dependence on workers' production knowledge and technique. It was for this reason that scientific management, or Taylorism, emerged: it expressed capitalism's need to remove all conceptual functions from the workers' tasks, leaving in their place only the functions of execution.

Much of the force of Braverman's analysis stems from its analysis of the confrontation between Taylorism and craft labor. In his view, management seeks to use time and motion studies and other tools of job analysis in order to "dissolve the labor process as a process conducted by the worker and reconstitute it as a process conducted by management" (1974:170). Yet he emphasizes that the imposition of Taylorism was merely an initial stage in the transformation of work, providing the organizational pattern that best corresponded to the needs of industrial capitalism. The full development of the capitalist labor process required the revolutionization of the productive instruments themselves. Closely following Marx, Braverman holds that advanced technologies in effect complete the subordination of labor, transferring workers' skill into machines and extending managerial control over the labor process to the fullest possible extent.[15]

To illustrate his thesis with respect to craft labor, Braverman invokes the case of the machine-tool industry, a branch of production in which workers had preserved much of their former craft control. Faced with continuing worker resistance to the intensification of their work, employers resorted to Numerical Control (NC) technologies, which enable engineers to use programmed means of controlling lathes, milling equipment and cutting tools, bypassing the machinist's skills entirely. Where numerical control equipment was introduced, Braverman argued, skilled workers were quickly replaced by "engineers on the one hand and factory operatives on the other" (1974:209), prefiguring similar changes that spread (however unevenly) throughout the various branches of the economy.[16] A similar fate befalls skilled craftworkers in other industries.

Although his theory is founded on the transformation of craft occupations in manufacturing industries, Braverman applies his reasoning to a broad set of white-collar occupations as well. In response to sociological arguments that the growth of office occupations signifies an increasing level of skill requirements and the growth of a new middle class, Braverman contends that office labor has fallen prey to many of the same changes that have degraded skilled manual occupations. In offices as in factories, Taylorism and mechanization combine to reduce employees to much the same class position. Thus, the traditional inequality between manual and mental labor tends to give way to a growing homogenization of *all* forms of wage labor, as there emerges a "secular trend toward the incessant lowering of the working class below its previous conditions of skill" (1974:129–130).

Braverman's analysis exerted a tremendous influence among social scientists in a number of fields. It prompted important studies on the material and ideological significance of Taylorism, the relative importance of efficiency and power as causes of the modern division of labor, as well as the relation between new technology, skill requirements, and alienation from work.[17] De-skilling theory also entered the vocabulary of activists in the trade union movement, at times promoting a more vigorous response to skill dilution than had previously been seen (International Association of Machinists, 1983). Perhaps its major contribution has been its contention that changes in work design and technologies are fundamentally social and political processes, rather than simple, unmediated expressions of technological imperatives or economic efficiency.[18]

Yet de-skilling theory stakes out a more ambitious set of theoretical claims than just this. It has advanced a number of assertions regarding the transformation of the labor process that have set off a continuing theoretical and empirical debate. Some writers have taken issue with the theory on primarily empirical grounds, claiming that repeated efforts have failed to produce any evidence of a de-skilling trend. For example, Adler (1988:3) alleges that the research literature has dealt a "resounding rejection" to the degradation thesis. Yet such portrayals of the empirical literature seem somewhat misleading, for they neglect a rich vein of case studies that lend credence to the theory.[19] Nonetheless, it is fair to say that the empirical literature has been contradictory and ambiguous at best. More substantively important, however, are the theoretical criticisms that have been leveled at the de-skilling thesis, often by Marxist theorists who find the degradation perspective gravely flawed in several important respects.

Some theorists contend that the de-skilling perspective exaggerates the prevalence of craft labor before the rise of industrial or monopoly capitalism (Monds 1976; Stark 1980; Form 1980, 1987). By defining the baseline for his analysis in terms of craft labor—a position that only a small minority of workers enjoyed—Braverman's analysis idealizes pre-capitalist labor processes, propounding a myth of the craftsman's 'lost paradise' (see Monds 1976). Other theorists have leveled their critique at the theory's excessive determinism. Because the theory defines workers as passive objects flung to and fro by the wants of capital accumulation, it ignores the degree to which workers' resistance actively shapes the labor process (Friedman 1977; Stark 1980; DiFazio 1985). Linked to this critique is the argument of Burawoy and several other writers who note the limitations in any theory that restricts its attention to the objective or structural aspects of work and class relations while excluding the subjective or experiential influences that may bind workers to their employers or otherwise affect management's efforts at control.[20] Finally, an increasing number of theorists have shown that the de-skilling perspective focuses solely upon *class* relations without acknowledging the impact of *gender* inquality on both the design and allocation of work. As Paul Willis (1977), Cynthia Cockburn (1983), and many others have shown, class inequality at work is typically overlaid with a second system of inequality based on gender. Neither system can properly be understood in abstraction from the other (compare with Hartmann 1976, 1984). Underlying these varying criticisms is the more general conviction that the de-skilling paradigm omits several decisive variables from its analysis.

Understandably, some scholars have responded by modifying the de-skilling paradigm in ways that retain Braverman's emphasis on skill as a critical object of struggle while remaining alive to those structural and ideological conditions that modify the working-out of the de-skilling trend.[21] One example of this trend is Wilkinson's analysis of several British metalworking plants that used varying types of Computerized Numerical Control systems (a later generation of NC equipment). Although in most of these plants managers clearly preferred that production knowledge and expertise reside in the office rather than on the shop floor, a number of factors affected their ability to realize their will. Among these were the relative power of particular occupational groups, the values and inclinations of managers at different levels of the corporate hierarchy, and the degree to which workers were able to participate in the introduction and debugging of CNC equipment. Similarly, Child and his colleagues found that the ways in which microelectronic technologies reshaped the labor process in banking, medical, and sales organizations depended on a number of contingencies such as the ideological resources that workers command in the public arena, the uncertainty of tasks prior to automation, and the opportunities workers have to influence the automation process itself. Finally, Kelley (1990) studied the use of programmable automation in a national sample of metalworking and machine-tool firms and identified a parallel set of contingencies that shape the use of new technologies. Large, unionized, multi-plant companies were least likely to allow blue-collar workers to program NC equipment on the shop floor. Smaller, non-union shops tend to adopt a more flexible, tolerant use of the same machines. What these and other studies have in common is their recognition that the de-skilling trend does not unfold mechanically in accordance with a pre-given logic. Rather, the outcome of technological change is at least partly *in*determinate—subject to modification by social, economic, and political forces that cannot be ignored.

MANAGERIAL HEGEMONY

A more complete break with the de-skilling tradition has emerged among Marxist theorists who have contributed to the emergence of what can loosely be called a theory of labor control systems. Advocates of this developing genre draw attention to the oversimplifications that inevitably result when we view the evolution of work as a transition from craft control to Taylorism. Such an approach overlooks the myriad forms of labor control that transcend the craft/Taylorist dichotomy—e.g., the putting out system, subcontracting, and many others as well. Indeed, one central goal of recent theory has been to develop a more elaborate set of conceptual tools with which to understand variations in the structure of labor control.

Much of this work has drawn upon notions of industrial segmentation to show how a firm's position within larger capital and commodity markets affects the resources it commands and the provisions it makes for labor control.[22] The most influential argument in this vein has been that of Richard Edwards, whose historical analysis of monopoly capitalism in the U.S. distinguishes three historically distinct types of control that persist within different sectors of the economy. Within smaller, competitive firms and industries there exists the initial and most rudimentary type—"simple control"—based largely on the personal rule of the manager or employer. In larger, monopolistic firms that produce for mass markets, control has shed its purely human guise and assumed a more structural form that Edwards calls "technical control," which relies on machines to enforce a given pace and method of work. Finally, in monopoly corporations that employ large proportions of office and techical labor, there emerges what Edwards dubs "bureaucratic control," which relies on the spread of internal labor markets and the formalization of managerial authority to maintain an appearance of universalism and industrial justice even within the very fortresses of the capitalist mode of production. This multiplicity of control systems is the key to working-class division and powerlessness, Edwards claims, in that different issues and inclinations are produced that make the achievement of solidarity all but unattainable.

Other formulations of labor control go further than Edwards. Burawoy (1985) has developed a conceptual apparatus that identifies an even more elaborate set of control systems. Among these are *patriarchal despotism* (in which men function as subcontractors and use their authority to exploit the labor of their own wives and children), *paternalism* (in which employers imbue their relation toward workers with the reciprocal obligations and deference that characterize the father/child relation), *market despotism* (essentially, the Taylorist model), and several others. Despite these differing formulations, theorists of labor control systems commonly agree on two important themes—first, that the mechanisms which maintain labor control lie beyond the labor process (or work methods and operations) and are lodged within the organization of the firm more broadly, and second, that the subordination of labor within the advanced capitalist enterprise depends particularly on organizational processes that serve to *legitimize* managerial power and to elicit workers' *consent* to the wage-labor relationship.[23]

Edwards (1979) develops this notion of the corporation as a crucible of consensus formation in his discussion of bureaucratic control. With the growing formalization of managerial authority and the articulation of internal labor markets, he contends workers tend increasingly to identify with the firm and to view its interests as identical with their own. Likewise, Claus Offe (1976) argues that the modern firm's provisions for individual mobility promote an ethos of individual achievement (the "achievement principle") that obscures the collective processes bound up with the production of surplus value. In much the same vein, Burawoy's early work (1979) argues that the social relations *in* production (informal behavior and workplace culture) tend to obscure the nature of cap-italist relations *of* production, even inducing workers to participate in their own exploitation. These theorists insist, then, that the organization of work within the monopoly capitalist firm produces more than mere commodities. In addition, it produces—as Bura-woy puts it, "manufactures"—the spontaneous consent of the workers to the *status quo*. Inasmuch as this 'hegemonic' concep-tion of work and authority is most fully developed by Burawoy, I will consider his formulation in some depth.

In his *Politics of Production* (1985), Burawoy introduces a sharp distinction between the labor process (the technical process of production) and the "factory regime" (the authority relations that shape workers' inclinations and capacities). Left to their own devices, workers would struggle to resist managerial control over their labor. However, factory regimes act to shape or circumscribe workers' actions and capacities, functioning to maintain the exis-tence of (or reproduce) the wage-labor system as such.

Burawoy distingishes between two broad forms of factory regimes—those based on *coercion* (despotic regimes) and those based on *consent* (hegemonic regimes). He maintains that classi-cal Marxism mistakenly viewed "market despotism" as the essen-tial form of authority relations under the capitalist mode of pro-duction. Breaking with this tradition, he holds that the emergence of this (or indeed, any) regime will depend on the specific political and economic conditions that surround the firm. Four such con-ditions are key to his model: (1) the economic organization of the industry, (2) the nature of its labor process, (3) the degree to which workers have been separated from the means of subsis-tence, and (4) the manner in which the state intervenes in produc-tion. In this view, the development of market despotism as a regime occurs only under highly specific circumstances: when employers face sharp competitive pressures from other firms, when workers have lost command over production knowledge and are also completely dependent on their employer for subsis-tence, and when the state refrains from setting any limits on the character of managerial behavior within the accumulation pro-cess itself. Where any of these four conditions are absent, Bura-woy contends, production politics will develop along different lines than Marx assumed.

Especially important in Burawoy's reasoning is the role of the state, which classical theories of the labor process typically ignore. Since the growth of social insurance programs provides workers with access to at least a modicum of economic alternatives, their dependence on the wage as their only means of subsistence historically declines. Once "the unity of production and reproduction" has been partly broken, workers can act with greater autonomy in relation to capital than before. Moreover, as the state begins to intervene directly ("internally") within the production process, proscribing certain types of labor practices, workers enjoy a further source of autonomy. Historically, then, market despotism becomes less and less frequent:

> Now management can no longer rely on the economic whip of the market. Nor can it impose an arbitrary despotism. The *despotic regimes* of early capitalism, in which coercion prevails over consent, must be replaced with *hegemonic regimes*, in which consent prevails...although never to the exclusion of coercion (Burawoy 1985:126).

Two hegemonic regimes are especially important in Burawoy's work. One is paternalism. Drawing on the work of Patrick Joyce (1980) and other historians of work, Burawoy notes the frequency with which textile firms in both New England and the English midlands imposed a form of authority on workers and their families that was unique in its breadth and character. By the *breadth* of the firm's demands I mean management's effort to impose its conception of morality and behavior on workers' domestic and community relations, whether through political or philanthropic apparatuses in the wider polity or through the firm's ownership of housing and commercial establishments. The *character* of the firm's demands stemmed from its effort to imbue the wage-labor relation with the reciprocal obligations and relations of personal dependence that are found (ideally at least) in family life.[24]

A second, less obtrusive form of hegemony is that which Burawoy views as characteristic of monopoly capitalist firms today. His most fully developed portrayal of this type of regime can be found in *Manufacturing Consent* (1979), a qualitative analysis of a Chicago machine-tool factory. The workers in this study performed jobs that were tedious and physically demanding, and their pay was subject to sharp variation, owing to piece-rate methods of payment. Nonetheless, management made few efforts to directly control workers' activities. The outcome was that workers' own shop-floor culture implicitly led them to participate in their own subordination.

Seeking to infuse meaning into otherwise boring tasks, workers engaged in industrial games, the most pivotal of which was the game of "making out"—that is, informally competing to see who could earn good wages even in the face of tight piece rates. Playing the game enabled workers to gain standing in the eyes of their co-workers and to demonstrate their personal triumph over the production process. In these ways the game of making out helped workers adapt to an onerous work situation. Yet at the same time, playing the game led workers to view themselves as freely acting subjects despite their subordinate position in production. In short, playing the game encouraged workers to take for granted the underlying rules of capitalist production, blinding them to the presence of class antagonisms at work. Ironically, the workers in Burawoy's study unwittingly helped to reproduce the very production relations that exploited them.[25]

Much of Burawoy's work was conceived before the economic crises of the late 1970s. His more recent work acknowledges the rise of an employer's offensive and increasing attacks on wages, working conditions, and labor organization. Yet he believes that workers' responses to management under these conditions will reflect their exposure to decades of managerial hegemony. Indeed, he uses the term "hegemonic despotism" to refer to management's success in gaining economic sacrifices from workers, to protect the viability or "health" of the firm. For this reason, Burawoy believes that even under conditions of economic retrenchment—*especially* under such conditions—factory regimes will continue to limit or regulate workers' capacity for resistance.[26]

More than any other recent theorist of labor control systems, Burawoy provides a rich conceptual schema with which to understand the varied forms managerial power can assume and the conditions that give rise to each. His concept of factory regimes is provocative and lends itself to historical inquiry. In spite of his contributions, however, his theoretical framework suffers from several limitations.

One limitation stems from Burawoy's tendency to assume that factory regimes inevitably succeed in reproducing capitalist relations, with little or no threat to managerial control (cf. Storey 1985:194). This is especially apparent in his treatment of managerial hegemony. In the context of a hegemonic regime, he asserts, workers can only develop a consensual culture on the shop floor. This claim can be questioned on empirical grounds, inasmuch as several recent studies have suggested that a more conflictual consciousness—a culture of resistance—can and often does arise in contexts where Burawoy would expect only worker consent.[27] Yet we have reason to question Burawoy's formulation even on theoretical grounds alone, for it fails to explain the rise of conflict or struggle within the firm. Because his theory is above all a theory of *reproduction*, it fails to allow for the emergence of *contradictions* within production politics, and for this reason cannot easily account for the transformation of factory regimes (see Staples 1987).

A second problem concerns Burawoy's conception of the labor process and its means of production. Burawoy criticizes previous theorists for their tendency to "underpoliticize" production—that is, to overlook the effect of the state on the production process and in turn on the workers' movement itself. Yet, inasmuch as Burawoy views the political apparatuses of production as the dominant element in the structure of managerial power, he himself tends to neglect the social and political character of the labor process, eventually viewing the latter as a set of technical relations that are external to the politics of production.[28] Moreover, Burawoy offers no compelling reasons why the dominance of the political apparatuses should be constant throughout all stages of capitalist production rather than a condition that is subject to historical change. In an era marked by sweeping changes in the material basis of wage labor, it seems reasonable to ask whether the very distinction between the labor process and managerial regimes might conceivably collapse, yielding forms of labor control that Burawoy cannot foresee.

THE EMANCIPATION OF LABOR?

As already noted, until the late 1960s, the prevailing assumption among most occupational sociologists was that modern industrial societies tends to require an increasingly well-educated and technically skilled labor force. The development of modern industrial societies, it was held, quite naturally tend to generate an upgrading of the worker's position within the class structure of industrial society. Some theorists based their analysis on the sphere of consumption, pointing to rising standards of living, greater enjoyment of leisure and exposure to mass media, and other such expressions of increasing affluence.[29] Other theorists based their analyses squarely in the sphere of production, however, claiming to find changes in the organization and technology of work that so ameliorated the workers' position in the firm as to dissolve the structural bases of working-class discontent.

Surely the most influential 'industrial' application of the *embourgeoisement* point of view was Robert Blauner's *Alienation and Freedom* (1964), which continues to inform research in the field. Blauner acknowledged that the *mechanization* of production had reduced workers' levels of skill and control over their jobs, generating the alienating forms of labor that Marx so forcefully critiques. Yet he insisted that the *automation* of work would eventually free workers from the contraints of the assembly line, give them a clearer view of the totality of the production process and integrate them into cooperative work teams alongside engineers and technicians. Thus, what modern industry initially took from the worker—the opportunity for meaningful, autonomous work and a sense of community while performing it—would eventually be restored.

The Blauner thesis was especially well-received in England and the United States, where applications and extensions of it quickly spread (e.g., Faunce 1965; Shepard 1971; Wedderburn and Crompton 1972; Hull, et al. 1982). During the 1960s, however, sociologists challenged the upgrading thesis on both theoretical and empirical grounds. Some critics chided Blauner and his followers for their adherence to a crude form of technological determinism (see Child 1986). Others questioned the fit between Blauner's data (largely survey data on job satisfaction) and the theory he wished to engage (Marx's theory of alienation and the work process). Still other critics noted that Blauner's study was largely ahistorical: it simply assumed that static differences between labor in the automobile and chemical industries in fact depicted real historical trends. On the basis of these and other criticisms, sociologists began to challenge the upgrading thesis as a species of utopian thought.

In recent years, however, several sociologists have advanced more theoretically nuanced and sophisticated versions of the upgrading thesis.[30] For example, Hirschhorn's (1984) study of continuous process industries concludes that advanced technologies are inherently more flexible than older, mechanized equipment and that automated systems increasingly require newer, more egalitarian organizational structures than did previous stages of production. Likewise, in her analysis of automation in the paper, insurance, and communications industries, Zuboff (1988) found that new information technologies make possible a profound upgrading of workers' jobs in ways that give workers a clearer and more transparent view of production than ever before. Finally, Adler (1988, 1990) suggests that the introduction of programmable systems into both the machine-tools and banking industries gives rise to a long-term need for a more conceptually skilled and responsible workforce, introducing certain "post-capitalist" tendencies into the modern firm. All of these authors are careful to note that managers may fear the loss of their traditional power and authority and thus resist the introduction of innovative forms of work organization. Nonetheless, these authors are confident that the rational utilization of automated technologies must eventually lead toward the development of "post-hierarchical" work structures that decisively break with the rigid models of work that industrial capitalism had spawned.[31]

These recent efforts to reformulate the upgrading thesis have moved beyond Blauner's account in certain respects. Rather than viewing technological change as an entirely autonomous force, these authors have acknowledged that the process of technological change will at least partly depend on management's preference for power and authority. Far more than their predecessors, these authors are aware that technological change may give rise to tensions or contradictions within the firm, as political and ideological pressures to maintain control over labor collide against purely technical and economic pressures to increase workers' skills (see Noble 1984). In the end, however, these authors assume that managers must pursue an economically rational course of action even if it means risking their own traditional power and authority. In an era of sharpening competition, the argument runs, management can no longer waste the productive potential that new technologies make possible.

Several problems can be identified with this emerging perspective. The first is that studies such as Zuboff's, which claim to detect evidence of the nascent "post-hierarchical" work organization, seem to provide a more convincing case for the continuing weight of hierarchical authority. A second is the perspective's reliance on technological determinism which, despite some allowance for the role of political structures within the firm, nonetheless explains the transformation of work processes through appeal to the imperatives of the new machines. A third limitation in this view lies in the ambiguous effects of economic competition. Although advocates of the new 'enskilling' theory suggest that sharpening economic competition will induce firms to *abandon* older forms of authority in an effort to maximize their return on new information technologies, competition might instead only *reinforce* employers' attachment to their accustomed patterns of organization, encouraging them to tighten labor controls even more. Conceivably there are various ways of maximizing the return on technologies, many of which are consonant with managerial power. This perhaps is the theory's most important limitation: the actors it casts as the major agents of worker empowerment are those who have the most to lose by taking such steps.[32]

DISCUSSION

Having sketched three of the most influential images of power in the monopoly corporation, we are in a position to extract from these views some of the more salient points of contention, and use these issues to guide empirical research.

One of the most central issues in the debate concerns capitalism's putative shift from a 'coercive' face of managerial power to a newer and more 'consensual' one. Interestingly, both hegemony theory and the upgrading approach emphasize the historical emergence of a consensual consciousness among workers in the advanced capitalist firm. Despite their differing explanations of this trend, for example, both Blauner and Burawoy have advanced a theory of working-class integration. One key issue that must be addressed, then, concerns this hypothetical shift in the nature of managerial power, from structural to normative processes and from coercion to worker consent. Has this shift in fact occurred, and if so, what processes—shifts in skill requirements, or shop-floor culture—have brought it about?

A further theme that arises here involves the emergence and transformation of labor control mechanisms historically. As we have seen, a number of competing formulations have been offered with which to interpret the structure of managerial control in the United States. Thus de-skilling theorists view labor control as involving the relentless spread of Taylorism as capitalism unfolds, while others (especially Burawoy) adopt a more historically contingent approach. What types of authority relations *have* been most prominent in this industry, and what conditions gave rise to them? What processes act to propel firms from one form of control to another? Focusing on a single industrial terrain, the present study aims to provide a clearer view of the social processes that underlie shifts in workplace authority over time.

A further theme relates to the specific locus of managerial control—whether it rests in the labor process (as both upgrading and degradation theory assume) or in identifiable regimes or labor control systems arrayed 'above' or beyond the content of work as such. As we have seen, Burawoy posits an invariant distinction between these two levels of analysis, with managerial regimes playing the dominant role. Has this distinction been constant over time, with managerial regimes providing the decisive mechanisms that shape workers' inclinations and capacities? Is this assertion equally true of the past and the present?

A final issue to be addressed concerns the implications of information technologies, not only for skill requirements and levels of alienation from work, but also for the exercise of power over labor. Has the introduction of programmable automation begun to erode class hierarchies at work, as upgrading theorists contend, or has it had other, less benign consequences? Has automation affected the work of men and women workers equally? Perhaps most abstractly, do information technologies in fact "revolutionize" the division of labor, or does the legacy of inherited divisions lend shape to the new, automated operations? To address these issues demands that we move deep into the workings of the monopoly core firm, exploring the character of historical trends in the structure of labor control as well as the specific mechanisms that bind workers to their employer within the contemporary context as well.

CHAPTER 3

The Old Regime at AT&T: Taylorism, Paternalism, and Labor Struggle, 1890–1947

The rise of the American Telephone and Telegraph Company coincided with the larger triumph of monopoly capitalism in the United States. Although the Bell system originated in 1876, it did not begin to establish its monopoly of the industry until after the turn of the century. From its relatively diminutive size in 1880, when it employed only 3,338 workers, AT&T expanded into a vertically integrated monopoly of unrivaled proportions. By 1920 the company controlled more than four-fifths of the industry's revenues (a figure that would remain constant until the dismantling of the Bell system in 1984) and employed 231,316 workers.[1] Much like the railroad industry, the Bell system became intimately involved in the spread of the market economy, reaching into virtually every city and town in the nation.

As with the expansion of other large monopoly corporations during this period, AT&T's growth brought in its wake the rise of labor struggle and organization, forcing the company to evolve mechanisms with which to subordinate and control its employees. For with the expansion of the Bell system there arose a growing challenge to management's unilateral authority, especially in the years between 1912 and 1923. My purpose in this chapter is to explore those mechanisms the company invoked to limit the spread of labor struggle and to maintain control over the workers it employed. My goal here is not merely to situate shifts underway in recent years (useful though that might be), but also to identify the strengths and weaknesses in previous efforts to explain why specific forms of labor control emerge, persist, and change within given historical periods.

The chapter begins by exploring the nature of the industry's work process and the forces which underlay the feminization of its work force during the end of the nineteenth century. It then examines the significance of both scientific management and mechanization, viewed as efforts to tighten management's grip on the labor process. As we shall see, for a time and to a limited extent, the pattern of labor control that emerged in the Bell system did conform to the model advanced by de-skilling theory. Between the years 1890 and 1915, the work situation of operators in particular changed dramatically as management applied the principles of Taylorism to switchboard work. Further rationalization and standardization occurred apace with the mechanization of telephone work. Yet the more thoroughly we examine the evolution of labor control within the Bell system, the clearer it becomes that the Taylorist model played at most a secondary role in the subordination of telephone workers. Until after World War II, the company's power over labor rested not so much on the distribution of working knowledge within the labor process as on the managerial regime that lay 'above' it. It was the evolution of a paternalistic form of production politics, not scientific management, that placed the most decisive limits on the class capacities of Bell workers.

WEAVERS OF SPEECH:
THE CHANGING CHARACTER OF TELEPHONE WORK

From the inception of the Bell system, its occupational structure encompassed three roughly distinct groups: (1) *operators*, who were employed in the Traffic department of each operating company and who comprised a majority of Bell workers until the middle of the twentieth century, (2) *skilled craftworkers*, located in the Plant department, many of whom were members of the electrical trades, and (3) a heterogeneous assortment of *managerial, sales,* and *clerical workers* distributed throughout several other divisions of each Bell firm. Few sources of data are available on the relative size of these three groups during the early years of the Bell system, but data for 1920 (the earliest year for which detailed statistics are available) are suggestive. In that year, operators made up 56.2 percent of the total work force, skilled craftworkers another 20.8 percent, while the remainder was spread among various office positions.[2] In the era of manual call switching, operators were the production workers of the industry.

During the telephone industry's first decade and a half, the labor process was organized in large part along lines inherited from the telegraph industry. This legacy influenced the character of telephone work in two important ways. One was the company's reliance on telegraphy's traditional source of labor—working-class boys seeking to learn a trade. The second was the persistence of a quasi-craft model of work which, until the end of the nineteenth century, left workers considerable latitude in the performance of their jobs. Both these inherited features came under attack as the Bell system began to stand on its own feet.

The Feminization of the Switchboard

Precise data are not available on the gender composition of the AT&T work force during its earliest years of operation, but when we rely on correspondence, reports, and photographs from this period it seems certain that in 1880, when roughly 2,000 of Bell's 3,381 workers operated switchboards, virtually all operators were male. (see figure 3.1). A company report later explained:

> It was the most natural thing in the world to use boy operators in the first telephone exchanges. Boys and young men had served as telegraph operators since Morse had ticked off his historic "What hath god wrought."[3]

The earliest telephone exchanges were apparently conceived as extensions of telegraph offices, with young men mastering the switching process, assisted by boys acting as messengers. Within a very short time, however, Bell managers began to abandon their dependence on inherited traditions and very rapidly recruited women in lieu of men.

Initially, women were hired only for daytime 'tours,' with men continuing to staff telephone exchanges at night. Thus, in 1882 the district manager of a Pennsylvania telephone exchange wrote a memorandum to one of his Chief Operators, giving directives that prefigured the emerging division of labor between the sexes:

FIGURE 3.1

AN EARLY SWITCHBOARD, WITH MALE OPERATORS, IN 1879.
COURTESY OF AT&T ARCHIVES.

Please secure a young lady at once and break her in, as we will put up a new board in two weeks. Her pay will commence as soon as she is able to run the board middling well. Also secure at once a young man or boy to be a night operator and to assist you if necessary during the day.[4]

Implicit here are certain doubts about women's capacity to work the board (her pay would be contingent on her competence) as well as an implicit denial of responsibiities reserved for her male counterpart.

Other managers were more explicit in voicing their doubts. Thus, in 1885 Thomas Lockwood, who would later become chief patent attorney, wrote to Theodore Vail, then general manager of the firm, questioning the wisdom of hiring women operators. By this time in Boston, Lockwood observed,

the [day] operators are all females, which of course has its advantages...which here it is unnecessary to comment on. [Yet] notwithstanding the pronounced opinion of resident authorities that female operators are much superior to males, the fact remains, viz: that the office manager, unless an unusually well-balanced man, is liable to form preferences, in favor of some to the exclusion of others. The young ladies also appear fond of airing their voices, and sometimes prolong conversations, to talk with subscribers, again losing time. On the other hand, they exceed the males in civility and general attention to the tables [early switchboards].[5]

Despite such reservations as Lockwood here expressed, the feminization of switchboard work proceeded rapidly, apparently owing to the "advantages" to which he alludes. By 1894, women made up a clear majority of the company's operators and fully 5,133 of the its 12,553 workers overall. Women were still rarely employed at night (the company feared for their safety during off hours), and all but 300 of these 5,133 women operators were employed during daytime hours.[6]

Yet this customary restriction on women's employment too began to fall away. Thus, a mere six years after expressing his doubts about women's fitness to work switchboards, Lockwood himself suggested to the president of American Bell Telephone that the company "let female operators do the night work as well as the day work:

I am well aware that a prejudice exists against employing females for night service, and that it has been deemed an unsuitable practice. Formerly, and in some localities, it may have been so. Now, and in the ordinarily safe and well protected offices of the New England Co., it seems to me that such an idea is not well founded; and that the objection to employing females for night service is purely a sentimental one.[7]

By the eve of World War I, the practice of employing men at night had in fact given way, as females had come to make up fully 99 percent of the firm's operators (Greenwald 1980:190). In the space of one generation, switchboard work had completely changed hands. It had been so completely redefined as an inherently 'female' job that a company report could later view the initial hiring of men as a historical mistake: "When one gets down to essentials, it was a job for which [boys] were not fitted by temperament or training."[8]

Recent efforts to understand the causes of occupational sex-typing have emphasized the economic reasons that underlying the feminization of jobs predominantly held by women. This emphasis is perhaps most notably developed in Margery Davies' *Women's Place is at the Typewriter* (1982). Seeking to understand why clerical jobs, a male domain before the Civil War, had been socially constructed as 'women's work' by the turn of the century, Davies stresses the role of wage levels and labor supply. In her account, the changing nature and scale of capitalist production dramatically increased demand for clerical labor, giving rise to new and more specialized office occupations not yet controlled by either sex. The supply of educated men was not sufficient to satisfy the demand, for men could typically gain jobs as managers, foregoing lower-level positions as clerical workers. Relatively well-educated women were, however, in great supply, as domestic and farm production released large numbers of workers for paid jobs in the nation's growing cities. Particularly inasmuch as women earned so much less than men, Davies concludes, employers enthusiastically used women to supply their growing office staffs. Although she does discuss cultural and ideological conceptions of women's temperament or 'fitness' for routine office tasks, Davies views them as justifications offered after the fact, only masking decisions made on economic grounds.

Samuel Cohn (1985) takes this economic approach even further, again arguing that economic interests explain the process of occupational sex-typing. Cohn contends that employers are typically biased toward the use of male labor, but that economic pressures force them to hire cheaper female labor whenever wages make up a substantial proportion of the cost of production. Cohn therefore views the feminization of office work as but one instance of a broader process whereby employers resort to cheaper labor power in labor-intensive work organizations. Like Davies, Cohn develops a model of sex-typing that stresses economic factors and pays little attention to the ideological categories managers invoked.

There is no doubt that economic forces played a role in the Bell system's reliance on women to staff its telephone exchanges. When Thomas Lockwood referred to the "advantages...which it is unnecessary to comment on" that accompanied the use of women operators, he probably had in mind the economic benefits that stemmed from women's lower wages. Elsewhere, he is more explicit, lamenting how "difficult it is to get the right person for such a position, for reasonable compensation." As Cohn (1985) would point out, in the manual era of call switching, telephone operations were in fact quite labor intensive, a fact that pressured management to use less costly, female labor wherever possible.[9]

At the same time, the evidence strongly suggests that the company's assumptions about the men's and women's temperaments were not merely a post hoc rationale, but actively informed its decision to substitute female labor for male. The evidence suggests that the factor uppermost in management's mind was its manifest dissatisfaction with the boys' insubordination and indiscipline. By relying on women workers, the company hoped not merely to gain an ample supply of cheap labor, but also to find a more submissive and compliant raw material with which to operate its telephone exchanges.

The point is apparent in abundant comments on the boys' comportment. One contemporary observer described male operators as "noisy, rude, impatient. [They] talked back to subscribers, played tricks with the wires and on one another." Another said that "a telephone call under the boy regime meant bedlam and five minutes; later, under the girl regime, it meant silence and twenty seconds."[10] Even Thomas Lockwood, the company official who initially favored the use of men, later observed that male operators were "often careless, and slow, and (if I may judge by my own experience) usually uncivil and discourteous; sometimes extremely so."[11] Boys sometimes even responded to real or imagined slights by threatening the well-being of subscribers:

> When [boy operators] had to report to a subscriber that a line he wanted was busy, they expected themselves to be believed. If their word was doubted, as it was not infrequently, there was an exchange of amenities over the wire which often involved a short and ugly noun.... There were reciprocal threats of punched heads and other bodily injuries and, now and then, an overt act of physical combat. They were a virile lot, those boy operators.[12]

It was behavior such as this (which management viewed as characteristically male traits) that led management to search for a supply of more obedient and better-mannered workers. In fact, management's earliest experiments with women operators promised to satisfy this need. Wrote one manager in 1881:

> Our experience has been [most satisfactory] with young ladies' help; the service is very much superior to that of boys and men. They are steadier, do not drink beer and are always on hand (quoted in Chapuis 1982:54).

In short, the firm began to rely on female labor at least partly because management assumed that "young women were capable of greater civility and could more easily tolerate monotonous work" (Norwood 1990:27).

The company's assumptions regarding women would ultimately prove faulty, as women operators failed to provide the docile labor force that management sought. Yet the company's conception of women as inherently different from men set in motion structural processes that would endure for over a century. The feminization of the switchboard at AT&T began a pervasive system of sex segregation that reserved virtually all rewarding, skilled jobs for men. It also reached into efforts to challenge the company's authority, introducing divisions into the workers' movement to establish trade unions at AT&T. Furthermore, the influx of vast numbers of women into the Bell system affected the company's relationship with its workers, inviting managers to adopt a protective and eventually paternalistic stance toward its largely female work force.

The Rationalization of the Labor Process, 1890–1915

Following hard upon such changes in the allocation of jobs between the sexes, there also occurred a thorough transformation in the structure of the jobs themselves, as the quasi-craft job structures inherited from the telegraph industry gave way to more fully rationalized and standardized work processes.

The basic unit of work in the telephone industry has historically been the production of voice connections between subscribers (see Mueller 1989:540). During the manual era of call switching, connections could be only fashioned by hand—manufactured—by operators using manual cords and jacks. In fact, but for its more confined character, telephone operating has long resembled the work of clothing and textile production. In both cases, workers tend machines—bobbins and spools in the one case, flashing lights and jacks in the other—responding to their constant demands.

Ironically, an advertisement for the Bell system that appeared in December 1915 sought to idealize AT&T's workers precisely by alluding to the kindred nature of textile and telephone work. The upper half of the advertisement showed a young operator holding telephone lines in her hands like so much yarn, laboring to make connections between factories, farms, and cities on the horizon. The text below the operator read:

> Upon the magic looms of the Bell System, tens of millions of messages are daily woven into a marvelous fabric.... Day and night, invisible hands shift the shuttles to and fro, weaving the thoughts of men and women into a pattern.... The weavers are the 70,000 Bell operators [who] sit silently at the switchboards, swiftly and skillfully interlacing the cords...

The painting used for the advertisement was entitled "Weavers of Speech."

As we shall see, by the time this advertisement appeared, few operators would have thought to describe their switchboards as "magic looms." Yet only a generation before, switchboard work had still accorded operators considerable autonomy and variety in their work. Until the early 1890s, operators still performed a broad variety of tasks quite apart from the handling of cords. In the industry's earliest years, male operators were expected to sweep out their offices, to keep coal on the fires, to run errands, and to relay messages for members of the community. Sometimes operators even helped with repair work. Thus one operator recalled straightening out telephone lines that were crossed during high winds, putting them back in service whenever the situation required.[13] A woman operator in a middle-sized Connecticut town wrote in her memoirs that during the first decade of this century:

> When the repairman was out of town, I would visit a subscriber's station and repair any trouble I was able to locate, and even fix things on the main frame of the switchboard (in Greenwald 1980:195).

In the absence of mass media, operators served as conduits of news, information about social events, and varied matters of concern to subscribers. Katherine Schmitt (1930:20), who worked for New York Telephone, recalled that "the questions subscribers used to ask me made my job a combination of personal service bureau and general guide to the city of New York." In return for good service, subscribers sometimes gave gifts to operators they came to know. As one worker recalled: "Subscribers used to send us boxes of candy and flowers, and drop in to see us."

The work process itself involved great uncertainty, partly owing to the primitive state of operating equipment. Careful coordination between several operators was needed to complete calls within the same local exchange; where calls involved subscribers in different exchanges, the process involved "all the thrills and hazards the radio fan experiences when he tries to tune in on London."[14]

In almost all exchanges, the work process divided the handling of incoming calls from their final completion. In the early 1890s, one commonly used system distinguished between the "case" (a long wall of electrical panels, each serving 100 lines) and "trunk tables" (tables that held the connecting points of telephone lines). When an operator at the case detected an incoming call (initially, with an annunciator, but later with signal lamps), she pulled a lever that opened the line and determined which number the caller wished to reach. She wrote it on a slip of paper and posted it near the case; a messenger then relayed the slip to the trunk table, where a second operator used plugs and jacks to close the circuit and complete the connection.[15] Often, operators at the case had to shout to their counterparts at the trunk table, informing them that an earlier call had been terminated and the line could be disconnected. In urban exchanges, where hundreds of calls were handled at a given moment, the usual state of affairs approached (in the words of an engineer at Western Electric) "perfect chaos."[16]

Such levels of uncertainty comprised a formidable obstacle to the standardization and rationalization of switchboard work. Yet as switchboards grew more sophisticated many of these obstacles were broken down. In the mid-1890s, apace with the development of electrical equipment in general, a number of important improvements in switchboard technology were introduced. Signalling lamps now replaced annunciators, enabling operators to see at a glance when callers had lifted their handsets and when they had hung up. A common battery system was developed at this time, providing a centralized source of power for each Bell handset (obviating the need for hand cranking and eliminating problems of transmission). These innovations ran parallel to (and facilitated) organizational changes in the structure of the work process. By the middle 1890s, AT&T management instituted a series of reforms that rapidly standardized the nature of each operator's job.

The historical record provides only patchy evidence of this rationalization process, yet it suggests that at least three important changes occurred. First, detailed rules governing both work methods and workers' behavior were established. Second, supervisory positions and procedures were standardized. And third, company training procedures were formalized. Taken together, these changes enabled management and engineering staff to approach traffic work performance more quantitatively than ever before, even using mathematical equations to estimate traffic loads and force requirements. The outcome exposed operators to a level of discipline and control that rivaled that found in any factory labor process.

There is no record of written rulebooks or employee handbooks in the Bell system before the 1890s, but the decade of the nineties saw many operating companies publish pamphlets of this nature. The earliest versions were abstract, speaking in general terms about principles and expectations the company sought to establish. A few years later, the same versions grew more detailed, providing a dense network of rules. Thus the "Instructions for the Guidance of Employes" published by the New York and New Jersey Telephone Company in January 1893 articulated over a hundred rules for employees to follow. Among them:

> No. 46. Operators will be expected to report promptly at the hours assigned to them and will cooperate with the office Manager in keeping their switchboards in a neat and clean condition.

> No. 47. Operators replying to calls will use only the words, "What number?" The number must be repeated back to the subscriber, that he may know it has been received correctly... and use the words proving the figure numerically, as follows: "Two-O," "Three-O," "Four-O," etc.

> No. 48. In making a call for a subscriber on a direct wire, the operator will give three distinct rings...[17]

To ensure that these rules were put into practice, operating companies began to adopt more standardized methods of supervision, establishing fixed hierarchies of authority that had been absent in many exchanges before. Indeed, the first announcement of the new authority structures was sometimes found in the employee handbooks. Thus, Rule No. 43 directs:

> In all offices where more than one operator is employed, a Chief Operator shall be designated, who shall answer all questions, receive complaints and be kept advised of any work being done liable to affect the proper working of lines or instruments.[18]

In larger exchanges, the Chief Operator (typically a middle-aged male) occupied a desk in the middle of the floor; his assistants (normally female) stood behind the operators, closely watching the women who had been assigned to them. As the photograph shows (see figure 3.2), first-line supervisors could often plug into

FIGURE 3.2
A CENTRAL OFFICE ON CANAL STREET,
MANHATTAN, IN 1928.
COURTESY OF AT&T ARCHIVES.

a given worker's board (depending on the equipment used) and monitor her compliance with the company rules.

The third change affected newly recruited workers, who now encountered a rigorous training program designed to inculcate the new work discipline the company sought to establish.[19] Operators' Schools, housed in the larger central offices, contained lecture rooms with blackboards and practice switchboards. A silent film intended for company training purposes that dates from 1920 shows new recruits being shepherded into the practice rooms, with supervisors paying great attention to their subordinates' movements even in approaching their boards. When seated in the school's classroom, the new recruits collectively practiced pronouncing their digits and the names of the local telephone exchanges (see Brooks 1977:18; Norwood 1990:41). Underlying these training practices was an ethos the company wished to impart—disciplined devotion to service in precise conformity with the Bell System practices.

Initiated in the 1890s, by the eve of World War I this process of rationalization had imposed a tight set of controls on the workers' speech, physical movements, and even posture. By 1915 one operator told an inspector for the federal government that she and her fellow switchboard workers were "not allowed to turn their heads—not even allowed to smile, to fold hands or to cross their feet, nor even to lean back in their chairs." The same inspector reported being told by another operator that:

> When a girl passes her plug to the girl next to her to complete a connection, her eyes must not follow in that direction. She must never turn her head to the side or look at anything except the board in front of her. The service must be kept up at any cost.[20]

The operator's job had been so thoroughly rationalized that one long-term Bell worker described her central office as a complex web of surveillance, with

> everybody watching somebody else and the whole gang watching the poor operators and trying to get more speed out of them. It's the greatest speed up system in the world (in Greenwald 1980:200).

Not surprisingly, as the social relations of production acquired a

Taylorist face, labor struggles grew increasingly frequent and combative.

Strikes within the Bell system had been recorded as far back as the 1890s, and demands for union recognition had not infrequently emerged among skilled craftsmen. Typically, the latter workers were electrical tradesmen who had been hired to install and maintain cabling, lines, and boards and who sought to establish craft control over the supply of skilled telephone labor. Save for isolated areas in the West, their struggles typically came to naught. Even when they tried to organize region-wide federations of telephone tradesmen, under the aegis of the International Brotherhood of Electrical Workers (IBEW), skilled workers found that craft unionism rested on too narrow a base to succeed.[21] By 1910 trade unions of Bell workers were restricted to tiny islands in Bell's ocean of non-union operations.

Partly owing to the transformation of work within the Traffic department, however, by the second decade of the twentieth century labor struggles gained strong momentum among operators for the first time. Faced with the larger structural changes just sketched, operators began to raise a number of specific demands relating to their terms and conditions of employment. The women worked six days under intense controls, and yet their wages were too low for single women to support themselves. Pay schedules were slow to reward increases in workers' proficiency, giving the firm peak output from operators with no improvement in pay. Many operators felt compelled to work overtime, yet Bell companies usually refused to offer overtime rates. A further source of discontent was the "split trick," which forced operators to leave work during slack periods of traffic, spreading their nine and a half hours of work out over a fifteen-hour period.[22]

By 1912, the Telephone Operators' Union, affiliated with the IBEW, began to organize telephone exchanges with great success, gaining a contract that provided for the eight-hour day and relief from the split trick. To defend their contract despite management intransigence, workers had to strike in 1913 (dubbed "the uprising of the 2,200"); their victory provided further impetus to unionization throughout the Bell system. With the entry of the U.S. into World War I, the federal government took control of AT&T's operations in 1918. Loathe to antagonize business, the

Wilson Administration resisted further unionization efforts. By 1919, however, when federal controls were lifted, the Operators' Union had gained sufficient support in New England to conduct the most successful strike against any Bell operating company up to that time (indeed, their 1919 strike was one of the few victories American workers won in the immediate aftermath of the war).[23] Sensing a opening in management's defenses, operators began to flood into locals affiliated with the Operators' Union, which reported chartering more than 100 such locals in 1919 alone (Greenwald 1980:225). Strikes extended into the Midwest and even the South. At the outset of the 1920s, IBEW leaders could claim "two hundred locals and 25,000 women in the U.S. and Canada," a fair-sized minority of all Bell operators. Labor struggle and organization had emerged in force within the Bell system.

Ironically, the mobilization of the operators posed an implicit threat to the position of skilled craftsmen in the Bell system and confronted them with a dilemma. On the one hand, the craftsmen needed to join with the operators in order to achieve their own goals. Yet by opening their unions to the operators, whose numbers far surpassed their own, they risked losing control over their own trade union organizations and even watching them evolve into what some craftsmen derisively called "petticoat unions." The men's great fear was that internal divisions and conflicts within the IBEW would increasingly be resolved along lines dictated by the women themselves.[24]

With such fears in mind, the IBEW constitution had explicitly barred women from joining affiliated locals until 1895. As late as 1918, a group of IBEW members introduced a motion at the union's annual convention to deny women voting rights within the IBEW. Arguing in favor of the motion, members of the IBEW Executive Board formally stated:

> We think there can be no rule of ethics or of human right which requires men handling the sting of electricity to submit forever to the rule of telephone operators in their methods and conditions of work simply because [operators] have tried that arrangement [paid labor] for a while (in Schacht, 1985:15).

This view saw women as untrustworthy migrants, intruding on male terrain.

Owing to the women's growing success at organizing, the motion failed to carry. In its place a compromise was reached: Operators were admitted into IBEW-affiliated locals, but their votes counted less heavily and their dues were set substantially lower than was the case for men. In exchange for accepting such second-class citizenship, the women were granted complete autonomy within their own division of the IBEW.[25] Although the schism between the two occupational groups lingered throughout the industry, with craftworkers occasionally crossing the operators' picket lines, this compromise achieved at least a modicum of labor unity. The threat which labor struggle posed to management, however, was less easily resolved.

There can be little doubt that the rise of labor struggle within the Bell system caused great alarm among the company's top officers. As early as June 1912, the vice president of the Bell system, H. B. Thayer, alerted the officers of each operating company that "trouble is being experienced at the present time with the operating force in Boston," where "progress has been made in the formation of a union of the operators."[26] Thayer was sufficiently concerned about such developments that in August of that year, when even further progress toward unionism had been made, he visited the Boston offices for himself, personally advising local management in its anti-union strategy.[27]

The workers' movement reached its height in 1919, when New England operators led a regional strike that brought New England Bell to its knees and gave enormous momentum to organizing among Bell workers. By the early 1920s, as company resistance was redoubled and the American workers' movement more broadly began to wane, organizing drives among Bell workers were thrown on the defensive and the newly founded locals soon began to disband. In its various pronouncements, management began to express a feeling of relief that the company had weathered its most violent storm. Yet the insurgence of Bell workers had breached the company's defenses, exposing a serious absence in the company's internal operations. Despite its prowess in the marketplace and growing sophistication in its laboratories, AT&T had failed to develop any clear mechanisms with which to maintain control over its own employees. Even before the workers' movement receded, management had begun to take steps to redress this situation. The question, then, is what sort of labor control mechanism evolved and why.

THE STRUCTURE OF LABOR CONTROL AT AT&T

Recent theories of work and authority lead us to expect managerial control to unfold at one of two very different realms. Deskilling theorists and others concerned with the labor process expect that machines will play a critical role in management's effort to maintain its control over labor, completing the division of labor that Taylorism began. By contrast, labor control theorists such as Edwards, Friedman, Burawoy, and others have stressed the importance of broader organizational and ideological structures superimposed on the labor process. The following analysis will explore the validity of these two approaches with respect to the structure of managerial control that unfolded in the years immediately following World War I.

A Little Robot of Steel: The Mechanization of Labor

In recent years students of workplace technology have viewed machines not as mere technical devices, but rather as social and historical products that inevitably incorporate political and ideological influences as well. This outlook is particularly clear in the work of David Noble. In his case studies of the machine-tool industry, Noble argues that large corporations such as General Electric and Westinghouse have favored Numerical Control (NC) technologies not merely because the latter are economically viable (in many cases they are not), but simply because NC systems promise to give management greater control over production processes, cordoning production knowledge off from workers on the shop floor and relocating it to computers that can be kept under lock and key. Noble speaks for many scholars when he contends that political interests (here, the thrust for control) are built into the design and selection of machine technologies.[28]

Given the widespread influence which this 'power' theory of machines has attained (Form 1980, 1987), it is incumbent on us to ask whether technological changes comprised a salient element in management's response to the rise of labor struggle in its midst.

When we consider the evidence, we find that technological changes did indeed unfold in the wake of Bell workers' mobilization, but they did not stem from management's thrust for control over the labor process. As the following analysis suggests, production politics by itself does not seem to have prompted massive changes in the technological foundations of the telephone work process.

From the industry's inception until roughly 1920, the provision of telephone service relied entirely on manual tools and equipment. As noted, operators 'manufactured' calls by moving cords, plugs, and jacks as each situation required. The manual character of the labor process gave operators a latent source of power, as the wave of strikes during the 1910s displayed. For once operators developed the organizational resources needed to engage in collective action, they could bring the industry to an immediate halt.[29] This state of affairs began to change dramatically during the years just after World War I, when management introduced electromechanical switching systems ("the automatic") to perform the operators' tasks.

There were several different variants of switching machines (Strowger systems, step-by-step systems, and eventually Cross-Bar technology), yet all involved massive grids of wiring and electromechanical equipment that occupied entire floors within each central office building. Interestingly, the famous Bank Wiring Group studied by Mayo and his associates had been producing precisely this equipment. To meet internal demand for the new switches, management had to enlarge the capacity of the Hawthorne Plant in 1919.[30] In offices that were "cut over" to the new systems, subscribers no longer needed the operator's assistance for the completion of calls. Now they could use dial telephones to activate the mechanical switches themselves. In telephone exchanges around the country, the sound of the operators' voices gave way to the metallic tapping of electrical switches clicking open and closed. From this point on, the machine and not the worker was the 'weaver of speech.'

Mechanization of course implied an increase in technical efficiency. Even as traffic sharply increased, the industry consumed far less labor time in handling the load.[31] Indeed, it is impossible to imagine modern communications systems—or for that matter, fully developed societies—without automatic call switching in one form or another (Mueller 1989). Yet technologies do not develop in a vacuum. They are introduced into specific social contexts and (many theorists insist) acquire a significance that transcends purely technical considerations. Certainly, participants in the change well understood that the character of an entire era of telephone work was fated to disappear if and when the new machines were introduced. The question of course was why the changes occurred and in what direction they led.

Many operators experienced the shift as an assault on the human character of the industry itself. Traditionally, even after management's application of Taylorism to their jobs, operators had found some compensation from the visible fact that it was *they* who conveyed scarce information to subscribers, responded to emergencies, and metaphorically wove their local communities together.[32] When *machines* began to perform this function, consigning operators to auxiliary roles in both the work process and local community, many felt a profound sense of personal loss. Wrote one operator who experienced the transition to electromechanical switches:

> Even old Cortlandt [a central office in New York] has joined the fast-moving procession and has been cut over to dial.... I stood in that old office and watched the last calls come in that would ever be made over that familiar board. Suddenly, at a given moment, the lights ceased to come in.... As I recalled the excitement, the lights, the rush associated with that place, I felt as though I had officiated at the last rites of a dear old friend.[33]

The leader of the Operators' Union, Julia O'Connor, resonated a widely felt set of sentiments when she scorned the cold, dehumanizing system she saw emerging before her. Said O'Connor:

> You have read stories of the telephone operators sitting at a switchboard until fire burned their fingers, in order that they might serve the public. The dial telephone removes that great human intelligence in times of stress and disaster, and substitutes a little robot of steel and metal, without capacity to respond to a human emergency (quoted in Norwood 1990:265).

In some cases, this humanistic lament also drew upon a more political critique of mechanization which resembles the 'power' theory of new technology alluded to. This was the case with Julia O'Connor, who believed that the new machines were motivated by more than economic considerations and were in fact meant to reduce telephone workers' newfound strength. O'Connor articulated her views in testimony before the Massachusetts Department of Public Utilities in 1933 (reported in Norwood 1990:262-63).

> LAWYER. Do you know or have you any information as to whether or not this [1919] strike and the possibility of another strike caused the company to enter upon the policy of machine switching development?
>
> O'CONNOR: It is my opinion that it did affect the policy of the company.
>
> LAWYER. And what effect would machine switching have upon the union organization and membership?
>
> O'CONNOR. It would reduce it, of course, and would reduce the importance of the operator as a factor in telephone service.
>
> LAWYER. And therefore make the union less effective?
>
> O'CONNOR. Yes.

The question is whether, or in what sense, O'Connor's thesis is valid. Was the mechanization of the switchboard a response to the rise of worker resistance throughout the industry?

In his study of labor struggle and organization among telephone operators, Stephen Norwood expresses a measure of agreement with the O'Connor thesis and views the company's conversion to automatic switching as "a method of controlling and disciplining the labor force."[34] Norwood points out that, in many areas, the introduction of the new machines took place in the aftermath of labor struggle, and he observes that "the first New England city to switch entirely to the dial system was Lawrence in December 1924—not coincidentally, the city with the most complete strike turnout in 1923."[35] Norwood also quotes from a May 1912 letter written by H. B. Thayer (who would soon become president of the Bell system). The letter was written before the mobilization of the operators, but appears to indicate that management was not unmindful of how mechanization would affect managerial control over the work process. When Thayer was asked why European telephone systems made much wider use of automatic (dial) equipment than did AT&T, he replied that the presence of "civil service rules with regard to the operators" in most European nations "makes the operator question much more serious than with us, and therefore the various European governments are *looking toward the automatic as a possible relief from trouble.*"[36] Norwood's interpretation of this evidence suggests that when the "operator question" arose in the United States, Bell management was forced to look toward the automatic as a "possible relief from trouble," much as the European nations had done before.

Certainly, mechanization followed hard upon the rise of labor struggle, and the introduction of automatic switching machines did limit the effect of labor struggle on the provision of service, as we shall see. On the face of it, O'Connor's thesis seems at the very least plausible, and is in accordance with the power theory of machines which so many recent theorists have found persuasive. The problem, however, is that the more we consult the evidence, the less tenable the O'Connor thesis becomes. None of the company's internal memoranda, reports and correspondence on the mechanization process suggest that the issue of control over work processes ever entered into the decision to introduce machine switches. Nor was the implementation process itself informed by considerations of power. In fact, the evidence suggests that management's use of machines was less a response to shifts in control over the labor process than to the rising cost of labor power as a commodity.

Gaps in the historical record render it difficult to reconstruct the company's decisions regarding the introduction and implementation of automatic switching machines with complete precision. Still, the evidence suggests that, until 1917, although Bell management was quite aware of the technical advantages of automatic switches, the company regarded their use as economically unwarranted. H. B. Thayer took precisely this position, as is made clear in the closing passage of the letter previously quoted. Thayer wrote in 1912:

> Our studies in this country of American conditions have led us to the conclusion that full automatic apparatus was not as economical [as manual service].... We are expecting to find that economies of the semi-automatic...will be sufficient to justify new installations, but, at present, are not expecting to find that they will justify changing over aparatus now in service.[37]

By 1917, however, the company had begun to view the economics of manual switching in a different light and had taken steps to explore the availability of patents for specific switching technologies.[38] The reason did not lie in management's struggle to control the labor process but in its effort to cope with rising labor costs, as shifts in the nation's economy during the American entry into World War I dramatically increased workers' wages.

Company documents indicate that Bell workers' wage rates rose by an average of 90 percent between 1914 and 1920. While the number of Bell workers increased by 58 percent during these years, its payroll ballooned by 175 percent, with almost all of the increase occurring between 1917 and 1920, when the United States entered the war.[39] This change prompted AT&T's chief engineer to observe in 1921:

> The almost complete substitution of machinery for the work of the operator was possible and was effected in some telephone exchanges outside of the Bell system over twenty years ago, but at the then rates of pay for labor, was not, in the judgment of our engineers, economical. *With the advance in the wage of female labor,* which came about through war activities and which still exists, and will exist for some time to come, *the situation changes* and in the natural evolution of the business these devices received increased attention and study and their economy in some places was demonstrated....[40]

In short, the decision to introduce mechanized switching systems was motivated by changes in the cost of labor power, not control over its use.[41]

Much the same judgment must be drawn when we explore management's plans regarding the implementation of the new switching technology as well. The company's research on the economic effects of mechanization was voluminous. By 1921 it had generated an elaborate projection of expected changes in revenues, operating costs, capital investments, and profits within a variety of locales under the assumption of both manual and mechanized production. This analysis yielded a detailed plan of action that selected specific types of switching technologies for different types of locales, with explicit reference to various cities (including Boston, the center of the operators' union). Yet *at no point does the question of control over work relations enter into top management's calculus.* The eyes of company officials were focused almost entirely on the flow of traffic, the operating costs of particular technical systems, and the flow of revenues specific types of telephone exchanges would generate.[42]

A final point regarding mechanization concerns its impact on the occupational structure of the industry and on overall shifts in its skill requirements. Most scholars who view technology as the product of social and political preferences within the firm tend to assume that mechanization replaces skilled, autonomous labor with labor that is unskilled and consequently more vulnerable to managerial control. Indeed, the notion that mechanization erodes craft labor is so widely accepted as to enjoy the status of an iron law. Yet we find that the mechanization of telephone labor gave rise to precisely the opposite trend. Rather than reducing the prominence of skilled craftworkers, mechanization instead expanded their role (in both absolute numbers and as a proportion of all Bell workers), while it depleted the ranks of the relatively unskilled operators. Thus, as switching machines reduced the company's need for direct labor (the operators), they required increasing numbers of workers performing *in*direct labor, most notably in skilled maintenance jobs. In this industry, then, mechanization actually promoted an *expansion* of craft labor (a matter discussed further in Chapter 4).

In light of this evidence, it becomes extremely difficult to portray the introduction of machine switching systems as part of management's evolving strategy for labor control. It is true that mechanization placed limits on the effect of strikes by allowing the company to maintain local service even when workers withdrew their labor power. Yet this effect was apparently an unintended byproduct of economically motivated decisions rather than an expression of managerial design. At most, mechanization served to strengthen the effectiveness of a system of labor control that developed external to the labor process itself. This system took shape as a paternalistic managerial regime.

Institutionalizing Paternalism

Even before trade unionism had shown its potential strength within AT&T, the raw materials of a powerful managerial regime had begun to emerge. One key ingredient lay in the familistic work culture that emerged throughout the Bell system.

AT&T's treatment of its employees had always been been closely wrapped up with their gender and family relationships. On the one hand, Bell managers often sought to use kinship structures to supplement the company's authority over its workers. Partly for this reason, the company took care to hire and retain only unmarried women, particularly those living in their parents' homes (Currie 1915; Brooks 1977) for in this way its employees would be (as one manager phrased it) "more carefully guarded, and generally surrounded by wholesome influences" (in Norwood 1990:42). In fact, the company "sometimes sent investigators to *check* on the domestic status of job applicants," in order to ensure that its workers were "enmeshed in family networks...that were domestic, matrimonial, maternal" in their character" and (Schacht 1985:28).

The company's reliance on kinship as a means of social control was further manifest in such events as Family Night, an annual event when operators' families were invited to visit their daughters' work locations, to hear speeches and presentations about the firm's practices and to confer with supervisors about their children's job performance. In 1919, for example, Family Night in Buffalo, New York, was attended by more than thirty-five hundred employees and parents, who enjoyed refreshments and dancing and then heard company officials give speeches on "the importance of telephone operating as a calling for young women." Similar events were held in Traffic departments throughout the country.[43] Through such ceremonial events, the company drew upon the hierarchical nature of family life to bolster its authority over its employees.

Yet the influence of kinship relations was not confined to the firm's environment. Instead, domestic themes and images entered into and shaped the character of the firm's production relations. As a brochure for AT&T Long Lines noted, the company hoped that its work locations would "reflect the character of a business home" by including "such furnishings as a girl might wish to have in her own living room."[44] Telephone exchanges commonly housed sitting rooms, parlors, and dining rooms, imparting a clearly domestic tenor to the worksite. Because the company felt that female employees working night tours needed special protection from the dangers that late hours posed, it provided lodging in company dormitories. To help care for the welfare of its young women, the company employed matrons at each telephone exchange. These "grandmotherly types" (as one manager described them) cared for the welfare of the company's girls, helping them to adjust to the rigors of work and advising them on their behavior. Indeed, an article published by the New England Telephone Company described the initial stages of employment by saying that "from that moment the new recruit is one of the girls—one of that mother's girls."[45] Although there are no data to support the conjecture, it seems likely that the term 'Ma Bell' had its origins in the image of the company's matrons.[46]

Thus, even before the end of World War I, Bell management had begun to imbue the wage-labor relation with the affective character and moral obligations that (ideally at least) prevail within family life. By defining its women workers as persons in need of protection from the harshness and dangers of the marketplace, Bell managers placed themselves in the position of surrogate parents, benevolently safeguarding the dependents who had been entrusted to them. So inspired, a recruitment pamphlet distributed by the Chicago Telephone Company assured the parents of prospective employees that the firm would provide their daughters with the "parental care" which they themselves would apply (Norwood 1990:48).

This paternalistic orientation toward the worker emerged spontaneously and constituted an enduring feature of the firm's culture by the turn of the century. Its advantage to management lay in its capacity to encourage a deferential relation between workers and the company, placing workers in a relation of personal dependence upon the firm. As occurred in textiles and other industries, management sought to justify the inequality of the employment relationship by wrapping it in the warm fabric of family life.[47]

Until the second decade of this century, however, this paternalistic relation between the firm and its workers was merely symbolic in substance: it was embedded in the normative milieu at work, but lacked any material or structural foundation. Perhaps the company sensed this deficiency in its labor control efforts, for the ensuing years were a period in which paternalism grew increasingly institutionalized, acquiring a firmer basis in the organization of the firm. The company took a key step in this direction in 1910 when it began to experiment with welfare capitalism.

As did many large corporations during the the Progressive Era (see Brandes 1976; Brody 1980; Edwards 1979), AT&T sought to demonstrate its concern for its workers and fend off union drives by distributing benefits of various sorts. The resemblance between AT&T's labor policies and those of other monopoly corporations should not be surprising, for Theodore Vail, president of AT&T from 1907 until 1919, actively participated in the National Civic Federation (NCF), an association which brought together the officers of the largest American firms who collectively sought to fashion an "enlightened" means of averting labor struggle and organization (see Weinstein 1968). In fact, AT&T both reflected and defined the NCF's labor control strategies.

Prior to 1910, several Bell firms had adopted de facto benefit plans, though on a limited basis. When AT&T took stock of its welfare provisions, it found that a few of its operating companies were "carrying on their payrolls old, long-service employees who were not required to report for duty," under the category of a "Special" or "Awaiting Orders" payroll. As a company report later acknowledged, this "was really an informal pension list."[48] Convinced that "the progress of social thought has placed upon industry certain responsibilities" that reached well beyond the wage, AT&T began to systematize the provision of such benefits.[49] By 1912 a committee made up of top management officers recommended the adoption of a uniform Benefit Plan, including pensions, sickness and disability pay, and life insurance, through which the company hoped to provide material evidence of its concern for the well-being of its employees, instilling in workers "a strong sense of fellowship and of partnership in the business."[50]

Although similar efforts in other industries stressed savings plans and other provisions to encourage thrift among workers, Bell managers found such plans distasteful. The reason apparently stemmed from their conviction that "benefits cannot take the place of individual thrift" and that any policy "which will tend to retard the development of responsibility and self-reliance on the part of the individual must be excluded."[51] This conviction seems ironic, for the firm's labor control efforts generally fostered the very ethos of dependence which management claimed to eschew.

Despite the company's implementation of welfare capitalist policies and its effort to 'domesticate' the culture of its workplaces, labor struggle and organization continued to gain strength during the years leading up to World War I. Indeed, the most militant confrontations occurred *after* the Benefit Plan was in place. Responding to its need for an even stronger mechanism of labor control, AT&T incorporated a third and final element into its evolving regime in 1919, when top management formally adopted the Standard Oil system of "employee representation" (company unions) that had emerged five years before.[52]

In June of 1919, during the New England Operators' strike, Vail wrote to the top officers of each operating company, outlining a plan that was announced in the company's annual report later that same year. Vail's letter alluded to the company's growing labor troubles and diplomatically observed that:

> The Bell system has lost some measure of that cooperation of the whole body of employees which previously existed. To restore that and restore it quickly, you are urged to encourage your employees to form associations which shall appoint representatives to discuss freely and frankly with the officials of the company any matters of concern to them.[53]

As Vail later stated, his hope (and that of his close associates) was that the system of employee representation "would assure a closer and more informal contact between the managing officials and the other employees." In his terms, the plan was designed to

> give to the management of the companies a more intimate knowledge and appreciation of the personal problems of the individual employee...[and] give to the employees generally a clearer and more general understanding of the policies and principles governing the administration of the business.[54]

In Vail's mind, the plan would provide employees with "the possibility of being heard" regarding the day-to-day issues that spring up in work organizations, yet without weakening the *"complete subordination of employee to organization and authority."*[55] In other words, the employee associations were designed to ventilate conflicts but to leave the fundamental structure of authority unchanged.

H. B. Thayer, who would be president of AT&T from 1919 until 1925, expressed much the same sentiments. Asked to explain the company's employees' associations, he replied:

> The [Operators'] union only thrives on the discontent of its members.... The plan we evolved, therefore, was to encourage *friendly* organizations of the employees.... It is our hope that...before very long, the employees of the Bell system throughout the country will have no affiliation with any outside labor organization and will cooperate thoroughly with management (in Norwood 1990:258–59).

A general manager at the Long Lines was even more blunt: "if this new thing worked successfully, it meant the finish, ultimately, of labor unionism."[56]

In its public pronouncements and reports, AT&T management was careful to present the associations in a democratic light. But in reality, management almost entirely dominated the character of the associations. Management encouraged its employees to fashion constitutions for their new associations, but the companies retained the right to reject or modify such documents.[57] Moreover, the company exercised the decisive influence in the election of each branch's officers. It provided letterhead, meeting space and other resources free of charge, relieving workers of the burden of any dues. Elections were held on company premises, and ballots had to be signed. There were no general meetings of the members, but only of smaller, local branches. Fearing the company's retributions, few workers dared speak out forcefully at meetings of the associations.[58]

The structure of the company unions mirrored the pyramidal organization of the operating companies. Local branches were based on each work location, but were limited to no more than a few dozen employees. Each branch sent delegates to district boards, division councils, and finally to the general board. In attendance at all association meetings were not only the delegates, who received suggestions and grievances from their fellow workers, but also local management officials. Whenever delegates raised issues and made suggestions, management retained complete authority: the company was free to disregard the recommendation of the association delegates, who could then only appeal to a higher level of management.

To understand the functioning of the company unions, we can appeal to a detailed summary of the activities of the Joint Plant Council of the Illinois Bell Employees' Association (Barbash, 1952:14-16). The most prominent entries in the council's list of its achievements that year involved relatively trivial changes in working conditions ("obtained bath towels for the use of employees," "established first aid classes"), as well as symbolic activities that placed the company in a favorable light ("demonstrated exhibits at the Pageant of Progress," "President appointed to the Vail Memorial Committee"; see Barbash 1952:15). Issues of material interest were not entirely absent from the activities of the associations, however. Thus, Illinois janitors gained a half day off on Saturdays, and some provisions were made for overtime pay. Yet when members raised issues of greater importance, as in their 1925 effort to safeguard their pensions, the management-controlled board of directors refused even to consider the association's suggestions and rebuked the members for spending "a great deal of time in an effort to revise something over which [you] have no control" (Barbash 1952:14). Workers quickly learned that one did not make demands at association meetings. Rather, one assumed the "posture of the petitioner, with the decisive power in the hands of management" (Barbash 1952:13).

While the company might occasionally chide its workers for abusing the employee associations, top management counseled patience in the handling of employees, at times even likening them to children who needed guidance. As one manager recalled, during the 1920s the relations between delegates of the company unions and the management

> reminded me of the relations between the typical inquisitive six-year-old and his Dad. [T]he careful, patient consideration and answering of every one of [the workers'] questions was just as much a part of the necessary education of the Association as Dad's answers [to his child].[59]

The company union system, in short, both reflected and enforced the company's paternalistic relation toward its workers.

With the company union structure in place, the elements of a powerful managerial regime had congealed into a unified system that successfully deprived Bell workers of the organizational and ideological capacities they needed to challenge management's unilateral control. By the middle of the 1920s independent unionism had almost entirely disappeared, and by the end of the decade company unions had completely replaced any stirrings of independent labor organization. By 1927 the president of the IBEW admitted the futility of labor struggle in the face of the company's plan:

> Our experience of the last few years convinces us that were we to attempt to organize the comparatively few in each company who desired organization, it would only result in their being discharged (Barbash 1952:9).

Workers who steadfastly maintained trade union consciousness seemed to this informed observer to make up only "a comparatively few in each company."

The emergence of a paternalistic factory regime was hardly unique to AT&T. In textile mill villages throughout the American south, an even more demanding species of paternalism emerged that kept workers in a position of near-total dependence upon their employers.[60] In much the same fashion, Ford Motor Company's famous Five Dollar Day was not merely an effort to motivate workers by means of the cash nexus; it was part of a far-reaching managerial effort to control the moral values and family lives of its employees (see especially Meyer 1985).[61] What proved remarkable about Bell paternalism, however, was its capacity to endure even as the same type of regime collapsed in other industries. By the early 1920s, paternalism at Ford had been completely abandoned (Meyer 1985), and pitched battles were being waged in Southern Piedmont mill villages by the end of the same decade (Bernstein 1964; Hall et al. 1987). By contrast, Bell workers were unable to shake management's ideological and organizational hegemony even during the working-class mobilization of the 1930s. Not until the coming of World War II did substantial cracks appear in the edifice of Bell's regime. The question that emerges here, then, is why AT&T provided so favorable a terrain for the growth of managerial paternalism.

Two Firms, One Regime

Typically, researchers have argued that paternalistic work organizations tend to be locally based firms whose workers are isolated from the wider system of urban-industrial capitalism, and whose limited size enabled employers to maintain personal ties with employees. Thus Newby (1977:66) writes that "stable paternalist rule tends to be a characteristic of somewhat isolated and/or self-contained work and community situations" in which employers are able to sustain a "solidarity of place" with their subordinates (Newby 1975:157). Likewise, for Norris the maintenance of paternalism depends on the local economic attachments of small capitalists (1978:478):

> In the final analysis then the maintenance of paternalist capitalism rests on the retention of local ownership by an identifiable group of individuals and families who have historical ties with the locality.

But a mammoth national structure such as AT&T could not be characterized as small or locally based, nor did its workers reside in isolated communities. Why then did paternalism persist here even as it decayed in other branches of production?

At least part of the answer can be found in Burawoy's theory of factory regimes. In his account, a paternalistic form of production politics is especially likely to emerge where workers are dependent on a given employer, have lost command over important production skills, and are employed by a firm that enjoys a monopolistic economic position. Under these conditions, Burawoy argues that employers can successfully exact deference from their workers, who cede the company broad control not only over their work situations but over their communities as well (Joyce 1980). By applying this reasoning to two instances in which industrial paternalism emerged but soon followed divergent paths—AT&T and Ford Motor Company—we shed light on both the strengths and weaknesses of this theory. As we shall see, Burawoy's reasoning does indeed help identify those factors that explain the reproduction of paternalistic factory regimes, albeit with important omissions.

Ford Motor Company of course differed from AT&T in many

salient respects. Ford produced manufactured goods rather than services; it was far newer, having been founded a quarter-century after AT&T; its operations were much more spatially concentrated than was the far-flung telephone industry; and, unlike Bell, it employed a predominantly male work force. Alongside these differences, however, were striking similarities that make comparison of the two firms intriguing. To begin with, both firms were giant corporations, each employing roughly 400,000 workers on the eve of the Great Depression (U.S. Dept of Commerce 1975; Lichtenstein 1989:1). Both succeeded by capitalizing on the growth of mass consumption: at the same time that Henry Ford introduced an "automobile for the great multitude," Theodore Vail evangelized the virtues of universal telephone service. Both firms relied quite heavily on the principles of scientific management, with large proportions of their workers engaged in unskilled, machine-paced work.[62] Most relevant here, both firms evolved a paternalistic form of production politics, but with results that quickly diverged.

Much as Burawoy's schema suggests, one decisive reason for this divergence stemmed from the trajectory of each firm's economic location. Despite Ford's early success with the Model T, the generalization of mass production techniques confronted it with sharp competition by the end of the First World War. Moreover, as Ford's work force grew, so too did the sheer cost of its factory regime. The profits component of the Five Dollar Day amounted to more than $26 million in 1917, not counting the administrative costs of its Sociological Department. As Stephen Meyer writes in *The Five Dollar Day*, this "represented a considerable financial expenditure" that became impossible to sustain "as the automobile industry became more competitive at the end of the decade" (Meyer 1985:167). Faced with a tight labor market that threatened to drive wages even higher, Ford abruptly terminated its profit-sharing plan and abolished its Sociological Department by the onset of recession in 1920–21.[63]

A very different set of economic conditions prevailed at Bell, whose monopoly power grew ever more secure during the first two decades of this century. Between 1917 and 1927 the percentage of the telephone industry's revenues controlled by Bell increased from 79.2% to 87.4%.[64] AT&T experienced little economic pressure to abandon its production regime: Insulated against declining prices and profits, its paternalistic structure remained in place.

The diverging pattern of production politics was also closely tied to the role of the state in the accumulation process. State intervention at Ford merely served to protect exchange relations external to the production process, without directly bearing on the firm's economic position as such. At AT&T, however, state intervention played a much more substantial role, helping the firm maintain its paternalistic regime by securing Bell's status as a regulated monopoly. This arrangement had been established in 1913, when the spread of antitrust sentiment led the Justice Department to impose a measure of accountability on the Bell monopoly. In what has been termed the Kingsbury Agreement (named after an AT&T executive), the Justice Department lent public sanction to the Bell monopoly in exchange for the public's right to regulate the firm's prices (rates) and profits.[65] Thus, state intervention at AT&T acted to suppress market uncertainties, enabling Bell to maintain a solid foundation on which workers could base their economic aspirations. Indirectly, then, the state reinforced the paternalistic authority structure that Bell hoped to maintain.

Stemming directly from these conditions were variations in the degree of dependence workers had on their employer. The economic structure of the automobile industry was marked by the existence of many competing firms ('many capitals'), each of which was led to adopt a 'drive' system of production. Yet such competition also provided workers with alternative buyers for their labor power, whether in auto production or in its various satellite firms.[66] By contrast, the skills and experience of workers in the Bell system typically had little or no transferability. Since Bell was virtually the sole provider of telephone service, workers' experience in the firm had almost no value in other branches of production. Hence, the more time workers had invested in the Bell system, the more they tended to align their interests with those of the firm (especially in an era when social insurance was not yet publicly provided). Thus, during the Depression, when layoffs had eliminated almost all of Bell's newly hired workers, the average level of seniority rose from 5.6 years in 1928 to more than 13 years in 1938.[67] So senior a work force was understandably loathe to risk its accumulated rights and benefits by engaging in industrial action.

Hence the market position of the firm, the pattern of state intervention, as well as the workers' degree of dependence on their employer all help explain the persistence of paternalism at AT&T, much as Burawoy's schema suggests. Yet they provide only a partial explanation.

Seeking to rebut cultural explanations of working-class consent, Burawoy views nonwork statuses as derivative attributes that have little bearing on the formation of factory regimes. The evidence however suggests otherwise: in one respect at least, the social composition of each firm's work force seems to have shaped the outcome of its factory regime.

The first question to pose in this respect is of course whether the greater representation of women at AT&T contributed to the persistence of paternalism. This issue has been explored in several other contexts, with researchers occasionally claiming that women are more susceptible to managerial paternalism than are men. Analysts of the textile industry, for example, have sometimes argued that women have historically been more committed to family and community and exposed to norms that counsel submission to male authority. Under these conditions, the argument runs, they are less apt to challenge managerial control (see Blauner 1964; Simpson 1981; Leiter 1982). In much the same vein, Tentler (1979) has argued that women's employment within sex-segregated occupations led them to internalize traditional conceptions of femininity that again restricted their tendency to rebel.

Certainly, AT&T management hoped that its strategy of employing women would deliver an obedient and deferential work force. As discussed, it was precisely this assumption that underlay management's decision to feminize switchboard work. Yet the history of labor struggle in the years immediately before paternalism arose suggests that women were no more likely to comply with management demands than were men. Indeed, the evidence suggests quite the reverse: "Telephone operators not only formed viable trade unions, but were more militant than the men [who worked alongside them]" (Norwood 1990:4). Particularly where political conditions allowed, women telephone workers led a movement to build the largest female-controlled union in American labor history. Moreover, although their employment in sex-typed jobs did immerse them in a rigidly sex-typed world, the conception of femininity held by female workers at AT&T is not easily described as traditional. As Stephen Norwood's analysis shows, the women of AT&T actively participated in the broader cultural shift symbolized by the 'flapper' and, in so doing, sought to *defy* the parental norms they encountered in their homes.[68] It is by no means straightforward, then, that gender differences explain the persistence of paternalism at AT&T.

Yet it seems that racial and ethnic ties *did* play a salient role. Although the data are far from definitive on this score, existing evidence suggests that *ethnic* politics leaked into *production* politics, affecting the divergent outcome of paternalism at Ford and Bell.   When the Five Dollar Day was announced in 1914, 75 percent of Ford's workers were foreign-born, and a significant proportion of the remainder were the children of immigrants. In fact, Ford paternalism originated at least partly in the company's condescending perspective toward Eastern and Southern European culture and its commitment to eradicate workers' ethnic and national identities. Thus Meyer observes that "the essence of Ford paternalism" was its tendency to view "the Ford immigrant worker as no more than a child to be socialized, in this case Americanized, to the reigning social and cultural norms of American society" (1985:159). While the female composition of AT&T was initially responsible for the rise of paternalism in that firm, then, it was ethnic and national identifications that had this effect at Ford.

When war broke out in Europe in 1914, national identification among Ford workers showed a remarkable tenacity despite (or perhaps even because of) the company's Americanization campaign. Confronted with the refusal of many foreign-born workers to support the wartime mobilization, Ford was forced to spawn a more coercive labor system, using an elaborate espionage and security apparatus to engage in surveillance of workers' loyalties (Meyer 1985:183). In this more repressive context, industrial paternalism found little or no room in which to survive. Ironically, if ethnic relations had prompted the rise of Ford paternalism, they also brought about its demise.

Ethnicity also figured prominently in the fate of paternalism at Bell, but in precisely the opposite way. In stark contrast with the ethnic composition of Ford, precious few among AT&T workers had immigrant backgrounds. In 1900, between 92 and 98 percent of the Bell work force was made up of native-born whites in 1900 and, remarkably, this proportion remained unchanged until the 1940s (Schacht 1985:27–28; Greenwald 1980:277). Although the company sometimes justified its recruitment practices on the grounds of technical requirements, claiming that communications work required literacy, linguistic skills, and craft experience that immigrant workers lacked, AT&T's exclusive selection policies were by no means based merely on technical requirements. The company typically excluded Jews and African-Americans, for example, no matter what their qualifications, and hired few workers with Polish and Italian surnames until the labor shortages of World War II. Apparently it was a patrician bias in favor of Anglo-Saxon groups that guided the firm's recruitment practices. What matters here, however, are not so much the firm's intentions as the consequences of its recruitment policies. Because the great majority of Bell workers shared the same ethnic heritage as the firm's managers and enjoyed higher status than other strata of the working class, AT&T found it that much easier to engender a "sense of exclusive mutuality and superiority among Bell workers...that made them highly resistant to outside organizers" (Schacht 1985:40). In short, social ties of ethnicity and nationality *differentiated* workers and managers at Ford, but had an *integrative* effect at Bell. Interestingly, the center of organization among Bell workers was in the southern New England area, where a high proportion of workers were Irish-American. This fact seems to have fueled the development of a sense of antagonism between workers and their primarily English managers.[69] In other parts of New England, however, workers shared much the same ethnic identification as their managers, eliminating "the ethnic antagonism toward telephone company management that was so important in the larger Massachusetts cities" (Norwood 1990:261–62). Thus the data begin to indicate that it was not only the political and economic structure of work that accounts for the divergent fate of paternalism at Bell and Ford; the ethnic composition of each firm's work force played an important role as well.

The Collapse of the Old Regime

So far I have concentrated solely on the conditions that help explain the *persistence* of factory regimes. Yet clearly a theory of production politics must also explain their *transformation*. What social factors impel factory regimes to change? More concretely, what conditions ultimately led to the demise of Bell paternalism?

The fate of Bell's paternalistic regime can be summarized briefly. The old regime proved sufficiently robust to contain labor struggle and organization even during the wider resurgence of the American labor movement of the 1930s. While workers in many other industries decisively broke with the AFL mold and participated in the building of a more militant and inclusive form of unionism (most notably in automobiles, electrical goods, and steel),[70] AT&T's workers remained in the grasp of the firm's system of labor control. By the late 1930s, however, Bell's paternalistic regime began to manifest subtle fissures and cracks as stirrings of trade unionism reappeared. With the coming of World War II, trade union consciousness and action finally overflowed Bell's system of labor control.

Much as in other industries, wartime strikes began to spread throughout the Bell system, as favorable labor market conditions enabled workers to impose their will on management. As these strikes forced the federal government to make wage adjustments and other concessions, workers grew more emboldened throughout the industry. By the end of the war, trade unionism at AT&T had grown so widespread that it forced the company to engage in collective bargaining on a system-wide basis for the first time. The movement culminated in the industry's first national strike in 1947, which in effect shattered the company's paternalistic regime.[71]

What social structural changes had occurred that made possible such a dramatic assault on Bell's managerial regime? Burawoy's theory of factory regimes contends that the sources of such change in production politics are purely exogenous. In this view, shifts in the internal structure of labor control reflect structural changes in wider political and economic conditions (see Staples 1987). When applied to the case of AT&T, Burawoy's perspective does indeed point toward important changes in the political economy which brought about the decline of Bell paternalism. One such change was a decisive shift in the relation between the state and capital, as the Wagner Act took aim at precisely the sort of company unions that existed at AT&T. A second change was the transformation of the industry's occupational structure, in response to the mobilization for war. Third, there occurred an influx of new workers into the Bell system who lacked any long-term exposure to AT&T's normative or economic controls. In addition to these exogenous sources of change, however, there also occurred a further, *endogenous* source of change in production politics that is not easily squared with Burawoy's perspective—the gradual metamorphosis of the company unions into vehicles of trade union consciousness.

Perhaps the most pivotal exogenous development that served to undermine the old regime at Bell was the transformation of U.S. labor law under the New Deal. Up until 1935, AT&T had enjoyed an almost unlimited freedom in the conduct of its industrial relations. When Congress passed the Wagner Act in 1935, section 8 (a) 2 of the law prohibited employer attempts "to dominate or interfere with the formation or administration of any labor organization, or contribute financial or other support to it." Bell and other employers fought against the measure and refused to honor it until the last judicial appeals had been exhausted. Once the Supreme Court upheld the law's constitutionality, the company was forced to make significant alterations in its labor control mechanisms to accomodate the shifting balance of political power within the wider society.

Initially at least, management's strategy was based on the assumption that minor changes in the employee associations could suffice. Almost in unison, the managers of each operating company advised the officers of the employee associations to modify their names and bylaws, hold new elections, and reconstitute themselves to comply with the letter (if not the spirit) of the Wagner Act. In several cases later brought before the National Labor Relations Board (NLRB), Bell companies were found to have provided the employee assocations with lump sums of money to guarantee their survival, or otherwise to have favored the former associations.[72] Bell's strategy was "to prop up a weak and divided union structure in order to forestall the possibility of strong unions moving in" (Schacht 1985:51).

Initially at least, this strategy seemed to bear fruit. Although workers took advantage of their newfound rights and reconstituted the employee associations, many of the new unions retained their traditionally deferential posture in relation to management. The fledgling union that represented craftworkers at Bell Laboratories in New York and New Jersey was a case in point. The officers of the new union were wary of adopting a militant union stance, fearing the occurrence of "strikes, loss of wages, and ill feeling between us and our employers."[73] Management viewed such officers as men they could deal with and apparently lent both moral and material support to their election (even paying their wages when they were later subpoenaed by the NLRB). The company viewed a rival organizing campaign, led by the more militant (and left-wing) United Electrical workers, as distinctly less desirable.[74]

Yet the company was not alone in its aversion to unionism. In 1937, when activists began to link the former employee associations into the National Federation of Telephone Workers (NFTW) they found that after long exposure to paternalistic arrangements, many Bell employees were likewise wary of embracing industrial unionism. One organizer reported at the founding conference of the NFTW: "the word 'strike' is repulsive to most of our people, and the entire subject will have to be handled very cautiously" (in Schacht 1985:66). Many Bell workers were reluctant to form a strong, centralized union structure with authority over its affiliates. Instead, they favored a federated structure that left each affiliate to its own devices, with the national leadership confined to playing a supportive role. Until the end of the 1930s, the union movement continued to manifest the ideological habits formed during a generation of organizational dependence on management.

The growth of union consciousness was hastened, hothouse fashion, by economic restructuring of the industry during World War II, that strained the delicate equilibrium between Bell companies and the former employee associations. With the entry of the United States into the war, AT&T was forced to devote virtually all of its resources to its Traffic departments and its Long Lines operations, foregoing capital investments and hiring in its Plant departments. This change rapidly increased the proportion of its workers employed as operators—the least rewarding, most tightly controlled jobs in the industry—while reducing the ranks of the more highly skilled crafts (see Chapter 4). Resources were scarce, and workers experienced "extreme difficulties" in their work, as they found they had "more business to handle than facilities to handle it with" (Schacht 1985:103). To make matters worse, wages and working conditions throughout the Bell system rapidly fell behind those in American manufacturing and construction industries. Lacking affiliation with either house of labor, telephone workers were denied representation on the War Labor Board, which set national wage guidelines.[75] Taken together, these economic developments began to test AT&T's ability to contain the new unions within the structure of the old regime.

The outcome was decisively affected by a further development that fostered the collapse of Bell paternalism, as war-induced shifts in the firm's labor force rapidly eroded the degree to which workers felt economically dependent upon the firm. As the war effort got underway, management was forced to hire tens of thousands of new employees to satisfy its labor requirements, particularly in its Traffic departments. Thus, in 1939 only 8.3 percent of AT&T's women workers had fewer than two years of seniority, but only four years later, that proportion had risen to 43.3 percent. In October 1943, nearly one-third of the company's operators had been employed less than one year, a figure that was five times higher than it had been in 1939.[76]

The effect was precisely the opposite of what had happened in the 1930s. Then, the work force was made up of senior personnel who were hesitant to risk the time they had invested in the firm and tended to align their interests with those of management. Now, however, because the Bell work force had less and less time invested in the system and little seniority to risk, they felt fewer constraints on their industrial behavior. Moreover, the growing ranks of new employees lacked any long-term exposure to Bell paternalism and were not steeped in the values of the old, deferential pattern of behavior.

These exogenous changes—shifts in state policy toward the production process, changes in the economic structure of the industry, as well as an influx of new workers who were not economically dependent on the firm and had little to lose from industrial unionism—enabled workers to press their demands to the fore, straining the old regime's capacity to the breaking point. But these were not the only conditions that promoted the collapse of Bell paternalism. An equally decisive factor was endogenous, stemming from the unanticipated consequences of company unionism itself.

Although management had long intended association meetings to disseminate the managerial point of view, historical records suggest that much more than this actually transpired.[77] First, by gathering workers together in groups of even modest size, the company unions provided an opportunity for workers to overcome their spatial and organizational isolation. Delegates were able to meet their counterparts in other areas and departments, for example, to exchange information on wages and working conditions (Schacht 1985). Second, by requiring workers to plan meetings, to organize membership rolls, and to verbally justify their actions before management, the company union experience "gave the leaders a basic training course in the skills of running an organization" (Barbash 1952:51; Schacht 1985:44). Third, as workers began to compare their experiences with their counterparts in remote work locations, they began to grasp the common sources of their complaints and to appreciate the degree of centralized control the company had amassed with uniform labor policies and practices in place. Finally, and perhaps most important, the company's effort to foster a relationship of 'exclusive mutuality' with its workers, based on the idea of the 'special mission' that united all telephone employes, began to evolve in a direction that management could not control. The old sense of a "common destiny" uniting all Bell employees began to evolve into a rudimentary awareness of the interests that *workers* shared as a collectivity. This is precisely what historian Jack Barbash (1952:51) meant when he wrote that "company indoctrination" itself helped promote a shared "consciousness of industry" and collective interest among Bell workers.

Taken together, these unanticipated effects of the company union plan encouraged workers to appropriate what had been mechanisms of managerial control and use them to achieve their own needs.[78] Ironically, the employee representation plan provided the vehicle for trade union consciousness and activity throughout the Bell system. Founded in 1937, the National Federation of

Telephone Workers (NFTW) steadily progressed from a loose assemblage of employee associations to a centralized industrial union structure that succeeded in overturning Bell's once-formidable regime.

The end of Bell paternalism came quickly. As occurred in industries throughout the United States, wildcat strikes began to break out in telephone locations. In August 1942, twenty-one hundred craftworkers in Ohio conducted an unauthorized strike, demanding that Ohio Bell match the Federal government's Little Steel formula of wage increases (Barbash 1952:41). Western Electric workers honored their picket lines, helping workers win their demands within the space of two days. Amid rising tensions throughout the industry, NFTW affiliates across the Midwest began to adopt the same tactics, forcing the national officers to appoint a strike director for the first time. Clearly, "the idea of the strike had begun to lose its strangeness" (Barbash 1952:41).

By 1944 strikes began to spread throughout the Midwest, with operators staging walkouts at Dayton, Chicago, Peoria, and other cities. The Dayton strike initially involved five hundred operators but quickly radiated outward into Ohio, Michigan, and Washington, D.C., involving upwards of ten thousand telephone workers. Again the strikers won their demands, forcing the federal government to appoint a national commission to examine wages, working conditions, and job structures throughout the industry.

With the end of the war in 1945, the mobilization of labor and capital rushed to its *denouement*. In October 1945, fifteen thousand Western Electric workers in the New York metropolitan area struck in defiance of the NLRB, seeking to demonstrate their support for their union. (This was the same union whose members had declared their aversion to "strikes" and "ill feeling between workers and employers" in 1937.) More than two hundred and fifty thousand telephone workers around the country conducted a brief sympathy strike in support of the Western Electric workers, completely disrupting long distance service during that time.

Ultimately, the rise of trade union consciousness and action proved impossible for management to contain. Immediately following the war, Bell workers forced AT&T management to bargain over wages and working conditions for its work force as a whole, yielding a dramatic victory which provided substantial wage and benefit increases. Most important, the agreement signaled management's de facto recognition of a national trade union representing Bell employees. A bulwark of anti-unionism for seventy years, AT&T had been forced to admit defeat. In 1947, the NFTW conducted the first national strike in the industry's history, seeking to secure its position. After a month-long walkout, the union's members were forced to return to their jobs in defeat, but a fatal blow had been administered to the edifice of Bell paternalism. Later that year the old federation of former company unions changed its name to the Communications Workers of America.

The abolition of the old regime did not occur everywhere at the same time. At New York Telephone, for example, whose members resisted affiliation with the CWA in 1947, the key change did not occur until the 1960s, when a series of strikes eventually dispelled the old system of labor control. Indeed, an interview with one of the leaders of unionization at this company recalled the event in these terms:

> Before the strike we had employees, older guys, who would never have thought about cutting cables or vandalizing the company's property. That was like spitting on the flag. But they did it. People just didn't care about the company after the strike. *It broke that paternalistic attitude.* That was out the window. It was an awakening on both sides.

Some residues of paternalism did linger for a time. Even now, in some smaller work locations where managers and workers have worked alongside one another for many years, some manifestations of deferential behavior can be found. But such manifestations are little more than vestiges of an older historical period. The question (explored in the next two chapters) then becomes what sort of new regime has emerged from the ashes of the old.

Conclusion

In this chapter I have sought to identify the social mechanisms that AT&T spawned in order to control the enduring problem of labor struggle and organization in its midst. In the process I have applied existing theories of managerial authority, premised on either the labor process or on forms of production politics more broadly. The analysis permits us to draw a number of important conclusions regarding the emergence, persistence, and eventual decay of labor control systems.

The rationalization of work methods and the use of scientific management—elements of work that de-skilling theorists often stress—were widely applied to this industry's work processes as early as the mid-1890s. Yet, much as critics of de-skilling theory have argued, the intensification and rationalization of work only exacerbated management's problem of labor control, promoting the spread of a union movement that gained particular momentum during the 1910s. In a sense, an "amber warning light" had flashed (Burawoy 1978), signaling the inadequacy of Taylorism and prompting management to seek alternative means of labor control. During this period, management did indeed introduce new, mechanized systems for the handling of calls, uprooting the older, manually based systems. But the evidence does not support the contention that mechanization comprised an element of management's control strategy. For mechanization was apparently aimed not so much at the *politics* of production (control) as at its *economics* (the rising cost of labor power). Although mechanization did tend to weaken labor struggle somewhat, the function of labor control was for the most part served by mechanisms that lay outside the labor process itself. Put simply, it was a paternalistic regime that successfully stifled worker resistance from 1920 until almost mid-century.

Partly informed by management's wish to shelter and protect its largely female work force, the company began to 'domesticate' its work locations, intermingling capitalist production with more traditional themes drawn from the sphere of family life. To provide a material expression of its paternalist orientation, the firm developed an elaborate welfare plan to provide for its employees' needs. Finally, it developed a national system of company unions, which both reflected and enforced its paternalistic relation toward its employees. By the early 1920s, these elements had congealed into a unified structure that deprived Bell workers of those organizational and ideological resources they needed to resist managerial policies. *This* regime solved management's problem of labor control, 'domesticating' Bell workers even as workers in other industries combined to build the CIO.

The foregoing analysis therefore lends support to Burawoy's theory of factory regimes. The usefulness of Burawoy's theory is particularly apparent when we seek to understand the relative success or persistence of Bell paternalism, compared with the outcome of paternalism at Ford. In line with Burawoy's suggestions, the stability of Bell paternalism rested in large part on the firm's monopoly power, undergirded by the state, which left workers especially dependent on Bell as the sole potential buyer of their labor power.

However, the analysis also reveals the need for important qualifications in Burawoy's theory of managerial regimes. One such qualification involves his insistence on viewing nonwork statuses as epiphenomenal or derivative influences that have little material effect on the persistence of given forms of production politics. In this respect, Burawoy has perhaps too rigidly adhered to classical Marxism's belief in the primacy of production. The data here are far from conclusive, but they begin to suggest that *ethnic* politics passes over into and mediates the effects of *production* politics. This was plainly the case at Ford, whose paternalistic regime quickly foundered on its workers' continued attachment to their national identities even in the face of management's Americanization campaign. While ethnic relations fostered the emergence of Ford paternalism, they also hastened its collapse. Conversely, the very tenacity of Bell's paternalistic regime lay at least partly in the company's recruitment of workers from the most privileged, overwhelmingly native-born quarters of the American working class, workers who were more easily brought to ally with the firm than with other strata of their own social class. Not coincidentally, the most important outposts of trade unionism among Bell workers developed in precisely those cities where the company's work force was most clearly distinct from management in its ethnic composition. While the role of ethnicity will vary across different contexts, with other influences perhaps taking its place, the point is that labor control does not occur in a social and cultural vacuum, and that non-work ties—here, ethnicity—condition the relation between workers and their employers.

A second limitation concerns Burawoy's insistence that the transformation of factory regimes occurs largely owing to exogenous factors. As we have seen, a potential problem with this view is that it tends to reify factory regimes, imbuing them with a solidity they may in fact lack. As the present analysis shows, production politics can equally well produce conflict and contradiction on their own account, giving rise to endogenous conditions that force significant changes in management's structure of control. This seems in fact to have transpired at Bell. In combination with other factors, management's company union system gradually manifested unanticipated consequences, evolving from a means of managerial domination into a vehicle of trade union consciousness. Eventually, then, Bell paternalism provided workers with precisely those organizational and ideological resources they needed to bargain on their own behalf. Apparently, under certain conditions, managerial regimes can contribute to their own demise.[79]

CHAPTER 4

Capital, Labor, and New Technology

If the period from 1900–1947 at AT&T was marked by the rise and eventual collapse of a paternalistic managerial regime, the period immediately following World War II marked a transitional period, an interregnum in the evolution of labor control. The presence of trade unionism was by now established beyond any reasonable doubt, and membership steadily grew from 54 percent of the industry's work force in 1950 to 68 percent in 1970.[1] For a time stability ensued: no definite system of labor control had yet emerged in place of the old regime, but the period's buoyant economy enabled ad hoc measures to suffice.[2] The question then is what sort of regime unfolded as the postwar years elapsed.

One answer to this question has centered on the dramatic transformations that have begun to occur in the technology used at work. As we saw in Chapter 2, critics of capitalism have argued that once modern corporations are equipped with information technologies and other microelectronic systems, they can uproot whatever residues of skill and productive intelligence workers command and in the process win unprecedented levels of control over production. The purpose of this chapter is to explore the validity of this argument on the terrain of the post-war Bell system. More implicitly, the analysis will pursue the same goal with respect to the rival, 'enskilling' perspective, searching for evidence of any latent trends toward post-hierarchical models of work organization.

An especially important issue here concerns the fate of craft labor within the industry. As noted, skilled manual occupations actually expanded in the wake of mechanization, as the growing mass of automatic switches required increasing amounts of indirect, skilled maintenance workers. The questions therefore arise: How have recent shifts in the organization and technology of production affected craft work? Has management tried to simplify skilled work and to transfer productive intelligence out of human labor and into metal and silicon? Or has the use of more sophisticated process technologies instead begun to increase the skill content of craftworkers' jobs? The chapter poses parallel questions with respect to clerical work, historically the preserve of women employees. The bulk of the following analysis is developed on the terrain of the operating companies, and more specifically their Plant departments, where the great majority of skilled manual workers are employed.

TECHNOLOGY, SKILL, AND POWER AT WORK

The collision between rival models of work, technology, and power can quickly be recapitulated. Upgrading theorists have reasoned that workplace automation tends to "relax the constraints" imposed on human labor.[3] The ethos of obedience that industrial capitalism created therefore gives way to one based on discretion, knowledge, and autonomy. In short, information technologies increasingly undermine hierarchical forms of work organization, giving rise to more flexible and egalitarian ones in their stead.

Early formulations of this enskilling thesis paid little attention to managers' preferences regarding power and viewed the division of labor as a simple outgrowth of technical requirements. Assembly lines demanded unskilled labor, while continuous-process work required the exercise of judgment and responsibility. Later incarnations were less deterministic and viewed job design as at least partly shaped by managerial values and preferences. Yet even the later versions of the upgrading thesis expect new technologies to promote more innovative and participative models of workplace relations. The end result, many have claimed, is a moderation of industrial conflict and "a relative lack of a management/worker cleavage" in technologically advanced firms, as rising skill requirements breed "a worker who is more middle class, in situation and perspective" than was previously the case (Blauner 1964:151, 153. Cf. Zuboff, 1988).

De-skilling theorists dispute virtually all of these predictions. They view the doctrine of technological determinism as a fallacy, arguing that managerial values and preferences actively shape the character of technologies and even influence particular machine designs (see Noble 1984; Wilkinson 1983). De-skilling theorists also dispute any notion of a qualitative 'break' or 'divide' between industrial capitalism and the current wave of scientific and technological change. Indeed, de-skilling theorists perceive a *continuity* between earlier and later periods of capitalism, and believe that information technologies will only deepen or perpetuate the influence of Taylorist models of work design. Armed with sophisticated information technologies, the theory holds, managers can shed their reliance on skilled workers and build the functions of control and surveillance into tools and machines themselves. The end result is what Marx termed the "real subordination" of labor beneath the means of production.

Empirical efforts to resolve the controversy between these two perspectives have suffered from subtle yet real problems of conceptual slippage and ambiguity (Attewell 1990; Vallas 1990). While researchers in different camps often seem to share the same set of concerns, they tend to use identical concepts in varying ways. For example, researchers in the two camps have often taken the term 'skill' to mean very different things. For researchers in the upgrading genre, the term has meant job complexity; for researchers schooled in de-skilling theory, it implies control, power, and technical authority. Not surprisingly, such disparate uses of the skill concept have given rise to a contradictory body of findings that points in several directions at once.[4]

A further problem is that researchers have commonly viewed upgrading and de-skilling trends as mutually exclusive possibilities. This view, however, is fraught with logical and empirical assumptions that may well be unwarranted. For one thing, varying processes may unfold at different *levels of analysis*. Thus, skill content may fall in many or even most occupations, but if more highly skilled jobs increase their share of the work force, then the net result may still imply an aggregate or compositional increase in skill requirements (Spenner 1983; Attewell 1987). Equally important, opposing or contradictory trends may easily develop with respect to different *dimensions* of skill. De-skilling theorists in particular have ignored this possibility, for they have assumed that possession of production knowledge is inextricably tied to control over work methods. Yet clearly this need not be the case.

Conceivably, the complexity and autonomy involved in workers' jobs can vary in any number of ways. For example, workers' jobs may become more complex and conceptually demanding even as management enjoys an increasing ability to control the method and pace of the overall production process.

The following analysis begins by exploring the nature of work relations at AT&T during the years immediately following World War II. To gain a more fine-grained sense for the social relations that underlay occupational restructuring, it pays special attention to the transformation of the labor process at one major Bell operating company during the second half of this century. The evidence, drawn from company records, fieldwork, and survey data, suggests that automation has indeed affected the pattern of labor control, but in ways not easily squared with either upgrading or de-skilling theory.

THE STRUCTURE OF THE BELL SYSTEM AFTER WORLD WAR II

Tradition Amidst Bureaucracy

The Bell system at mid-century was a mammoth, vertically integrated monopoly that controlled its own manufacturing complex (Western Electric), research and development facilities (Bell Laboratories), long distance division (the Long Lines division) as well as twenty-two local operating companies spread throughout the United States. Although each operating company was nominally independent, its internal structure and functioning were subject to highly centralized controls emanating from AT&T's headquarters at 195 Broadway in New York. As I noted in Chapter 3, the rules and practices employed in the provision of telephone service were largely standardized across the Bell system. This standardization of the company's operations eased management's problem of coordination and planning and enabled the company to deploy resources from its disparate parts without fear of incompatibility. Thus, virtually all operating companies manifested the same pattern of internal differentiation, dividing their operations into Traffic, Plant, Commercial, Accounting, Engineering, and other such departments.

The hierarchy that arose to control the Bell system's operations was labyrinthine in its complexity and rivaled only by the military. Crews of craftworkers or operators routinely reported to first-level supervisors, whose evaluations depended on the performance of their subordinates. First-liners reported to second-level managers, who in turn reported to District Managers. These District Managers oversaw part of their department's operations throughout a given geographic area. Above the District Managers stood a fourth link in the chain—the Division Managers—who controlled an entire department's operations within each geographic region (for example, managing the Traffic department's operations in downstate New York). Only at the fifth line of supervision—the General Manager's position—did control over the operations of several departments converge. A sixth level of authority—Assistants to the Vice President—approved major decisions made by General Managers and set policy guidelines for them to enact. Ultimately, authority reached upward to the Vice Presidents, and finally the President, of each operating company. Beyond this corporate demiurge stood the parent firm, whose officers oversaw decisions made within each Bell firm.

AT&T's internal structure, then, reached as high as any of the company's skyscrapers and was as vertically differentiated as any major bureaucracy in the nation. Yet, owing to a combination of circumstances affecting Bell firms (such as their insulation from market competition, the legacy of paternalistic authority relations as well as the recruitment of managers from within the firm itself), there remained considerable room for customary or traditional forms of behavior between the various levels of managers and the work force they sought to control. In the Traffic department, the work remained highly routinized. But even there, managers sometimes sought to demonstrate some personal concern for their workers—for example, by bringing in snacks made at home or making sure fans were available on hot summer days. One senior operator I interviewed recalled having her manager bring lemonade around to the girls. "They made you feel like a person to some extent," she recalled. "It wasn't all rules and numbers then." The maintenance of informal social relations and customary procedures was greatest in the Plant department, however, where craftworkers enjoyed substantial degrees of control over their work.

Retrospective interviews with older workers and retirees who entered the Bell system in the 1950s were virtually unanimous in depicting a set of work relations that remained highly traditional in character. Virtually all of the older Plant managers I interviewed recalled that during the 1960s craftworkers retained their customary ability to influence the pace and method of their work. Often, supervisors lacked detailed knowledge of their subordinates' work methods and were unable to directly supervise their work. This was especially true in older central offices, where repeated rewiring left frame equipment impenetrable to all but the local craft force. Thus, one second-line manager suspected that his craft personnel intentionally caused troubles in their switching equipment, "to make sure there was enough work to go around." Given his limited grasp of the equipment and work methods, he could not say for sure.

Respondents in office occupations commonly recalled working in locations where people of different rank shared holiday dinners together and where children's hand-me-downs were exchanged between supervisors and their workers. Symbolic of this set of social relations was the social fabric established at the district headquarters of New York Telephone's Nassau County operations. This office, a large complex in Hempstead, New York, was a bustling community whose members went fishing together, attended the weddings of their co-workers, and came to know one another's children as well. Despite the overarching formal structure within which telephone work was performed, then, the bureaucratic structure of many Bell firms was overlaid with substantial residues of personal or communal social ties.

That such recollections are more than a romanticized image of the past is partly attested to by data bearing on changes in AT&T's degree of bureaucratization. Presumably, any trend toward increasing bureaucratization during the postwar years would be evident in the relative growth of the system's administrative overhead—the ranks of its managerial, supervisory, and technical personnel. Detailed occupational data on this question are limited to the years 1945–1960, a period of dramatic economic growth for the firm and the wider economy. Yet we find little evidence of any trend toward increasing bureaucracy within the Bell system during these years. As Table 4.1 reveals, even as the Bell system expanded by more than 200,000 employees, the proportion of its work force made up of executive, technical, and supervisory personnel remained constant, fluctuating between 15 and 17 percent of the firm's employees. One change which the data do reveal is the steady expansion of technical specialists—mainly, electrical engineers and professionals in kindred fields—who accounted for an increasing proportion of Bell's administrative personnel (rising from 24 percent in 1945 to 41.4 percent in 1960). This growth of technical professionals apparently stemmed from the system's growing use of mechanized switching systems (as mentioned in Chapter 3) and the consequent need for specialists to oversee the modernization of each operating company's equipment. Such engineering personnel were rarely involved in the day-to-day operations of plant or traffic work, however, and remained peripheral to the line of authority.

TABLE 4.1

MANAGERIAL, TECHNICAL, AND SUPERVISORY PERSONNEL
AS A PROPORTION OF ALL BELL EMPLOYMENT, 1945–1960*

Employment Category	Year			
	1945	*1950*	*1955*	*1960*
Bell System Workforce	355,167	514,819	598,014	572,628
Administrative Category: Managers and Executives	3,033	3,415	5,101	5,089
Supervisors of Business Offices or Clerical and Craft Employees	44,460	59,337	50,485	54,304
Technical Professionals	15,033	23,843	35,395	41,937
All Administrative Personnel as Percent of Bell Workforce	17.60	16.82	15.21	17.70
Technical Professionals as Percent of Administrative Personnel	24.04	27.53	38.90	41.39

Source: *Bell System Statistical Manual 1945–1962*, AT&T Archives
*Includes engineers, engineering assistants, and staff specialists employed by Bell operating companies and AT&T long lines. Excludes legal, medical, and accounting professionals.

When asked to recall the 1950s, many Bell employees and retirees used language that faintly echoed Toennies' conception of *Gemeinschaft*. Because many worksites were located in workers' communities, employees often brought locally formed friendships with them into work. Women workers in particular liked working close to home, for it eased the travail of combining paid employment and family life. In their positive regard for the warmth and affective relations that persisted at this time, however, what workers ignore is the heavy price that custom and tradition imposed on many workers, even after Bell paternalism had been shattered. Perhaps the highest price of all was paid by the company's female employees.

As we saw when discussing the feminization of the switchboard, AT&T managment historically regarded women as more submissive and docile than men—attributes it believed uniquely qualified women for employment as operators until such time as they married. This view of female employees endured even when women's behavior defied management's assumptions (as when operators mobilized a national trade union movement) and even after the collapse of the company's paternalism. Consequently, a caste-like system of occupational sex-typing emerged that channeled men and women into separate and inherently unequal jobs.

The depth of the firm's sexual division of labor is immediately apparent in Table 4.2, which shows the occupational distribution of men and women in the Bell system in 1950. As Column D of the table reveals, the bulk of the overall Bell work force was distributed into three major occupations—operators (42.7 percent of all Bell employees), craftworkers (24.1 percent), and clerical employees (18.3 percent). Each of these occupations was comprised almost uniformly of one sex or the other. Indeed, the occupational distribution of men and women workers generally had few points of similarity.

The great majority of male workers (68.3 percent) was concentrated in the skilled crafts, but significant numbers of men were scattered throughout all of the industry's occupations. Men were underrepresented in clerical jobs, however, where they were only one-fifth as likely work as were women employees. They were severely underrepresented in switchboard jobs, the most firmly sex-typed occupation in the industry. In 1950, only seventy-eight of the Bell system's 181,635 men were employed as operators. Ten years later, the proportion of men employed as operators had actually declined, for in 1960 only nineteen of Bell's 247,630 male employees worked in Traffic locations (not shown). Eleven of these nineteen men held supervisory positions.

Women in the Bell system were concentrated in only two job categories—operator and clerical worker—which together accounted for 91.5 percent of all female employees. These two occupations were the lowest paid in the industry and offered little or no chance of promotion. In the more desirable positions—most clearly, in management and skilled craft jobs—women were gravely underrepresented. As Table 4.2 indicates, only sixteen of AT&T's 333,184 women held positions as company officials. When we explore the departmental location of these sixteen female executives, we find that thirteen of them were employed in legal and financial staff positions. Hence there were only three women throughout the Bell system who occupied positions of substantial line authority, all three of whom held middle-level jobs in the traditionally female Traffic Department. Hence, of the 843 executives who managed the overwhelmingly female Traffic department, 840 were male.

Women's representation in skilled craft occupations was correspondingly small. While roughly a quarter of the Bell work force was employed in craft occupations, only sixty-nine of 333,184 female employees (or fewer than two-hundredths of one percent) held skilled craft jobs. The rigidity of this pattern of segregation becomes even clearer when we look at the distribution of the sixty-nine women who *did* hold craft jobs. All 69 were employed in central office crafts; not one held a position in a heavier craft job such as cable splicing and line work. In short, there was a nearly one-to-one correspondence between normative definitions of manliness and skilled manual work.

By the mid-1960s a coalition of women's organizations and civil rights groups began to focus attention on AT&T's employment practices (Wallace, 1976). The issue assumed all the more importance because of AT&T's status as the largest private employer of women in the United States. By 1973, the company announced the terms of a consent decree, in which it agreed to implement a vigorous affirmative action program with the goal of

TABLE 4.2
EMPLOYMENT IN THE BELL SYSTEM BY OCCUPATION AND GENDER, 1950

| Occupation | Males | Females | Total (A+B) | Percent of Total Employment | Percent of Men | Percent of Women | Females as Percent of Occup. (B/Cx100) |
	A	B	C	D	E	F	G
Officials	3,399	16	3415	.66	1.87	.005	.47
Prof. and Semi-Prof.	22,878	2,735	25,613	4.98	12.60	.82	10.68
Business Office and Sales	8,416	20,332	28,448	5.52	4.63	6.01	70.42
Clerical	9,170	84,875	94,045	18.27	5.05	25.47	90.25
Operators (including Chief operators)	78	219,887	219,965	42.73	.04	66.00	99.96
Craft and Kindred	123,996	69	124,065	24.10	68.27	.02	.06
Other	13,698	5,570	19,268	3.74	7.54	1.67	28.91
Total	181,635	333,184	514,819	100.00	100.00	100.00	64.72

Source: *Bell System Statistical Manual 1945–1962.*

equalizing gender representation in all its major occupations. In addition, and even more important for our purposes here, the firm agreed to institute a formal system of job bidding that would guard against bias and favoritism in the distribution of job assignments. This system, termed the Upgrade and Transfer Program (UTP), established an elaborate set of rules governing the distribution of positions among the firm's employees. In lieu of the older, customary mode of operation, the firm now began to establish a more universalistic and bureaucratic structure of job ladders, replete with formal rules governing employees' rights. This shift began to tug work relations at AT&T away from their traditional, pre-bureaucratic mode of functioning and toward a newer and more highly formalized style. This may in fact be among the most important effects of the consent decree.[5]

Thus, movements of aggrieved groups seeking to uproot the inherently biased nature of the company's employment practices began to erode the role of custom and tradition within Bell firms. Other sources of change also made themselves felt. Along with the spread of labor organization, informal patterns of accomodation between workers and supervisors began to give way to contractual stipulations, increasing the centralization and the formalization of authority at AT&T. The rise of economic competition also forced management to introduce a rationalization campaign, further weakening the role of informal customs and traditions. Yet no source of change has exerted a more dramatic influence than the introduction of programmable automation and other information technologies that, beginning in the 1960s, began to shift the very ground on which telephone workers stood.

Technological change began gradually as electromechanical switching equipment spread from local service into AT&T Long Lines. By the late 1960s, it accelerated to a breakneck pace as one after another generation of technologies moved into previously manual work processes. In many cases (as with the development of computer-based or 'stored program' switching systems), the new technologies prompted a growing concentration of labor in large, more formally organized offices, as the small, community-based bureaus of the fifties were closed. Increasingly, telephone work came to resemble continuous-process work. Automated control centers monitored the functioning of remote work units, detecting troubles electronically and sounding audible alarms whenever malfunctions occurred. With the advent of such new information technologies, the traditional character of telephone work rapidly gave way as the industry became one of the most heavily automated in the United States. The following analysis begins by considering the transformation of work in the Traffic bureaus, and then considers the fate of craft and clerical jobs in the Plant departments.

The 'Real Subordination of Labor' Revisited

Advocates of de-skilling theory can readily point to the work situation of telephone operators as the living embodiment of what Marx called the "real subordination of labor" (a system in which machinery enforces the method and pace of production, palpably subjugating workers to capital equipment).[6] Indeed, management has used automated technologies to achieve an intensification of labor in the Traffic department whose power and sophistication far transcend management's efforts earlier in this century.

Managerial concern with work measurement and the enforcement of production standards in the Traffic department is of course far from new. As noted previously, by the 1910s and 1920s, supervisors in telephone exchanges commonly sat behind their subordinates, using a monitor's cord to listen in on a given operator's board. Bell firms introduced a somewhat more sophisticated arrangement by the 1920s, relying on "observation boards" located in the corner of each telephone exchange, where monitors could listen in on and evaluate each worker's job performance (Norwood, 1990:33–40; Cameron 1926). While in theory, supervisors could use these methods for surveillance of their subordinates, in practice such methods proved clumsy and unreliable. Operators could commonly detect the opening of their lines by the firm's monitors, and the task of generating data on each worker's productivity proved so time-consuming as to be impractical. These limitations were scarcely affected by the shift toward electromechanical switching systems, for those operators who were still employed continued to use manual equipment. Until the 1970s, for example, directory assistance bureaus still relied on heavy-bound telephone directories, much as their predecessors decades before them.

This state of affairs began to change during middle 1970s. Then, manual directories gave way to microfiche equipment (an interim arrangement) and eventually to microelectronic information systems. Since the end of that decade almost all Traffic bureaus have been equipped with small consoles (custom keyboards and monochrome displays) connected to database systems running on remote mainframe computers. The new systems are of course far more powerful than the old manual methods and have made possible dramatic improvements in productivity. Whereas an acceptable working day in the early 1920s involved between 120 and 130 calls, computerized information systems enable operators to handle six or even seven times that number every day. These productivity gains have required a sharp intensification of labor, however, which largely rests on the new system's capacity to generate reports on each operator's work performance, enabling the company to enforce uniform production standards more easily than ever before.

Working the Switchboards   Directory assistance operators face extremely high levels of specialization and routinization: Virtually all incoming calls are of the same type, varying only by locale. There is somewhat greater uncertainty at Call Completion Service (CCS) bureaus, however. Here, incoming calls may involve anything from a toddler playing with the phone to a potential suicide. Yet even in CCS bureaus, the overwhelming majority of calls involve the same repeated operations. Much of the time, callers wish to report problems reaching their parties, repeated busy signals, or the failure of coin-operated phones. Just as frequently, customers wish to bill their calls either to credit cards or to third numbers. Finally, callers often dial the wrong type of operator, as when they dial 'zero' when they need directory assistance. In almost all cases, the operator's console contains a specially designed set of keys to handle each type of call. This fact, combined with an operator's training in uttering the same phrases in given situations, imparts a mechanical character to almost all the operator's tasks. For this reason, many operators report feeling like they "become part of the machinery" when they come to work.

An operator's tour starts when she chooses a cubicle (or "position") to use for that day. (The company does not assign

operators positions of their own, for most offices must accomodate workers on different shifts). One position is identical to all
others, symbolizing the impersonal nature of almost all Traffic
bureaus. Once an operator plugs in her headset and keys in her
identification code, calls immediately begin to stream in. The act
of logging in, then, is equivalent to punching a time clock, except
that the 'clock' (the computer console) not only indicates the time
operators have put in; it also provides data on the efficiency with
which that time has been used.

Although Public Service Commission studies take note of each
worker's courtesy and responsiveness in performing the job, the
single most important criterion of work performance is the Average Work Time (AWT)—a computer-generated measure of the
mean number of seconds an operator takes to handle each call.
AWTs manifest themselves in three different ways. First, each
worker's AWT is displayed in the corner of her computer screen,
providing a constantly updated ('real time') measure of work performance. After an especially difficult or time-consuming call, a
worker's AWT can appreciably increase, prompting the operator
to work more quickly thereafter. Second, each operator's AWT is
recorded on the office log at the end of the day. In most offices,
supervisors look at the dailies to see which of their subordinates
did well and which poorly. Finally, AWTs are also printed out in
paper form, particularly for the formal "skills and knowledge
review" that supervisors hold each month. At these times, workers receive formal evaluations not unlike report cards, with
numerical performance ratings coded in varying ways.

In offices where the second-liner feels especially secure in her
position or is nearing retirement age, the office milieu tends to be
more relaxed than elsewhere. In one such office on Long Island,
the manager has earned considerable standing in the firm after
thirty-five years of service and feels little need to demonstrate her
competence. This manager has disabled the AWT displays on her
operators' consoles, signalling her concern for the dignity of her
subordinates. Yet such offices are rare. Most second-liners in
Traffic face great pressure in monthly district meetings, as third-
liners emphasize the dollar amounts the company stands to lose
from incremental increases in an office's aggregate AWT. This
pressure trickles down to first-line supervisors, whose promotions

and raises stand or fall on their ability to deliver low AWTs. Thus the technology of work measurement is interwoven with the organizational hierarchy in ways that ensure that operators work at their maximum intensity.

Not surprisingly, a profound sense of alienation pervades most Traffic bureaus. One operator I interviewed had held a factory job before starting work at New York Telephone. Here is an excerpt from the transcript:

> AUTHOR. If you could decide all over again, would you take the same job you have now?
> PAT. I'd stay in factory work.
> AUTHOR. Would you? How come?
> PAT. I had more freedom. I was not confined. If I had to go to the bathroom I could. If I wanted to say 'Hi' to someone, I could take a few minutes to do that. [Here] it's confining. It's a choking situation at times....
> AUTHOR. What keeps you from leaving?
> PAT. Financial obligations, really.
> AUTHOR. Anything other than that?
> PAT. No, nothing.

I asked Evelyn, an operator in her late forties who works in lower Manhattan, what she likes best about her job. She answered:

> My days off. [Laughs] And that's the truth.... All I look forward to is my days off. I don't want to be there. It seems like I'm fine until I get to that building, and then I get sick.... All I look forward to is the time when I can get away from that board.

That these sentiments are in fact broadly representative of operators' attitudes emerges when we explore the survey data. Just under two-thirds of the operators in the 1985 survey "often" or "always" felt that "the only thing I look forward to on my job is getting paid" (62.3 percent). Roughly the same proportion (63.5 percent) felt that "on my job I feel as if the machines and equipment control me" rather than the other way around. Few operators dare voice such sentiments openly, however, for most (57.1 percent) report that they are frequently "afraid to say what they think because of what the supervisors might do." These proportions are far greater than in any other occupation.

Thus, although the operator's job has been highly structured since the early decades of this century, there can be little doubt that automation has only contributed to the intensification and subordination of labor within the Traffic bureaus. *Yet at the same time that such adverse changes have occured, Traffic work has rapidly dwindled away as a proportion of the industry's work force.* If automation has introduced a powerful form of machine pacing and evaluation of these workers' jobs, it has shifted a growing proportion of workers *out of* jobs as operators, and *into* relatively skilled craft and clerical jobs.

Technology and the Occupational Structure   We can begin to understand how the overall structure of communications work has historically changed by inspecting statistics on the distribution of the industry's work force among the various occupational categories over time (see Table 4.3). Such an effort must be approached with great caution, for the construction of job categories often reflects social and ideological forces quite apart from the technical content of workers' jobs (Steinberg 1990; Attewell 1990). The qualitative and survey data that follow will be indispensable for precisely this reason. Nonetheless, occupational statistics enable us to detect changes in job structures over relatively long periods of time.

As discussed in Chapter 3, switchboard work during the years prior to 1920 was entirely a manual affair. The industry's growth during these years therefore caused immediate increases in the employment of Traffic personnel. Since the advent of mechanization in the early 1920s, however, the structure of work has dramatically changed, and switchboard jobs have steadily eroded as a proportion of the industry's work force. Reflecting the increasingly capital-intensive nature of the industry's work process, skilled craft jobs have tended to expand (though somewhat erratically) in both relative and absolute terms.

This trend was first apparent in the 1920s, when large numbers of central offices were first cut over to dial equipment. As Table 4.3 shows, during this decade there was an enormous surge in demand for service, but there was scarcely any increase in the employment of operators. The growth in demand for craftworkers far outstripped that for Traffic personnel, apparently for the first time. This trend was temporarily masked by the mobilization for war in the 1940s (when investment in Plant equipment and

TABLE 4.3
OPERATORS AND CRAFTWORKERS AS A PROPORTION OF THE BELL WORK FORCE, 1914–1960

	1914	1917	1920	1929	1939	1945	1950	1960
Total Employment in Bell System	NA	NA	228,656	358,011	259,930	387,300	514,819	572,628
Operators (N)	74,234	104,613	128,530	139,328	93,353	154,078	183,780	124,065
Percent of Bell Workforce	—	—	56.2	38.9	35.9	39.8	35.7	21.7
Craftworkers (N)	40,308	45,293	47,599	94,392	70,102	71,306	124,065	163,611
Percent of Bell Workforce	—	—	20.8	26.4	30.0	18.4	24.1	28.6

Sources: Data from 1914–1945 are from *Bell System Statistical Manual, 1914–1945;* Those from 1950 on are from *Bell System Statistical Manual, 1946–1962*, both in AT&T archives.

Note: To maintain comparability across the different series, figures on operators exclude chief operators and other supervisory personnel, while those for craftworkers include foremen.

maintenance was cut to the bone). It continued, however, into the postwar period, fueled by the mechanization of switching in AT&T's Long Lines operations. The effect of subsequent changes in work has been to deepen this shift of communications workers out of the least skilled jobs and into more highly skilled occupations. By 1980 the absolute number of operators had actually fallen below its 1917 level, making up fewer than 16 percent of the industry's workers (not shown). By contrast, craft occupations continued to grow. By 1980 some 280,000 craftworkers comprised 35.4 percent of the Bell work force as a whole. The trend is clear: the more automatic the system has become, the larger the proportion of workers who hold relatively skilled positions.[7]

The magnitude of this trend demonstrates the danger involved in basing conclusions about skill requirements purely on the *content* of workers' jobs. Further, it provides clear reason to guard against the widely held assumption that mechanization necessarily leads to the substitution of unskilled labor for skilled, for in this industry precisely the reverse has occurred. The question that confronts us, then, is how the substance of skilled craftwork has fared over time, especially in an era marked by the introduction of microprocessor-based technologies into virtually every corner of this industry.

The Nature of Plant Work in Manual C.O.s

Plant departments within Bell operating companies have long functioned as the very nerve centers of the nation's local telephone network. It is here that the great majority of skilled craftworkers have been employed in occupations involving the installation of trunks, cables, and lines as well as the diagnosis and clearing of troubles throughout the local system. These functions have also required the maintenance of enormous amounts of information on the use and the condition of the system's various elements, with this last task falling to the department's clerical employees.

Until the late 1960s, the most fundamental of all organizational units within the Plant department were the thousands of Central Offices (C.O.s) distributed throughout the nation's neighborhoods. Red brick buildings that resembled grade schools, C.O. buildings once housed nearly all of the functions needed to provide telephone service within the local area. The trunks and cables that knitted subscribers together converged in the cable vaults located in the basement of each C.O. From there, the wires reached up to the first floor, which generally contained the frame and electromechanical switching equipment used to connect different telephone numbers to one another. On the second floor of a typical C.O. were located a number of separate offices, the most vital of which was the Repair Service Bureau (RSB). Reports of malfunctions ('troubles') anywhere in the local network flowed into this office, prompting workers to begin the process of identifying, diagnosing, and clearing problems in the Plant department. The key function of the Plant department—that of maintaining and expanding local service—was largely controlled by workers employed in the RSBs (see Figure 4.1).

These workers fell into two distinct occupational groups. The first of these was a clerical group, overwhelmingly female, called Repair Service Attendants (RSAs). These employees fielded incoming reports of trouble from callers and kept detailed service records on each subscriber. As shown in Figure 4.1, RSAs worked in close proximity to a second occupational group of overwhelmingly male craftworkers. These workers, called Test Deskmen (or Deskmen), were the most strategic craft in the operating companies. They were responsible for determining the location of troubles anywhere in the local network, diagnosing each trouble and then helping other craftworkers to perform the final repair. To accomplish these tasks required broad mechanical and electrical knowledge and a familiarity with Plant equipment both inside and outside the C.O. The bulk of the Deskmen's skills, however, were analytical, requiring virtuosity in the manipulation of electrical meters and troubleshooting devices installed at the Test Desk position. Deskmen turned dials that ran small amounts of current through remote cables, and then interpreted the test results. Knowing the guage of the wire at issue, its resistance, and the technical context of remote cable boxes and switches in the field, Deskmen could usually determine both the nature of given troubles and even the location of the fault as well. Sometimes Deskmen could diagnose the state of a cable simply by listening to the tone it carried.

Deskmen occupied an especially strategic position within the Plant department. No repair could begin until they completed their diagnostic work and forwarded the trouble ticket to a worker in the

FIGURE 4.1

A REPAIR SERVICE BUREAU IN MID-TOWN MANHATTAN, 1930.
COURTESY OF AT&T ARCHIVES.

relevant repair craft. Deskmen still played an important role even after the trouble had been located, performing tests and conveying information in league with the worker actually completing the repair. When a given trouble was 'dispatched in' (referred to workers elsewhere inside the C.O.) for repair, Deskmen used remote loudspeakers to direct the efforts of workers at the switching equipment itself, providing highly visible evidence of their authority. "They really ran the show, and they made a lot of money," recalled one former switchman. "They were the hub. Everyone had to go to them." Because workers in the repair crafts depended on the Test Desk for information, the former group was sometimes called (somewhat unfairly) *"the tester's arms and legs."*

Thus, a distinctly hierarchical relation existed among the crafts which placed the Deskmen in a roughly aristocratic position. Photographic evidence suggests that the superiority of their position was particularly clear in earlier decades (see Figure 4.1). In the 1930s, for example, Deskmen dressed more like managers than workers, even wearing jackets and ties. Retrospective interviews suggest that their aristocratic position endured even as late as the 1950s and early 1960s, by which time they had adopted a more casual or common style of dress. One worker recalled that even in these latter years the Deskmen "thought they were bosses. I mean, *they were worse than the foremen.*"

Although workers in other crafts occupied subaltern locations in the labor process, they nonetheless commanded a substantial body of technical knowledge and expertise in their own right. When a trouble seemed to lie in a faulty cable or a pair of wires outside the C.O., the task of locating and clearing the trouble fell to members of the outside crafts—usually, cable splicers. Splicers worked out of garages that served each C.O., driving repair trucks equipped with electrical tools and equipment such as tone generators, electrical test sets, cable books (maps of the local grid), and headsets with which to listen in to the line. To find an aerial (above ground) trouble, a splicer used many of the same techniques as did the Deskmen, taking ohm and voltage readings and adjusting for the wire's resistance to estimate where the current seemed to fail. A common technique was to send a surge of electricity through a specific pair of wires, causing them to short out at the precise location of the fault. By attaching a tone generator to successive places on the wire and listening to see where the tone faded away, splicers could identify the faulty portion in the cable and then set about completing the repair.

Although splicers and Deskmen used many of the same diagnostic skills, there were three major differences between their jobs. First, splicers worked only with the outside portion of the network—the portion of the cable that ran from the customer's premises up into the basement of the C.O.—while the Deskmen oversaw the entire network in the local Plant installation. Second, the splicers were physically engaged in the repair process, while the Deskmen had left their manual skills behind.[8] In fact, the 'manual' skills required in a splicer's job were extremely important. For example, after opening a cable to repair the wiring it contained, a splicer had to use an acetylene torch, solder, and lead insulation to forge a weatherproof seal. In underground jobs, where the danger of sewer gas ruled out the use of torches, splicers had to fashion metal insulation by hand, pouring hot lead over the wires and molding the metal into an insulation sheath (a technique called "wiping a sleeve"). A splicer who was skilled in this technique could form sleeves that were smooth enough to show his own reflection.

Given the differing levels of manual involvement, a third difference between the two occupations arose involving workers' shared conceptions of themselves. Given its physical demands, the job of the splicer gave rise to an occupational identity that emphasized the worker's physical toughness and willingness to clear troubles others could not find. By contrast, the occupational identity of the Deskmen stressed the members' mental acumen and capacity for precise analysis. One Deskman said: "On the outside you only had to be right within six feet. On the inside there was hardly any room for error at all."

In addition to the splicers, a second subaltern group that worked with the Deskmen was comprised of workers in the switching crafts, who located and repaired troubles that occurred inside the C.O. itself. Until the late 1960s, virtually all such workers were employed at C.O.s equipped with Cross-Bar switching systems, a variant of the same electromechanical equipment that first supported dial telephones. Such C.O.s had two distinct parts: the frame, usually located on the first floor of the C.O., whose function was to support the myriad wires that stretched upward from the cable vault; and the switching equipment itself, where each pair of wires attached to the network could be connected to the electrical destination the caller had defined.[9]

Frames in Cross-Bar C.O.s were composed of long arrays of upright metal columns called verticals which stretched twenty feet from floor to ceiling. Each vertical contained hundreds of wires arrayed in horizontal rows. Both the verticals and their rows of wire were numbered, enabling craftworkers to locate connections involving particular cables and pairs of wire. The number for each "cable and pair" in a given area provided a sort of mechanical address, identifying the equipment used to serve each subscriber's telephone. When a trouble occurred that was traced to the C.O. itself, an inside craftworker had to find the specific cable and pair of wires dedicated to that telephone number and locate what part of the frame or switch had malfunctioned and where. Workers in the switching crafts used many of the same principles and techniques that were used by splicers to pinpoint troubles in the system. Yet given the cramped contexts through which the wiring flowed as well as the intricacy of frame equipment—a medium-sized urban frame handled 100,000 lines—finding and repairing troubles inside the C.O. was often an exacting task.

The older the frame and the more often it had been rewired, the more incomprehensible it became to outsiders. Particularly where craftworkers had been lax in recording changes made to the equipment, schematic diagrams became nearly useless. Customarily, supervisors could not make sense of the labyrinth of wire that ran through the frames and had to depend on the will of their subordinates to keep the system up and running. This situation gave switching workers considerable autonomy over the methods and the pace of their work. Said a former frameworker who has since been promoted to middle management:

> The craftsman for the most part ran the job. If I was a frame-man today and behaved like that, *I'd fire me*. Things were routinely done that were unacceptable. Craftsmen'd look at a job and say, 'That's overtime.' So they'd go slow during the day and finish the job on time and a half!

This remark referred to the late 1960s, when a tight labor market and high demand for new service enabled craftworkers to expand their control even beyond its customary level.

Often, troubles that had been dispatched 'in' occurred not in the frame itself but in the switching equipment installed on the second floor, where the C.O.'s wires converged for interconnection. In such cases, Switching Equipment Technicians had to locate the source of the trouble, again working in league with the Deskmen. During the heyday of Cross-Bar equipment, each connection was formed using mechanical contact points (much like those in old automobile ignition systems) which repeatedly opened and closed in response to dial equipment. Cross-Bar installations therefore tended to be quite noisy, especially during hours of heavy telephone traffic. The busier the system, the greater the number of switches that clicked open and closed at any given time. In fact, switchmen who knew their equipment well could sometimes sense the occurrence of troubles simply by using their ears: if the relays in a given vertical all clicked at the same time and then locked up, the switchman knew a cable failure had just occurred.

Usually, however, switchmen learned of troubles via reports that streamed in over teletype machines. Switching troubles could have any number of sources: the wires leading into a switch often shorted out, power supplies sometimes failed, and the contact points in a switch eventually wore out after years of constant use. The switchman's task was to determine which component in the switch had failed and then to replace the faulty part. The task sometimes required coordination with the tester, but often left the switchmen on his own, using smaller and more portable versions of the meters found at the Test Desk position. There was sufficient autonomy and expertise involved in the process that good switching workers could take pride in clearing troubles that had confounded other workers. Said a former switchman who worked alongside seventy other craftworkers: "I could walk up to any job, any installation, look at that job and within five guys I'd know who did that job."

Workers often learned the fundamentals of specific methods and machines at company schooling sessions, but the equipment changed so often and varied so widely between different suppliers that informally produced knowledge was critical to the effective performance of their job.[10] This fact placed further distance between supervisors and the labor process they sought to command. As one worker put it: "Most first liners haven't picked up a tool in fifteen, twenty years." They were therefore quite literally out of the loop.[11]

One final group of workers whose labor undergirded Plant work was made up of clerical employees in varying occupations. As we have seen, these jobs were overwhelmingly held by women, whose general function was to file and retrieve information that was essential to the department's work. This was precisely the job of the Repair Service Attendants (RSAs) depicted in Figure 4.1. These workers recorded service histories for each piece of equipment attached to the network, filing the data in large wooden tubs. At times, RSAs could play a role in the diagnostic process. For example, when a number of troubles began to stream in from the same location, an experienced RSA would suspect a common source, and alert the Deskman to the possibility of a cable failure. RSAs also came to develop some familiarity with the vocabulary of repair work. Yet because they were denied any experience out in the field, RSAs possessed only the most tenuous knowledge of Plant equipment. Usually, they were expected merely to process and retrieve information with neatness and accuracy. In some respects, their jobs required them to play roles as metaphoric "wives" of the skilled craftworkers, providing support for the men controlling the tools, but themselves remaining distant from the technical aspects of the labor process.

A second type of clerical occupation in the manual C.O.s was found in the Loop Assignment Centers (LACs), where women filed and retrieved information needed to install new equipment on the network. Essentially, LACs served to process new orders and to assign each new telephone number a definite physical location on the network—that is, a specific cable and pair of wires.[12] LACs were usually small, community-based offices that employed two dozen women in several different job categories. Service Clerks performed simple functions such as the recording and retrieval of data on index cards. Assignment Clerks used cable books to give each telephone number an appropriate cable and pair of wire, and thus needed some knowledge of Plant equipment. A very small group called Back Tap Assignors assisted engineers who made modifications in the area's cable grid. Save for this last group, work in the LACs was highly routine, requiring memorization and application of a set of equipment codes and procedures. As with the RSAs, clerical work in the LACs required women to dutifully record data on Plant equipment, working as neatly and accurately as possible.

These arrangements prevailed until roughly the early 1960s. As noted, C.O.s were the critical organizational units in the Plant department during its manual era. Although each C.O. might include two or more levels of line management, control over the day-to-day functioning of the C.O. traditionally fell to the skilled manual workers themselves. Informally generated knowledge of the local equipment converged with customary patterns of autonomy in ways that left Plant work largely in their hands. This system largely excluded clerical workers from the technical operations of Plant work and assigned them only those tasks that were deemed unsuitable for craftsmen to perform. Virtually all of these arrangements were overturned by the late 1960s, however, as both the structure and the functions of C.O. units underwent a series of dramatic transformations, altering the nature of the work process beyond recognition.

Rationalization and Resistance

The manner in which these changes were introduced and the response they provoked from workers varied across Bell firms, depending on the social and economic context in each locale. The general process, however, shared certain essential features. Economic pressures (described more fully in Chapter 5) forced management to seek greater control over the internal operations of the firm and to rationalize the work process wherever possible.[13] Where workers had established a strong and relatively cohesive structure of representation, they sought to resist such measures, seeking to stay management's hand. Such resistance can most clearly be seen at New York Telephone, whose workers engaged in a growing wave of rank-and-file job actions throughout the 1960s (including dozens of unauthorized strikes) to defend their traditional control over production. Eventually, when their backs were to the wall in 1971, workers in New York walked out for seven months, defying calls for moderation from their own national union leadership, but in the end suffering a massive defeat. In this context, a wave of organizational and technological changes swept over the firm's operations, most of which workers have been unable to forestall. These conditions seem enormously favorable to de-skilling theory and should therefore provide an especially strong test of its claims.

The events of this period are still relatively fresh in the minds of senior craft personnel at New York Telephone. Most of the workers I interviewed recall the workplace of the sixties as marked by great turbulence, and published accounts confirm their claims. The *New York Times* reported fourteen different strikes of New York Telephone Plant employees during the 1960s. Interviews with workers as well as company and union officials, however, indicate that these were mainly the larger disputes, comprising a small fraction of the work stoppages that occurred. Asked how often the smaller job actions occurred, a former chief steward in New York City who led many of them replied, "Oh Christ. At least once a month, and that was the minimum. They'd last a day, two days, three days." Another respondent recalled:

> Sometimes we'd call our men out for an hour, and walk around the corner. They'd come looking for us, and we'd have gone back into the C.O.! They didn't know *what* we were gonna do. We were having a great time, keeping them guessing.

The issues that provoked these walkouts were varied. As one participant in these battles related in an interview, "They could be for anything, but mostly because the company had too heavy a hand." The most important issues stemmed from the company's effort to formalize its internal operations, to tighten work discipline and generally gain greater control over each departments' functions. This effort often forced middle managers to abandon customary modes of operation. Thus older methods of assigning holiday work schedules or of dealing with the safety of workers in ghetto neighborhoods were subject to change, disrupting what local stability had existed.[14] As a pattern of industrial conflict developed, larger issues also surfaced, such as the company's insistence on the right to subcontract work and to use supervisors' labor. Each abandonment of custom and tradition provoked small-scale work stoppages, as when a dozen men in a repair garage would walk out in defiance of what they viewed as management's arrogance. The company typically responded with suspensions and dismissals. As news of such discipline leaked out, conflicts that had been confined to single work locations quickly mushroomed into battles affecting an entire local union (two thousand workers) or even the entire firm's unionized work force throughout the state (upwards of forty thousand workers).[15]

The more workers engaged in such behavior, the more management grew determined to impose its will. Recalled New York Telephone's Director of Labor Relations at that time:

> Management said, 'We're not gonna stand for this. We can't continue down this path. *We're* gonna run this business!' There was a strong anti-union feeling at the time, a feeling that the workers were taking advantage of us.

Partly because of these conflicts, but also because of an unforeseen explosion in demand for service, the company was plunged into a service crisis that caused widespread discontent among callers. Unable to rely on the good will of its own workers to help cope with this situation, New York Telephone unilaterally decided to import telephone workers from Texas and Illinois, lodging them in hotels and promising them unlimited overtime, without seeking their own workers' consent. Understandably, the New York workers viewed this as an affront to their own position and a corporate effort to undermine their strength, and they conducted a series of strikes in their own defense. It was precisely the use of imported labor and subcontracting that provoked the long and bitter strike of 1971, the culminating battle in management's struggle for control.

Plant workers had traditionally viewed their skills as indispensable, assuming that management could not long maintain local service in their absence. The strike put this belief to the test. Workers in other departments of the company were represented by other unions and still had contracts in force, which meant that only Plant workers went out on strike.[16] Yet the firm was able to draw on engineers, managers, and technicians from inside and outside the company and succeeded in maintaining service (albeit with long delays for installations and repairs) for the duration of the strike. After seven months on the picket line, workers were forced to accept a crushing defeat, reluctantly voting to accept the very contract they would not sign before.

A third-line manager recalls the scene when the workers at his C.O. returned to work.

> When the union people came back, they marched into the central office in two lines, you know, to show their solidarity. And when they saw the frames looking better than before, everything looking even more neat and orderly than when they were in charge, their faces dropped to the floor! They learned that *we didn't need them to run the show.*

Having won this tug of war, management was well situated to introduce a series of changes that recast the nature of the labor process workers had known.

The initial wave of such transformations was organizational, growing out of the company's campaign to institute what it called "functionalization"—a process of dividing job functions that had been combined in a single office and removing them to larger units dedicated to a single task. The goal of such organizational changes was to increase work efficiency at every point in the productive circuit. The second wave, which often followed in the wake of such organizational restructuring, centered on the transformation and modernization of the firm's technology, chiefly through the introduction of programmable automation throughout the Plant department.

INFORMATION TECHNOLOGY AND WORK PROCESSES

There was much to modernize. For roughly four decades after the 1920s, the tools and methods of Plant work had scarcely changed. Beginning in the mid-1960s, however, Bell Labs had begun to announce a series of new technologies that promised sweeping changes in the nature of communications work and which were quickly adopted across the Bell system. The most prominent of these were electronic or "stored program" switching systems (which revolutionized switching operations), Mechanized Loop Testing equipment (which automated the testing of lines), and various computerized systems for the management of Plant information that recast the nature of clerical functions. Initially, these changes were limited to isolated departments. By the end of the 1970s, however, more and more work locations were caught up in a movement toward electronic integration, as the labor process began to evolve into a complex web whose elements are electronically interwoven by mainframe computers located far from any given worksite.

To show how these changes have reshaped skill requirements and managerial control during the past two decades, I shall first present data gathered from field work and interviews conducted at New York Telephone's Plant department. I will then use quantitative data to model the precise interrelation among new technologies, skill requirements, and alienation from work.

The Automation of Craft Labor

Management's campaign to rationalize its operations began, logically enough, at the most pivotal unit within the C.O.—the Repair Service Bureaus. Beginning at the end of the 1960s, the company introduced two decisive changes directly bearing on the RSBs. The first involved the organization of the RSBs: management began to separate the functions of craft and clerical workers, distributing them into two distinct organizational units. This change enabled the company to consolidate the labor of the Repair Service Attendants into larger and more concentrated bureaus that served much wider geographical areas, in this way reducing the the number of offices the company needed to maintain. As will soon be discussed more fully, this reorganization enabled the company to establish what it called "a traffic environment" in the consolidated trouble-reporting bureaus.

A second change centered on the technologies used to test and interpret troubles. Hard upon the reorganization of the RSBs, the company installed microelectronic equipment called Mechanized Loop Testing (MLT) systems, which translated the Deskman's testing and interpretive skills into computer programs. No longer dependent on the Deskmen as the supplier of testing skills, the company promoted lower-paid clerical personnel who lacked any technical knowledge of electrical circuits to take the Deskmen's place. Typically, the clerical personnel assigned to run the MLTs were recruited from the ranks of the RSAs, the very clerical workers whom the Deskmen had previously overseen.

In the old RSBs, trouble reports were literally handed to testing personnel by the RSAs standing adjacent to them. Now testing personnel receive trouble reports electronically, from consolidated 611 bureaus that are often hundreds of miles away. As RSAs forward trouble reports into a testing office (now called Installation and Maintenenance Centers, or IMCs), clerical workers type the suspect telephone numbers into programmed interfaces ("masks") on their screens. Once the clerk presses the enter key, the system *automatically* tests the relevant cable and pair, outputting the test results in roughly forty seconds. A screenful of data comes up, showing the circuit's ohm and volt readings, AC and DC signatures, the status of the dial tone, as well as other data. Yet the only unit of information that concerns the clerical worker is the VER code, which indicates the apparent source of the trouble. A VER code of 3, for example, indicates a probable trouble in the switches; in this case, the clerk forwards it to a switching control center, where the system assigns it to a craftworker's log. When the VER code indicates a cable problem, the clerk sends the trouble to a repair garage where a splicer is assigned to locate the trouble and close it out. Virtually all elements of judgment and interpretation have in fact been encoded into the algorithms of the MLT system's software; clerical workers have little or no substantive knowledge of what the tests actually mean.

From management's perspective, this arrangement reduces the variable or contingent nature of the labor process. In the words of a top technical manager at New York Telephone, MLT technologies ensure that

> a VER code of 3 will *always* go to the switching location. A certain handle number will *always* get the right cable and pair. There are no decisions to be made along the way. *That's the way we want the work to be.*

Repercussions from the new technologies echoed throughout the Plant department, beginning a process that affected both the outside workers and switching crafts alike. One immediate impact of the MLTs was to introduce sharp conflict and tension between clerical workers (mainly women) in the automated IMCs and the craft personnel (men) who actually completed the relevant repairs. Such conflict typically occurred under two circumstances. One was when the MLT reports were erroneous or vague, and craftworkers had to call in to the IMC for further information. Because the company's aim was to reduce its labor costs, it kept its IMC staff to a minimum, often forcing craftworkers out in the field to wait long periods of time before getting through. Indeed, the splicers in one garage heard from their counterparts in the city that they had better brush up on their reading skills, for the new technologies would mean long delays. "Boy, were they ever right," he noted.

A second source of conflict occurred when craftworkers *did* get through, as workers in the skilled crafts now had to deal with workers who had been denied all but the most rudimentary knowledge of telephone circuitry. One splicer expressed a widespread feeling with particular force:

> These M.A.s [MLT operators] have *no idea* what it's like to hang up on a pole when it's ten degrees out, with your knees hurting and legs turning to jelly, with some bimbo fiddle-fucking around!

As splicers observed, the MLT operators passively read the results on their screens without adjusting for weather conditions or the age and type of the equipment. As a result, what they saw on their VDTs often had only the most tenuous bearing on the actual state of Plant equipment. With few other means of defense, MLT operators often clung to the organization's rules, insisting on the validity of the system's results and forcing craftworkers to "clear" troubles that sometimes didn't exist. As one splicer reported:

> An M.A. says the pair's no good, but I can see with my own eyes that it tests fine. I can get tone on it. The trouble was in the C.O., not in the pair! She [the MLT operator] is just not experienced enough to know what to do.

To some extent these conflicts reflected the organizational tensions that often accompany the restructuring of work methods. For one thing, the task of automating the Deskmen's job was extraordinarily complex; many of the tacit skills Deskmen had accumulated were not (could not be) incorporated into the MLT systems. This posed enormous threats to the validity of diagnostic work. Recalled one Deskman who works with the MLTs in a different department of the firm:

> See, when you test you're also *listening* to the circuit, and you can detect certain things that the [computer] system can't, because it can't hear the line. Also, when a machine tests a circuit, it doesn't have a memory, at least not in the same way we do. Like when we say, 'Oh, I remember there was something like this before...' It can *try* to duplicate that. But it simply doesn't have the human capacity of relating a lot of different things together into one.

The results were sometimes highly wasteful. In one case, as many as a dozen workers were dispatched to the same location when the system failed to "see" the common source underlying several kindred troubles.

These technological sources of uncertainty were exacerbated by the company's effort to minimize its training and staffing costs. The automation of testing work had been undertaken to speed up the flow of work through the Plant department and to reduce the cost of shooting troubles in Plant equipment. When the new systems yielded an *increased* need for communication between the clerical workers and outside workers, however, the restructured system was more poorly equipped to handle such needs than ever before. The resulting tensions were directed at the MLT operators, who bore the brunt of the workers' resentment.

Even more important than these factors, however, has been the role of gender ideology and politics, which intensified the conflict between male outside workers and female MLT operators. Much as in printing, metal trades, and many other crafts, outside craftworkers had infused their tasks with the trappings of masculinity, defining their skills in terms of what Paul Willis has called the "manly controntation with the task."[17] Peering out through this gendered lens, many of the men viewed the women in the testing offices as inherently incompetent in the analysis and interpretation of troubles. By pointing to the women's manifest lack of knowledge of Plant operations, moreover, the men could reaffirm the importance of their own skills. For these reasons, many outside craftworkers viewed the women as interlopers, in effect blaming them for organizational developments that were in fact well beyond the women's control. Only recently has such conflict begun to abate, as the company has taken steps to correct the problems it had itself created.

The problem management faced was how to increase both the quality and the speed of information that flowed to the outside craft force. There were only two means of doing this. One was to enhance the skills of the MLT operators and increase their staffing levels, thereby resolving the problems that had emerged.[18] However, this approach obviously ran counter to the very goal that had inspired the introduction of the MLT systems—that of reducing the cost of shooting troubles. A second approach, the one management pursued, was to automate the process even more.

From management's point of view, the problem was to facilitate the flow of information from the MLT system to the craftworkers out in the field. This was of course the function of the MLT operators, who ran the testing program and conveyed its results to craftworkers who performed the final repair. To open the sluice gates and enable test results to flow directly to the point of repair, management has introduced new technologies that give outside craftworkers the ability to access the testing system directly, without having to rely on MLT operators at all. To do this, the company has distributed Craft Access Terminals (CATs) to its cable splicers and other outside craftworkers. These workers can now log on to the system *independently* of the MAs. Using small video screens and pointing devices on their CATs, splicers can access data on each trouble and generate test results for themselves. In effect, the company has shifted the "window" on the testing process outward, away from the MLT operator and toward the craftworker out in the field.

This change has enhanced the conceptual skill requirements of the outside force, who now have more testing and knowledge-generation capacities at their fingertips than ever before. In a sense, where splicers could once be called the "tester's arms and legs," the distribution of CATs has given them their own pair of "eyes." Because most splicers have accumulated a store of practical knowledge about the Plant equipment they repair and can now run tests to explore its functioning, the CATs have expanded their view of the cable grid they must repair. Coupled with other changes in outside Plant equipment (e.g., Subscriber Loop Control [SLC-96] systems, which use microelectronic circuitry to expand the carrying capacity of cable installations), the effect has been to *in*crease the level of skill which management requires of its outside craft force.

The use of CATS has had the opposite effect on the MAs, however. Since the company's need for them has begun to erode, the consensus is that their days as a new and growing occupation have come to an abrupt end. Few craftworkers seem likely to mourn their fate.

The Automation of the Switching Crafts   The deskmen had played a central role in the detection and analysis of switching troubles, but the actual repairs were performed by switching craftworkers assigned to each frame location. The clearing of troubles within each C.O. required little outside intervention, as C.O.s were largely self-sufficient units. This arrangement began to shift in 1965, when Bell Laboratories announced the development of Electronic Switching Systems (ESS), more generically known as "stored program" equipment. In contrast to mechanical installations, ESS equipment uses digital technologies to store switching codes in memory, in effect assigning each telephone number an electronic address. In this way the computer views each telephone as a logical device attached to a wide area network. When a subscriber inputs a telephone number to be reached, the computer processes the call as an input/output operation, calculates the optimal path for the call, and establishes the connection electronically.[19]

The technical advantages of stored program switching systems are unmistakable. With such systems installed, Plant managers can achieve far greater flexibility in the use of their equipment, changing the assignment of particular cables and pairs without any manual intervention. Digital systems usually detect faults before customers ever become aware of them. Failing components can be automatically taken off line, achieving a level of fault tolerance not possible before. Finally, because digital systems make little or no use of mechanical devices, they require far less maintenance than their mechanical predecessors. From the perspective of the workers, however, stored program switching has had several less beneficial effects.

The *first* has been a virtual depopulation of most C.O. frame and switching installations. Before, in a large switching hub as existed in the Hempstead district office, switching craftworkers maintained their own miniature society, with playful rivalries between workers skilled in different systems. Each frame often required as many as twenty-five workers, who rotated on and off different shifts in order to keep service up and running. Now a typical frame location requires no more than a half-dozen of switching workers. Many workers have been transferred to other locations (e.g., to the computerized control centers) or else are retained on a roving basis (making repairs wherever they need to be dispatched). Still, when New York Telephone's switching services in Nassau County were cut over to digital equipment, the area's force requirements in switch fell by 40 percent between 1982 and 1991 (from 992 to 605).

The introduction of digital switching equipment has promoted a *second* and even more pronounced change in the work process—management's centralization of its switching operations—which has placed control over each territory's switching equipment in a new type of office, Automated Switching Control Centers. Much as in automated process industries, the Switching Control Centers constantly monitor the operations of the area's switching and frame installations, alerting workers to changes in the state of the system's functioning and even adjusting the network's behavior as the situation demands.

Before the shift toward Control Centers, New York Telephone maintained twenty-four distinct frame installations in Nassau County, each of which was a relatively autonomous organizational unit. By 1982, stored program switching systems enabled the company to establish ten Control Centers to oversee all of its switching installations. Three years later, the number of Control Centers had shrunk to four, and by 1990 to only one. While there remain twenty-four frame and switch installations in this county, a single highly automated complex located in the company's district office now 'manages' their functioning from afar.

This shift toward more centralized controls has split the switching crafts in two. Some craftworkers continue to work in remote C.O.s, as system needs require. Other switching workers have been assigned to the Control Centers, working in entirely new situations. This had led to a *third* effect of the new technologies: switching craftworkers in the Control Centers have exchanged their older, physically based knowledge for a set of abstract, "intellective" skills (Zuboff 1987).

To be sure, there were important analytical skills required of inside craftworkers even before the introduction of ESS equipment. To find a trouble, switching craftworkers often had to run a battery of tests at their local installations, using schematic diagrams and manuals to interpret the results. Yet these tests were always conducted alongside the switching machines themselves, and workers had previously been part of a mechanical, hands-on working environment. The practical test of their diagnosis was physically present before their very eyes. For switching personnel who have been assigned to the Control Centers, however, the material trappings of their craft have all but fallen away. Increasingly, switching craftworkers conduct their tasks at computer screens far removed from any concrete referent.

Workers employed at different sections of a Control Center perform varying sorts of functions. In one section, for example, workers oversee the operations of specific types of equipment— for example, maintaining Northern Telecom DMS switches, AT&T ESS-5 machines, or the few remaining Cross-Bar switches in the district. In a nearby area of the same office, workers run tests on troubles that have been reported to the 611 bureau and which have been traced to malfunctions in a switch. In yet another area, workers are assigned "control and surveillance" functions, analyzing computer-detected faults in the district's switching operations. What unites these workers is their constant use of computer systems in the conduct of their tasks.

One system that is commonly used in New York Telephone's Switching Control Centers is an installation called CIMAP (Circuit Installation and Maintenance Assistance Package). Pronounced SEE-MAP, the acronym reflects the system's goal of helping workers peer into the operations of the switching equipment distributed throughout the local terrain. In the words of one supervisor, CIMAP "is our universe."

Workers in the Control Center receive their tasks in different ways. A routine source of work stems from CIMAP's nightly test-ing of circuits in the district's switching systems. As the system locates components whose ohm readings violate acceptable thresholds, it routes calls around faulty circuits, flags them as troubles that need repair, and electronically sends each task to a given worker's log. Craftworkers then access their work logs and bring up each task, using an array of diagnostic programs to see what produced each trouble report. This type of assignment is called "programmable load work." A less routine source of work happens when CIMAP detects the sudden occurrence of a fault which is a potential threat to some portion of local service. In such situations, CIMAP sounds a bell and outputs the trouble report to a line printer, where it receives immediate attention. Whether they are performing programmable load work or responding to alarms, workers now receive their work assign-ments from CIMAP itself. *The computer system itself informs workers which of the system's parts to repair.*

When a switching craftworker accesses his work log, he opens a trouble report to see what type of fault he or she has been assigned. The worker then calls up a circuit history of the equip-ment involved, uses CIMAP and other, supplementary diagnostic systems to run a set of testing routines, and locates the trouble on the basis of the results. Sometimes, the trouble stems from a soft-ware error. In such cases, the trouble can be cleared electronically, simply by issuing a set of commands from within CIMAP. More often, the worker finds an open circuit, meaning that a specific electronic component has failed within a remote C.O., indicating the need for manual repair. In the latter case the craftworker for-wards the test report (usually including a short narrative describ-ing the trouble) to a repair worker out in the field.

Although a yawning distance now separates workers from the objects of their labor, few craftworkers have experienced the feel-ing that Zuboff called "epistemological distress," in which older ways of knowing are rapidly overturned, resulting in confusion and uncertainty about the actual condition of the production pro-cess. Even so, most switching workers feel a sense of discomfort with the increasingly abstract character of their jobs. Said one young Hispanic woman working in a Manhattan Control Center:

Part of the problem with working with the computer is that you have little view of what you are actually testing, and you need that. You see, when you're testing on the tube [using the terminal], the computer tells you what *it* sees, not what *you* would see with your own eyes. You don't have that same pulse on the circuit as you had before, when you'd hear certain irregularities on the line and kind of sense things that way.

This inability to "see" and "hear" the switching systems themselves persists despite the most sophisticated programming efforts to overcome it. This was clear in a Control Center that has experimented with a visually-oriented alternative to CIMAP. This new system, called Vision, graphically displays the functioning of the entire area's C.O.s on large computer monitors, with a rectangle representing each remote C.O. Blinking rectangles signal the existence of a troubled C.O., while a steady-state condition indicates normal functioning. Using a mouse, a switching worker can click on each rectangle, windowing into data on the operation of each C.O., even showing several trouble conditions on the screen simultaneously. Such systems do make it easier to *figuratively* 'see' the conditions that prevail in remote C.O.s, but most workers still prefer work in the C.O.s, where they can *literally* see their tools in front of them and feel a sense of material connection with the objects of their work. One worker explained:

> At the SCC you're responsible for *everything*, the whole system, so you don't get a proprietary sense about anything at all. You can feel really removed from what's going on out there. But at the C.O., there's a feeling of *owning your own switches* that you can't get at the Control Center.

One might easily conclude that this preference for the older, mechanical style of working is an expression of traditionalism that is destined to fade away. Yet the evidence suggests otherwise, indicating that workers' preference for the C.O.s is more than an irrational attachment to tradition. Rather, it reflects their aversion to the *fourth* and final effect of computerization—its establishment of an increasingly structured, more tightly constrained set of work relations within the Control Centers. Put simply, workers chafe at the tightened discipline the company has achieved in the Control Centers and prefer to work in the C.O.s, where they feel a greater sense of independence from managerial control.

No one could reasonably suggest that management has sought to introduce a "traffic environment" in its Control Centers. The work is still too varied and complex to allow for such complete standardization. For example, although the introduction of computers has automated the routine testing of circuits, workers must still set the program's ohm thresholds themselves, and to do this they need considerable knowledge of different types of equipment. (If the thresholds are set improperly, the system will report an excess of troubles, generating much more information than workers can possibly use). Given the differing types of equipment in use (mostly from Northern Telecom and AT&T), months of active use can go by before workers begin to understand the rudiments of each particular system. Despite the continuing complexity of workers' skills, however, systems such as CIMAP have quite clearly enabled management to establish a stricter set of production standards than had ever existed before.

When CIMAP allocates tasks to each technician's work log, it also establishes a "price" for each job that depends on its type, in this way maintaining an ongoing record of each worker's efficiency rating. If a worker's total number of production units falls below the value expected for the week, the worker's efficiency rating begins to suffer. Workers assigned to programmable load work, for example, are expected to achieve "96–99 percent completeness" as a matter of course. Ironically, the very system that detects "faults" in the switching network performs the same function with respect to the *human* network that keeps the system on line.

The importance of technology in maintaining an expected level of work discipline emerged clearly in the remarks of middle- and lower-level managers. Said one first-line supervisor:

> I don't need the machine to know who's not pulling their weight. I knew who wasn't pulling their weight even without it. *But it helps*. It makes a real difference. It means there are fewer confrontations. I have something *real* now I can show people to back up my point. *They can't argue with the hard copy*.

Almost every manager was quick to justify the use of performance measurement, portraying it as a tool that helps them develop their subordinates' skills. One supervisor told me:

> When one of my people is having a problem, I can see it more quickly now. I can sit down with him and determine what's wrong. Maybe there's something he hasn't tried yet that would help, some method that will bring his performance up a few notches.

This view of performance measurement as an aid in training and development contains an important element of truth. Yet it conveniently ignores another, less friendly function of the new technologies: with the new systems in place, the task of maintaining given levels of production became that much less dependent on personal forms of supervision. When asked how stored program technologies had affected his control over the work locations under his authority, a third-level manager of switching services alluded to precisely this point. He shook his head and identified an anomaly: "It's funny. Each office is much less supervised now, *but it's much more controlled.*"

This development is at times made graphically clear, as in one major Control Center that oversees the switches in a suburban New York county. The supervisors in this Control Center have installed a video projection system that magnifies a computer screen's display and projects it onto the front wall of the office. The image, involving data from CIMAP's tracking system, shows each outstanding fault in the Control Center, the name of the worker assigned to it and the time the worker has spent on each outstanding task. The effect is to "publicize" each worker's ongoing work performance, which is now apparent for all to see. A supervisor explained why he liked this arrangement:

> Now I don't have to constantly ask people how their work is coming. And I don't have to log into the system to check. I can see for myself *just by looking up at the wall.*

Even this office could not reasonably be called an electronic sweatshop. Workers have too much discretion for that term to fit and can still engage in casual conversation if their trouble schedules allow. As suggested, their work remains highly complex. Yet methods such as this serve to put switching workers on notice that the clock is ticking, and that the same computer system that assigns them their tasks is measuring their efficiency in handling each one.

The Automation of Clerical Work

My analysis thus far begins to suggest that the fate of craft occupations has in fact been a varied one. In one case—the Deskmen—craftwork has been subject to sharp skill degradation, much as de-skilling theory forewarns. In a second case—the switching crafts—craftwork has experienced a different and more contradictory fate. As switching workers have lost their manual skills, they have gained a new and more intellective set in their place. Still, their levels of autonomy at work seem to have declined. In a third case—the cable splicers—craftworkers have actually enjoyed a mild upgrading trend. Splicers have apparently inherited at least some of the testing functions previously performed by the Deskmen, now acquiring "eyes" to complement their "arms and legs." In sum, if automation has often adversely affected skilled crafts, the overall effect has been to *reproduce* craft occupations as a distinct occupational category.

Recall that as part of its rationalization campaign, management separated the clerical and the testing functions of the RSBs into distinct organizational units. The function of recording trouble reports, performed by the Repair Service Attendants (RSAs), was moved to larger, consolidated service bureaus that served much wider geographical areas than before. This process eliminated the limited involvement in the maintenance process that RSAs had formerly enjoyed and imposed a "traffic environment" on their labor. In terms that faintly echo Adam Smith's pin manufacturers, a technical manager at New York Telephone recalls:

> It was a conscious decision. You began to functionalize the operation and move toward centralized work locations. We used to have ten people in ten different offices. But once we went to one large office we found that *we didn't need* a hundred employees to handle the work any more.

So great were the gains in output that eventually only four centralized service bureaus were needed to serve the entire state of New York.

In fact, a typical centralized repair bureau houses roughly one hundred workers, although only half that many are on the job at any given time. As in traffic, the overlapping and often rotating shifts that workers are assigned rule out the establishment of personal work areas. When an RSA arrives at work, she selects one of the fifty-odd cubicles to use that day, plugs in her headset, and logs in her ID code. From that point on, the work is almost indistinguishable from that performed in Traffic bureaus. Calls automatically flow to the first available RSA. Just as in Traffic bureaus, work performance is measured using the AWT system.

The starting pay for an RSA is low (only $249 per week), but doubles within five years' time. Still, turnover is high, and many RSAs leave before this period elapses. The reasons are clear. The job involves friction with aggrieved subscribers, who often vent their frustrations at the company's workers. It offers little autonomy or discretion, for workers' tasks are highly standardized: they use a few structured questions to elicit data which they enter into computer fields on their screens. As in traffic, workers' performance is timed; expected AWTs hover at about 110 seconds per call. Finally, force requirements lead to strict enforcement of the rules governing absences and sick leave. As the second-line manager of a 611 bureau put it: "If I need 6.5 bodies, they've got to be there. If not, my service is impacted. So you better believe we're strict!"

Events in this manager's office are especially revealing. Despite the company's strict absence-control policy (or perhaps because of it), absenteeism has remained quite high. This fact, coupled with levels of turnover and poor performance, began to indicate to management that their rationalization efforts might have gone too far. Beginning in the late 1980s, third line management began to advise their second liners (including the manager of this office) to ease up on production standards and to emphasize quality more. The second-liner recalled,

> We used to beat them over the head with the AWTs. Literally. But now I've been told to relax things, to raise the AWT and to look at my Telsam ratings [service evaluations commissioned by the state] and not just the AWTs.

Nonetheless, this man is quick to point out that his office's AWT has loosened only slightly, moving from 110 to 120 seconds per call; he is proud that other offices have let their AWTs slide even more. Apparently, the calculus of productivity still informed his behavior.

Management has applied elementary Human Relations techniques to this office, to improve work attitudes among the RSAs. On Employee Recognition Day, the company presents awards to those RSAs who have performed especially well. At the last such event, workers were allowed to rotate off their positions for an hour or so on company time and to share hero sandwiches and cake, while middle- and top-level managers heaped praise on them, dubbing them the company's "unsung heroes." At the end of the festivities, commemorative mugs were distributed to the attendees. A party atmosphere prevailed for much of the day, with workers straggling in as their shifts allowed.

A further effort to counter employee alienation in this office has been the establishment of the Sunshine Club, a small group of supervisors and workers who try to enliven social relations at work by throwing parties on holidays and employee birthdays. On such days, members of the club affix crepe paper streamers to the ceilings and lay out a spread of cookies and soda. The evidence suggests, however, that none of these efforts—minimal relaxation of the AWT or the various Human Relations efforts— has had any appreciable effect on workers' attitudes. Workers eat the company's cookies and take home its mugs, yet feel little change in their orientation toward their jobs.

A small number of RSAs employed at the office described above was included in the 1985 regional survey of two Bell operating companies. Because the number of such workers was small, caution is clearly warranted in drawing inferences about this particular clerical group. Nonetheless, a relatively clear and consistent pattern emerges in the work attitudes and perceptions of these RSAs.

It is useful to view the workers in this industry on a continuum that ranges from the most highly alienated group (the telephone operators) at one end, to the least alienated group (craftworkers such as the splicers) at the other. When we locate the RSAs on this continuum, we find that their attitudes are now almost indistinguishable from those of their counterparts in the Traffic department. In light of their work attitudes, it is hard to believe that they are employed in the same industry as the splicers (see Table 4.4).

TABLE 4.4
RESPONSES TO SELECTED INDICATORS OF ALIENATION
FROM WORK BY OCCUPATIONAL GROUP

| | *Occupational Group* | | |
Percent who "often" *or "always" report* *feeling the following:*	*Directory* *Assistance* *Operators*	*Repair* *Service* *Attendants*	*Cable* *Splicers*
	%	%	%
	(N)	(N)	(N)
On my job I feel as if the machines and equipment control me*	68.0 (103)	82.3 (17)	6.0 (50)
When I'm working I feel like just another part of the machinery.*	71.0 (107)	76.5 (17)	22.0 (50)
I really have to force myself to go into work.*	51.9 (106)	70.5 (17)	18.0 (50)
The only thing I look forward to on my job is getting paid.*	67.9 (103)	76.4 (17)	32.0 (50)

*P < .0005 using chi square.

Only 6 percent of the splicers usually feel controlled by their machines, yet more than four-fifths (82.3 percent) of the RSAs "often" or "always" feel this way. Like the majority of the operators, most RSAs (76.5 percent) have come to feel "just like another part of the machinery" when they are at work, a sentiment accompanied by a clear sense of aversion toward the work itself. The same proportion of RSAs report a clearly instrumental view of their jobs, where only the pay serves as a motivating force; the comparable proportion among the splicers (32 percent) is less than half as large. Clearly, the work situation of the operators has reappeared in a newer context—the centralized Repair Service Bureaus.

There are at least some indications that clerical workers in other organizational units may escape the fullest development of this process, as countervailing trends have to some extent offset the de-skilling effects RSAs have felt. The automation of the Loop

Assignment Centers, for example, has abolished the most routinized and repetitive functions (those of the data entry clerks),
chiefly because the electronic integration of the labor process has
reduced the need to re-enter the same data at different points in
the productive circuit. In highly automated LACs (called Loop
Data Maintenance Centers, or LDMCs), the great bulk of the
information processing work that clerical workers had performed
is now conducted automatically, as computers search their
databases and assign cables and pairs to new equipment with little need for human intervention. Although such processes have
tended to eliminate the least skilled clerical tasks, the bulk of the
work in automated LACs remains highly routine. Workers perform auxiliary tasks, picking up whatever residual jobs the computers find too awkward to conduct. The programs that manage
the flow of work through automated LDMCs contain routines for
the measurement of each worker's performance, though they are
not yet widely used.

While still preliminary, these observations begin to suggest
that the de-skilling trend has been imposed with greater force on
clerical than craft occupations, as workers in lower-level office
jobs have felt the full effect of the rationalization trend. Clerks
have at times been used as a wedge in management's battle against
craftworkers, as when they were used to de-skill the Deskmen.
More generally, clerical workers have tended to experience what
the company calls a "Traffic environment," involving the use of
machine-pacing and electronic surveillance to maintain desired
production standards.

Estimating the Linkages among Technology,
Work, and Alienation

Taken as a whole, the analysis begins to reveal a pattern which is
not easily squared with de-skilling theory. Some crafts have
indeed been simplified and diluted, with management exercising
increasing control over the use of workers' labor time. Yet many
craftworkers have also found their older, manual skills replen-
ished by new and more 'mental' demands, in some cases actually
benefitting from an apparent upgrading trend. In lieu of a simple
de-skilling trend, then, these changes suggest that craft labor has

been transformed and its skills have been redistributed, without uprooting or degrading craft skills as such.

Clerical workers, however, have not been so fortunate. As office work has grown increasingly specialized and machine-paced, many lower-level white collar workers have encountered the full weight of the de-skilling trend. This trend is especially visible in the case of the Repair Service Attendants. Formerly employed in small, relatively personal settings as clerical adjuncts of skilled craftworkers, the RSAs have been subjected to sharp functional specialization that has intensified the work process and generated markedly increased levels of alienation. In sum, the qualitative evidence begins to suggest that the older dualism between skilled manual and routine clerical occupations has persisted despite massive changes in the organization and technology of work. In the following discussion I shall make use of the survey data, seeking to provide a firmer empirical mooring for the qualitative analysis outlined above.

Ideally, we should like to use longitudinal data to assess the impact of the new technologies.[20] The static, cross-sectional nature of the survey data fall short of this ideal. They do, however, permit us to approximate the nature of the changes at issue by creating a 'synthetic cohort' of jobs situated at varying points in the automation process. The strategy adopted here has been to compare the content of similar jobs at low, medium, and high levels of automation, deciphering technologically related variations in job complexity and autonomy. To understand the attitudinal effects of these changes, we can explore data on alienation from work as well. In the following analysis, then, I shall fit the survey data with a structural model that reveals the nature of the links among new technologies, work content, and alienation from work for both craft and clerical occupations.

Figure 4.1 displays the model used to guide the analysis. Similar heuristic devices have been commonly used by studies in the the upgrading genre (e.g., Blauner, 1964; Faunce 1965; Shepard 1971; Hull, Friedman, and Rogers, 1982). In using the model, I make no assumptions that technology is an autonomous force, standing above or beyond social influences (as upgrading theorists have often assumed). I assume only that the introduction of new technologies has enabled management to reconfigure the work process in ways that the model can unearth. The dependent variables which the model employs include both structural and attitudinal variables (that is, both work content and levels of alienation). The measures I have used in the analysis can briefly be described as follows.

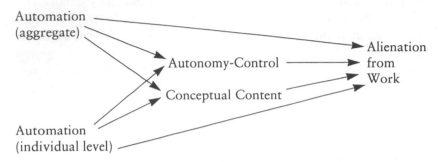

FIGURE 4.2
A MODEL OF THE LINKS BETWEEN THE DEGREE OF
AUTOMATION, WORK CONTENT,
AND ALIENATION FROM WORK

Alienation.   Alienation from work is a much-embattled concept whose meaning and analytical value have been enormously controversial (Blauner 1964; Horton 1964; Seeman 1975; Althusser 1971; Archibald 1978; Erikson 1990). Ironically, positivistic and Marxist theorists have at times implicitly converged, viewing the alienation construct as a prescientific notion laden with idealist philosophical baggage. Others, such as Seeman (1959) and even Kohn (1976) have advocated alienation research, yet subtly changing the concept's Marxist moorings, imbuing it with Durkheimian themes of *anomie*.

My own view has been that the alienation concept can provide a much-needed antidote to the objectivism and scientism that plague purely structuralist analysis, but only if we seek to restore the concept's original theoretical substance.[21] Toward this end I have defined alienation from work in terms of a relation between the worker and the job that generates two subjective conditions: (1) the worker's feeling of separation or disengagement from his or her work, which comes to acquire a merely instrumental meaning, and (2) the worker's perception that he or she has become an *object* of the production process, falling under the control of his or her own tools. While multiple dimensions would ideally be developed to measure this construct, a more parsimonious, one-dimensional scale has been developed on the basis of five survey items.[22]

Autonomy and Conceptual Content.   My approach to studying work content follows Spenner's lead (1983), recognizing two distinct dimensions—autonomy-control and complexity (or conceptual content). By autonomy I mean the extent to which workers are free to direct the method and the pace of their work. By the conceptual content of their tasks I mean the degree to which their work requires "independent thought or judgment" (Spenner 1983:828), rather than what Braverman called the labor of execution alone. The analysis that follows uses multiple items to measure each dimension of work content, with indices that achieve reliability coefficients that were deemed at least acceptable.[23]

Automation.   The degree of automation, finally, is defined in terms of the extent to which digital or other advanced technologies have replaced older, mechanical tools and machines. To measure this variable I have used a set of occupation-specific items that asked how often workers routinely use specific types of equipment. These items enable us to distinguish between workers using relatively primitive or manual equipment (coded as 1), those using equipment at intermediate or mechanical levels (coded as 2) and those using relatively advanced, digital technologies (coded as 3).[24]

One further point remains before presenting the results. The research design was planned in a manner that used distinct *workplaces* (rather than the individual *worker*) as the primary sampling units. (Once a workplace was selected for inclusion, questionnaires were administered to all the workers in it). This approach makes possible the use of a fuller, more structurally oriented measure of automation than could be done merely using individual automation scores. By aggregating the degree of automation that prevails in each workplace, we can form a measure of automation at two distinct levels of analysis—the structural or systemic level of the office as a whole, as well as the individual level of each worker's specific job. Presumably variations in work content and worker attitudes will be shaped by automation at both levels of analysis.

To form the contextual measure of office automation, workers' individual responses have been aggregated by work location (Kendall and Lazarsfeld 1955; Coleman 1969), yielding the mean level of automation that exists within each office. To separate out the individual effects of automation, I have constructed a term that represents each worker's deviation from the office mean (see Tannenbaum and Bachman 1964; Alwin 1976; and Lincoln and Zeitz 1980). The following analysis thus includes both contextual *and* individual measures of technology, enabling us to unravel the effects of automation at the two levels of analysis.

To form the 'synthetic cohort' of jobs at different stages in the automation process, we must be able to compare occupations that are similar in all relevant respects save for their degree of automation. For this reason, I have broken down the regression equations into occupational subgroups, showing the links among automation, work content, and alienation within each specific job category. As we see in Tables 4.5 through 4.7, the results lend support to the qualitative analysis outlined above.

Consider first the effects of automation on the autonomy of the two craft groups. Table 4.5 begins to show that the effects of automation are not homogeneous across the craft categories. The autonomy of the inside craftworkers does indeed decline when workers are employed at automated switching systems, much as the qualitative data suggest. Among the outside craft group, however, automation has the opposite, upgrading effect: outside craftworkers who install and maintain the most sophisticated equipment tend to report significantly *greater* autonomy than their counterparts employed in less advanced contexts.

When we consider apparent shifts in the conceptual content of craft work, we find no evidence that automation brings about any simplification or loss of conceptual functions with respect to the switching crafts (Table 4.6). In fact, Equation 1 (which predicts conceptual content for the inside crafts) fails to attain statistical significance. Among the outside crafts, however, automation again acts to enhance work content: outside craftworkers who work in the most technically advanced contexts again report significantly *greater* conceptual complexity in their work than their counterparts in less advanced contexts.[25] Thus, while the work situation of the inside craft groups does seem to suffer (at least with respect to

TABLE 4.5
WORK AUTONOMY REGRESSED ON THE DEGREE OF
AUTOMATION AND CONTROLS, BY OCCUPATION GROUP.
UNSTANDARDIZED COEFFICIENTS (BETA IN PARENTHESES)

Predictor	(1) Inside Crafts	(2) Outside Crafts	(3) Clerical Employees
Size	.70***	-.50	-.05
	(.34)	(-.12)	(-.02)
Seniority	-.02	.02	-.02
	(-.05)	(.05)	(-.03)
Gender	1.52	2.25	.26
	(.12)	(-.11)	(.15)
Automation (individual)	-1.56*	-.19	-1.54***
	(-.18)	(-.03)	(-.28)
Automation (contextual)	-2.27	2.87**	-2.57***
	(-.08)	(.30)	(-.26)
Constant	15.10	9.45	9.77
R^2	.21	.08	.18
N	(133)	(103)	(249)

***$P < .001$
**$P < .01$
*$P < .05$

work autonomy), the functions of other groups are apparently enhanced. Hence we find no evidence of any wholesale erosion or destruction of skilled manual occupations. What seems to occur is the *transformation* or reproduction of craft work.[26]

Again supporting the qualitative analysis, the data suggest that automation has strong and consistently adverse effects on the content of clerical workers' jobs. The autonomy of the clerks declines apace with automation at both the contextual *and* the individual levels of analysis (see Table 4.5). Likewise, the conceptual content of clerical work quite clearly falls as computerization proceeds (Table 4.6). What these data suggest is that the experience of the RSAs, whose labor has been fully rationalized, does indeed hold wider relevance for the clerical work force as a whole, for the de-skilling process seems to bring its full weight to bear on this occupational group.[27]

TABLE 4.6
CONCEPTUAL CONTENT REGRESSED ON DEGREE OF
AUTOMATION AND CONTROLS.
UNSTANDARDIZED COEFFICIENTS. (BETA IN PARENTHESES)

	(1) Inside Crafts	(2) Outside Crafts	(3) Clerical Employees
Size	.09	.11	.02
	(.06)	(.04)	(.01)
Seniority	.03	-.01	.06**
	(.10)	(-.04)	(-.15)
Gender	1.24	-.54	1.49**
	(.12)	(-.04)	(.15)
Automation (individual)	-1.09	.29	-1.00***
	(-.17)	(.07)	(-.21)
Automation (contextual)	1.65	1.61*	-1.04
	(.08)	(.24)	(-.12)
Constant	6.34	8.74	9.21
R²	.07	.10	.10
N	(133)	(103)	(249)

*P < .05
**P < .01
***P < .001

The differential effects of automation on craft and clerical work grow even more apparent when we extend the analysis to include the subjective experience of work—that is, levels of alienation from work (see Table 4.7). By combining the results in the three tables we can estimate the total effects of new technology on alienation, including both its direct and indirect effects (i.e., those which operate independently of work content, and those which are mediated by shifts in job design). When we do this, a number of important conclusions emerge.

As we have already seen, the introduction of advanced technologies increases the autonomy and conceptual content of the outside crafts, in turn reducing their level of alienation. The total effect of such changes on workers' attitudes is, however, quite modest: on average, a standard deviation increment in the degree

TABLE 4.7
ALIENATION FROM WORK REGRESSED ON DEGREE OF
AUTOMATION AND CONTROLS.
UNSTANDARDIZED COEFFICIENTS. (BETA IN PARENTHESES)

	Inside Crafts	*Outside Crafts*	*Clerical Employees*
Size	-.03	.62*	.01
	(-.02)	(.19)	(.00)
Seniority	.00	.03	.00
	(.00)	(.09)	(.00)
Gender	1.64	1.33	.23
	(.15)	(.08)	(.02)
Automation (individual)	-1.64**	.36	.93**
	(-.23)	(.08)	(.18)
Automation (contextual)	2.51	.32	.00
	(.11)	(.04)	(.00)
Autonomy	.37***	-.41***	-.28***
	(-.43)	(-.52)	(-.31)
Conceptual Content	-.20*	-.10	-.25***
	(-.18)	(-.09)	(-.23)
Constant	10.22	7.80	12.20
R^2	.251	.34	.27
N	(133)	(103)	(249)

*P < .05
**P < .01
***P < .001

of automation is expected to reduce worker alienation by a total of .18 standard deviations.

Somewhat more surprising are the overall effects of automation on the inside crafts. As noted, the use of programmable automation reduces the autonomy of the switching crafts, indirectly increasing worker alienation. However, as Table 4.7 reveals, the direct effect of automation on alienation serves to *offset* this indirect, alienating effect: After adjusting for variations in work content, we find that automated switching technology tends to *reduce* workers' levels of alienation.[28] Because the direct and indirect effects of alienation move in opposite directions, the result cancels out any trend toward alienation that switching craftworkers might otherwise feel. Overall, we therefore find no pronounced changes in alienation among the two skilled craft groups.

As we have seen, automation exerts a pronounced de-skilling effect on the content of clerical labor, which in turn heightens these workers' alienation from their jobs. In addition to this indirect effect, automation also exerts a direct effect on clerical workers' attitudes, which in this case only *exacerbates* the trend toward increased alienation. Given the consistency and strength of these effects, we find that automation has an especially strong and adverse effect on work attitudes among the clerical group. Thus the model estimates that each standard deviation increase in the degree of office automation elevates clerical workers' alienation by an average of .40 standard deviations—an appreciable effect.

Hence the data largely conform to the qualitative observations just sketched and shed further light on the limitations of the de-skilling thesis when applied to skilled manual work as a whole. We again find evidence of a deterioration in the work situations of certain crafts (those in switching and frame locations) where programmable automation has reduced workers' autonomy. Yet we find no evidence of any overall trend toward the simplification or dilution of conceptual skill requirements. In fact, the only significant trends involving conceptual content are among the outside crafts, whose jobs demand *in*creasing levels of conceptual skill as automation rises. Again, the automation process seems not so much to *abolish* as to *recast* the nature of craft work. Where the position of one craft seems to weaken, that of another craft group is enhanced, redistributing skills among the various crafts (Penn, 1985). At the same time, automation seems to foster a clear de-skilling trend among clerical employees. The net effect is to reflect or reproduce the pattern of inequality that exists between craft and clerical workers. In fact, this pattern of inequality seems if anything to have grown more pronounced, as clerks have experienced the brunt of the rationalization process.

CONCLUSION

The transformation of the labor process at New York Telephone during the years after 1971 provides us with an especially useful means of testing de-skilling theory. Here, after all, is a case in which management enjoyed considerable latitude in the reorganization of work, following a major victory over its unionized work force. Furthermore, the company had at its disposal a wide array of highly sophisticated information technologies with which to uproot craft skills. Despite these conditions, however, the processes underway in this firm only partly conform to the de-skilling paradigm and indicate the need for substantial qualification of its claims.

First, we find no evidence of any widespread simplification or dilution of skill requirements, nor of any leveling or homogenization of labor to the same unskilled condition. We do indeed find instances of such phenomena, most notably in the case of the Deskmen. Yet their fate—as classic a case of de-skilling as can be found—does not reflect the fate of skilled crafts in the industry writ large. For it appears that management has been *unable* to reduce or eliminate the need for conceptual skills in workers' jobs. Often, as with the increasing access to data which the outside crafts now enjoy, the company has merely shifted the locus of expertise. This process has implicitly served to reproduce or replenish workers' skills, redistributing them among various claimants and reconstituting skilled manual work as a distinct occupational category.

The same cannot be said for workers employed in routine office jobs. As we have seen, these workers have been reassigned to larger, consolidated offices in the search for greater efficiency, a process that has led management to impose much the same "Traffic" environment on their work as the operators have long known. What seems to have occurred, then, is that the introduction of information technologies has not transformed or abolished the schism between skilled manual and routine office jobs, but instead only reflected and reproduced it.

We can speculate on why this is so (although limitations in the data prevent us from drawing any definite conclusion). One possible explanation stresses the neglect of the union in protecting the nature of women's jobs. This view ought not to be dismissed out of hand, least of all in an industry in which male workers and their organizations have historically shown a tendency to favor their gender over their class interests.[29] Yet this view seems to overstate the power of workers' unions in shaping the labor process, especially at a time of their gravest weakness (the post-1971 years).

A second explanation for the reproduction of inequality within the Plant department centers on managerial biases toward so-called "female" work. Again, this view conforms to the history of the industry and seems to explain why women reaped so few benefits from the de-skilling of the Deskmen's craft and eventual use of CAT systems. However, interviews with technical planners and managers found no pronounced tendency toward the singling out of "women's" jobs as candidates for automation, and it is by no means clear that the eventual erosion of the role of the MLT operators stemmed from any managerial bias in favor of male labor.

A third explanation stresses the cumulative or indirect effects of gender segregation, and seems most plausible here. This view suggests that the tendency of automation to reproduce women's unequal position within the labor process flows not from the conscious agency of either management or labor at the present time, but rather from the working out of historical processes set in motion decades before. Insofar as women were excluded from skilled jobs and concentrated in largely routine occupations during earlier periods, *their jobs were left more fully susceptible* to the rationalization process than workers in other, more highly skilled occupations. In such a context, even the application of technology in a gender-blind manner will reproduce schisms and inequalities laid down before.

A final consideration that emerges from the study of workplace automation in this industry concerns its effects on *all* groups of workers, regardless of occupation. To say that craft occupations have for the most part been reproduced as a functionally distinct category is by no means to suggest that these workers continue to hold the same position within the firm as they did before the 1970s. In fact, the spread of the new technologies has transformed the relation between the company and its workers in several unprecedented ways. These can best be sensed by juxtaposing the social relations of production that prevailed at mid-century with those which have only recently emerged.

As noted at the very outset of this chapter, despite their bureaucratic trappings, Plant departments at Bell operating companies were remarkable for the room they accorded to informal, customary patterns of social behavior, leaving substantial residues of discretion in the hands of their employees. Even workers employed in a district headquarters during this period—Nassau County's office in Hempstead—worked in the context of customs and traditions that muted or constrained management's relations with its employees. This is no longer true. The county's present district office—a large complex in Garden City, from which much of the network is controlled—is a far more highly structured or controlled environment than before. As observed the middle manager quoted above, offices now tend to be "less *supervised,* but more *controlled.*".

It is difficult to imagine workers at New York Telephone conducting the same rank-and-file job actions today which they routinely conducted a quarter of a century ago. Of course, a variety of organizational, economic, and political factors explain this fact. For one thing, the workers' unions have grown more highly bureaucratic, with local unions far more beholden to the union's District office than before. This has meant that primary and secondary union leaders, who played a key role in the struggles of the 1960s, have lost substantial amounts of power over the union's affairs. The labor market too has changed, with good-paying jobs far more difficult to find. And of course, the political climate is less conducive to labor protest, as the workers' movement as a whole has been forced into retreat.

Yet it seems clear that new technologies *have* played a pivotal role in shifting the overall balance of power within the firm. Increasingly, automation has enabled management to transcend workers' informal sources of power and to substitute software-controlled processes for the give-and-take of an earlier day. As programmable machines come to lodge decision-making rules within computer algorithms, workers find that information technologies play an ever-more central role in production, regulating the rhythms of the work process from afar. A top technical planner for New York Telephone put the point this way:

> Now you *know* how the work is being performed. The machine guarantees you that the job you always *thought* was being done, *is* being done. What automation does is to begin to ensure that *one hundred percent of the work is processed by the norm.*

The increasing use of information technologies to regulate production has not, we have seen, required any overall trend toward the simplification or intensification of work. Indeed, the process has begun to show the weakness of a key assumption on which de-skilling theory rests: the belief that increases in managerial control demand the progressive removal of skill from workers' hands. This assumption may have been appropriate in prior periods, when workers' possession of production skills conferred important elements of control over the labor process. With the coming of automation, however, this link between skill and power has apparently declined. For once information technologies have dislodged workers from the most strategic points in the labor process, relegating them to peripheral or auxiliary locations within the labor process, even craft workers find that *their skills confer less power* over production than was the case a generation ago.

CHAPTER 5

The Limits of Managerial Hegemony

The previous chapter focused on the transformation of the labor process in an effort to understand the structure of labor control that has evolved at Bell firms during the postwar period. The analysis has drawn attention to some of the limitations inherent in de-skilling theory, while at the same time showing ways in which technology bears on the regulation of labor. As many theorists have pointed out, however, it cannot suffice to study the objective structure of the labor process alone. To understand the mechanics of labor control, we must also examine workers' conceptions of their roles as producers and their attitudinal and behavioral responses to the labor process. It therefore becomes incumbent on us to explore the normative or *ideological* influences that shape workers' responses to managerial control. More specifically, the question is whether workers are indeed subject to organizational processes that elicit their tacit consent to the relations of production, as theorists of managerial hegemony have claimed.

The thesis of hegemony takes many forms. Burawoy's own analysis holds that the postwar period is notable for the rise of hegemonic regimes, rooted in the informal relations that emerge in production. He further contends that rising economic competition and restructuring only strengthen management's ideological predominance, as troubled times pose growing threats to workers' livelihood, inducing workers to align their interests with their employers and to make concessions when the firm demands. A second variant of hegemony theory emphasizes the rise of what have come to be called Firm Internal Labor Markets (FILMs)—job structures and promotion ladders—which promote an individualistic ethos of mobility (Doeringer and Piore 1971; Edwards 1975, 1979; Kalleberg and Sorensen 1979; and Littler 1983). A third, less fully developed version centers on the rise of workplace reform efforts, which sustain the appearance of democratic participation even amid the persistence of unilateral managerial control (Parker 1985; Grenier 1988; Fantasia, Clawson, and Graham, 1988).

These and other variations on the theme of managerial hegemony have grown increasingly influential among industrial sociologists. They have an obvious relevance in an industry whose workers enjoy relatively high wages and who are exposed to both internal labor markets and workplace reform efforts such as the Quality of Work Life process (QWL), which aim to kindle a spirit of cooperation between workers and management. Mindful of the industry's characteristics, several hegemony theorists have explicitly invoked the case of AT&T to illustrate the labor control system they have in mind. As noted above, Edwards (1979) drew on the case of AT&T—especially its elaborate bureaucracy and system of job ladders—to develop his theory of bureaucratic control. In the same manner, Cornfield (1987) has viewed the industry as especially favorable soil for the growth of labor/management cooperation (Batten and Schoonmaker 1987). Remarkably, however, few hegemony theorists have actually explored the link between the hegemonic mechanisms they stress and the substance of workers' consciousness.[1] Instead, they are content to assume that the articulation of internal labor markets and other such work structures must logically have the ideological effects imputed to them.

Several important objections to the hegemony thesis can be raised even at the start of the analysis. First, there now exists a fair-sized literature that suggests that workers have by no means uncritically embraced the tenets of managerial ideology, but instead have viewed its premises with great skepticism.[2] Second and more theoretically, the hegemony perspective seems inclined to stress ideological controls when other, more structural or material influences may better explain the phenomena its advocates would address. Finally, as is true of de-skilling theorists, advocates of hegemony theory typically neglect workers' resistance to the firm, and may therefore reify management's ability to shape the values of the workers they employ.

In this chapter I will explore the adequacy of hegemony theory as a model of labor control within the monopoly corporation.

The chapter begins by examining the substance of hegemony theory, turning first to the nature and effects of QWL reforms. It then discusses the ideological consequences that have flowed from rising economic austerity and inter-firm competition. Such economic developments are especially important in the communications industry, of course, in the wake of the historic process that divested AT&T of the operating companies it formerly owned and controlled. As we shall see, the breakup of the Bell monopoly has shattered the economic assumptions workers had taken for granted. To understand the full range of workers' responses, I will broaden the analysis beyond workers in the Plant department (my major concern with respect to the labor process) and now include workers in the Traffic and Commercial departments as well.

THE DOMINANT IDEOLOGY AT WORK

Hegemony theory traces its lineage to those sections of *The German Ideology* in which Marx and Engels outlined a nascent theory of ideology whose central thesis was that the ideas of the ruling class play a decisive role in perpetuating the subordination of the working class (see Marx and Engels 1976:57–67). Developing this reasoning two generations later, Antonio Gramsci (1971) theorized that the defeat of the workers' movements after World War I was due to the failure of socialism to contravene the moral and cultural dominance of the bourgeoisie within the sphere of civil society (see Anderson 1976). Soon thereafter, with the rise of fascism and the stabilization of Western capitalism, members of the Frankfurt school bemoaned the growing strength of bourgeois rationality, which they felt had insinuated itself into even the most private spheres of social life.

None of these formulations of hegemony theory emphasized the direct role of the commodity production process. In recent years, however, students of work have in effect 'industrialized' the theory, rooting the production of working-class consent within the labor process itself. In certain respects, this has turned Marx on his head. While Marx believed that commodity production processes would precipitate an oppositional consciousness among the working class, recent theorists of managerial hegemony instead contend that the social relations of capitalist production themselves help explain the weakness of the workers' movements in the advanced capitalist world. Thus, if "notions of exploitation and unpaid labor are even more removed from everyday life on the shop floor" than during Marx's time (Burawoy 1979:29), the reason must lie within certain aspects of the capitalist firm that induce workers to accept the authority relations they confront.

As discussed in Chapter 2, Richard Edwards (1979) argues that within monopoly core firms a system of "bureaucratic control" has emerged that not only formalizes managerial authority (imbuing company policy with a quasi-legal aura) but also ensnares workers within internal labor markets that foster a careerist orientation among their ranks. The result is that workers tend to identify more with the *firm* than with their own social *class*. A somewhat different perspective can be found in Burawoy's early work (1979), which holds that the "social relations *in* production" blind workers to the presence of conflictual relations *of* production, engaging workers' productive energies and inviting them to participate in their own exploitation. For both theorists, the internal structure of the monopoly corporation secretes an ideology that not only impedes the formation of working-class consciousness, but actively encourages workers to embrace the status quo.

Edwards in particular is careful to suggest that the precise workings of bureaucratic control vary at different organizational levels (1979:147–52). However, he believes that essential to its effectiveness are the ideological constraints it imposes on virtually *all* monopoly core workers. "The new system has transcended its white collar origins," he writes, and has encompassed both manual and mental employees within the monopoly capitalist firm (Edwards 1979:132). In the end, "workers use the first person plural differently: 'we' now means 'we the firm,' not 'we the workers'" (Edwards 1979:148).

Although both Edwards and Burawoy contend that ideological mechanisms are critical to the reproduction of managerial control, there are important differences between their accounts that are important to acknowledge. Perhaps most obvious, Edwards is mainly concerned with the *formal* properties of the modern corporation (written rules and procedures), while for

Burawoy the key to managerial hegemony lies in the *informal* realm (principally, shop-floor culture). For our purposes here, an even more important distinction between their respective analyses lies in their contrasting interpretations of how economic competition and austerity affect managerial hegemony.

In Edwards' view, economic crises, when severe enough, force management to renege on the implied contract that underpins bureaucratic control: as layoffs spread and career opportunities vanish, the structure of bureaucratic control begins to develop widening cracks that may even portend an emerging crisis of managerial control. In this view, economic uncertainty spawns disillusionment with managerial ideology. For Burawoy, however, growing economic competition and austerity have precisely the opposite effect. Particularly where workers have been conditioned to align their interests with their employers, as under hegemonic regimes, they are likely to consent to the austerity measures their employers demand (a system he terms "hegemonic despotism"). An important issue to be addressed, then, is precisely how economic competition has affected worker consciousness.

There is a further species of hegemony theory that will also concern us in this chapter, and that centers on the link between worker participation programs and the character of worker consciousness. As industrial sociologists have increasingly pointed out, the rhetoric of participation, combined with programs of limited organizational reform, can provide a potent means of controlling workers. Thus Fantasia and colleagues (1988) find that despite managerial pronouncements favoring workplace democracy, worker participation programs are often part of a larger effort either to avoid or to undermine the presence of trade union organization. Likewise, Guillermo Grenier's (1988) case study of Quality Circles at a Johnson & Johnson plant in New Mexico finds that management systematically used the rhetoric of empowerment to mask a determined effort to extend its control over work groups throughout the plant.

Such critical analyses are by no means confined to the academy. In fact, the union officials who were involved in the inception of this study were deeply concerned that Bell's QWL program might interfere with the workings of collective bargaining or otherwise undercut workers' support for union representation.

Although CWA stewards, staff, and union officials often saw in QWL a host of new opportunities, many at all levels in the union opposed the new program, viewing it as a Trojan horse.

Interestingly, a number of managerial consultants and organizational analysts such as Kanter, Zuboff, Hirschhorn, and others have found virtue in worker participation efforts, often celebrating precisely the same conditions that have prompted criticism among others. Such writers often argue that workplace reform prefigures a new mode of authority that will overcome capitalism's legacy of industrial conflict, rekindling a sense of commitment and community within the firm, and in so doing making labor unions unnecessary and obsolete. Indeed, Zuboff (1987) goes so far as to outline a model of managerial authority that quite consciously denies independent labor organization any space at all.

I begin by asking whether the QWL process does indeed comprise a potent means of incorporating workers into the firm.

THE IDEOLOGY OF PARTICIPATION

The 1980 collective bargaining agreement between AT&T and CWA was the product of frustration on both sides. As AT&T's corporate vice president explicitly acknowledged, the company's comprehensive Work Relations Surveys had for some time documented disturbing levels of alienation and poor worker motivation. And Glenn Watts, then-president of the CWA, admitted that the union had enjoyed little success in dealing with its members' work-related discontents and had even begun to share in the workers' assignment of blame.[3] In an effort to deal with lagging productivity and work satisfaction, the company and the union signed an agreement that established a joint National QWL Committee, empowered to outline a statement of principles that would guide the national QWL process in the ensuing years. In keeping with prior QWL efforts in other industries, the statement was careful to avoid generating fears on either side of the class divide. Especially noteworthy were statements that defined the terrain on which the QWL process was to operate, statements which took pains to note that "the process of implementing an improved quality of life at work shall not infringe upon existing management rights."

By 1981 the National QWL Committee had taken steps to ensure that QWL radiated outward and downward throughout the Bell system. To do this it appointed coordinators at regional and district levels, who helped establish steering committees at each operating company. These steering committees in turn fostered local steering committees, made up of middle managers and union officials who oversaw the establishment of QWL teams at given work locations, supporting their activities by designating facilitators and other 'resource people' to train team members in the goals and methods of worker participation, QWL-style. Thus QWL embodied a clear contradiction: itself a heavily top-down process, its avowed goals were to "increase worker participation in decisions which affect the job."[4]

Teams established at each work site have typically been composed of five to ten members who participate on a voluntary basis. Where teams develop roots, membership is placed on a rotating basis to allow broad, inclusive representation. Meetings are usually hour-long affairs held each week during working time, typically in the presence of facilitators drawn from both management and the local union. Although procedures vary in accordance with local preferences, most teams solicit input from the broader population of workers at each site and take steps to define and address issues on their own account. They do so with the understanding that their actions are not to intrude on contractual agreements and in the knowledge that their proposals are merely that—non-binding recommendations that must be forwarded to the relevant officials (usually, middle- and upper-level management), who may decide to reject, accept, or merely ignore them.

Despite misgivings among both company and union officials, support for the QWL process was strong enough to ensure its growth. By the end of 1981 there were 150 teams in existence; three years later this figure had grown to more than 1,200 nationally. AT&T and CWA management were emboldened by their success in initiating the process, but completely in the dark as to its actual consequences. Many teams faltered soon after their establishment, sowing mistrust and even resentment. In a few widely publicized cases, members of QWL teams crossed picket lines during the national strike of August 1983, raising questions about QWL's effects on collective bargaining. Despite such difficulties, a study conducted by the U.S. Department of Labor's Division of Labor/Management Cooperation sought to evaluate the QWL process at AT&T and found what it called "encouraging signs" that the effort had begun to bear fruit. Conducting an in-depth analysis of ten QWL teams drawn from the Bell system nationwide, the study found evidence of improved relations between workers and supervisors, reductions in the number of grievances, and other signs of a newly cooperative relation between local management and its workers. The study took pains to note that even these indications were both modest and fragile. Often, teams that undertook too ambitious a program of reform encountered resistance from above and soon grew discouraged, leading to the collapse of the local effort in toto (U.S. Department of Labor 1984).[5]

Officials at New York Telephone and District I of the CWA participated in the national effort. Beginning in November 1981, a CWA/NYT QWL Committee was established, which soon succeeded in propagating local steering committees wherever the host milieu proved favorable. The first QWL teams were initiated in Buffalo and soon spread throughout New York, including the downstate area. By 1985, when this study began, thirty-six QWL teams had been established in New York, and more were introduced each month.

The Labor of Participation   To read existing records of QWL team meetings is to encounter reports that could easily be mistaken for archival records of the old company unions at AT&T. Much like the report from the Illinois Bell Employees' Association of the early 1930s quoted in Chapter 3, workers' efforts seem mainly to revolve around technical and hygienic issues. A recent compendium of team achievements cited such improvements as these: "provided training to service clerks to ensure uniform work procedures," "relocated noisy air dryers that are used to pressurize cable," or "instituted field trips where assignment clerks accompany installers to see how their jobs impact field assignments."[6] The QWL team meetings I observed usually addressed issues such as smoking policy, provisions for keeping corridor floors dry during inclement weather, and methods of improving communication between departments.

It is all too easy to trivialize these concerns. Obviously these issues bear little resemblance to syndicalist battles for workers' control. Yet for workers such issues as these often involve enduring sources of irritation and discomfort in their working lives, and their resolution may take on a symbolic importance that is often neglected by outsiders. The point is that if and when the QWL process works, it can harbor a subtle ideological importance: Arguably, QWL can impart a vocabulary premised on cooperation and compromise, as did the old company unions, defining the search for common ground as the proper avenue down which class relations ought to move.

Hence the question is whether QWL contains the seeds of managerial hegemony in a new guise. Sites included in my 1985 survey of workers in New York and New Jersey included nine QWL teams representing a total of 321 workers in three major occupational categories. Mirroring the national experience, outside craftworkers seemed unresponsive to the QWL effort, and no QWL teams had been established among their ranks. Hence, the nine sites include only operators, clerical employees, and craftworkers at frame and switch locations.

To assess the effect of QWL on workers' attitudes and behavior, I have made two types of comparisons. The first involved the attitudes of workers in similar occupations, whose work locations are distinguished only by the presence or absence of QWL teams. The second included workers employed at QWL worksites and compared the attitudes of team members with the broader population of workers they are asked to represent. The analysis is of course hampered by its cross-sectional design and by the relative 'youth' of the QWL teams. Yet most of the teams had been functioning for more than a year and a half, and some as long as three years. Presumably evidence of any ideological effects will have begun to appear within that span of time.

Six outcome measures were employed, including levels of alienation from work, perceptions of supervision, frequency of union attendance, and three dimensions of workers' attitudes toward management—their conception of the firm, their support for worker control, and their propensity to strike.[7] Using analysis of variance techniques to explore how the presence of QWL affected attitudes among workers in each of three occupational categories (operators, clerks, and switchworkers) yielded a total of eighteen tests of significance. In addition to these comparisons of workers at QWL and non-QWL sites, comparisons for team members and nonmembers at the same work location yielded an additional eighteen tests. The results, summarized below, are almost entirely negative, casting strong doubts on claims that the QWL process weakens working-class consciousness. Indeed, QWL seems to have had little discernible effect of *any* type on workers' attitudes or behavior.

The presence of QWL teams has no significant effect on the attitudes of operators. Operators remain highly critical of their employers' treatment of them even at offices where QWL teams have been established. Even team members betray little indication of an attitudinal or ideological effect. Of the 130 operators employed at sites with QWL teams, perceptions are evenly divided as to how worthwhile the effort has been; no variations in union attendance obtained. For most operators, the critical issue in their working lives—the intense pressure to keep working—remained unchanged with QWL teams in place.

The results are much the same for the clerical employees and switching craftworkers. In no case did statistically significant differences emerge between the broader population of workers at QWL and non-QWL sites. Only in the frequency of attendance at union meetings did team members differ from nonmembers: contrary to hegemony theory, team members were *more* frequent attenders (a difference that likely preceded the establishment of QWL itself).

Field work at QWL meetings yields evidence that is firmly in accord with these data. Although most team members seemed committed to the participatory goals implied in QWL, few were terribly sanguine about the process in which they were engaged. Often, team members openly expressed varying levels of fatalism, sometimes leavened with humor, when questions were raised about the outcome of their efforts. At one team meeting held at a clerical work site, a team member who had been out with a broken leg returned after several months and asked what had happened to the team's recommendation that management allow assignment clerks to wear new and more comfortable headsets while handling the phones. A fellow team member replied tersely, "It got the usual response." When I looked puzzled a third member explained, "It's still on Jim Winkler's desk," referring to the second-line manager at that location. "Isn't democracy wonderful?"

A further issue involving QWL concerns its relation to technological change. Advocates of 'post-hierarchical' models of workplace authority often suggest that innovative forms of workplace authority are most likely to develop within automated production processes. We might therefore expect that QWL would be best suited in work settings that employ advanced information technologies (see Zuboff 1987; Hirschhorn 1984). In keeping with this suggestion, preliminary analysis of the survey data indicates that QWL teams *are* in fact significantly more prevalent at highly automated work locations. Only 28 percent of the sites at more primitive levels of technological development, compared with a majority (52.8 percent) of the highly automated worksites, had established QWL teams (p < .0001). However, further analysis suggests that this association is entirely due to the disproportionate location of QWL teams at Traffic worksites, where alienation and discontent have traditionally been highest, and where automation has been taken to its extreme. Among the other occupations included in the analysis, there is no evidence of any affinity between automation and QWL. If QWL was intended to provide an alternative means of labor control, in short, that attempt has apparently failed.

ECONOMIC COMPETITION
AND THE WORKERS' RESPONSE

A second variant of hegemony theory argues that the rise of external threats to the economic position of particular firms or whole industries often induce workers to align their interests with their employers. This is the thrust of Burawoy's argument (1985) concerning 'hegemonic despotism'—a term he uses to describe the growing capacity of large corporations to dictate the terms and conditions of employment to workers who feel compelled to make concessions for the sake of the firm. It is further developed by Daniel Cornfield (1987), who sees such a pattern as especially likely in firms whose workers are unionized and who have made a long-term investment of their working time in a particular company. When their firms encounter external economic threats, says Cornfield, workers in these situations will close ranks behind their employers and embrace a newly cooperative pattern of work relations.

Economic restructuring and growing competition are obvious features of the communications industry. Even if we restrict our attention to the postwar history of economic organization in this branch of production, we find that competition has steadily grown during the past three decades, not only predating the breakup of AT&T, but actually driving divestiture forward. In fact, much of the impetus toward competition had its roots in the 1956 Consent Decree, in which the Justice Department dropped its antitrust litigation against Bell, thereby agreeing to leave the Bell monopoly unchallenged. In return, Bell was forced to forego any involvement in the nascent computer industry, and to place a long list of transmission and relay technologies in the public domain as well. At this time, state policy was being used to maintain boundaries between different branches of the economy—communications and computers. Eventually, however, the technologies which the Consent Decree secured (radiotelephony, microwave transmission designs, and so forth) themselves acted to undermine this industrial boundary and played a decisive role in the economic restructuring the industry would undergo.

Two economic effects of these technologies were apparent before the 1956 Consent Decree was even a decade old. First, they dramatically reduced the cost of production of long distance services. And second, they reduced the capital investments firms needed to enter the long distance market. The first of these effects could not help AT&T profits in the least, for the FCC forced AT&T to use any cost savings within its Long Lines division to subsidize local telephone service. The second of these effects directly hurt AT&T, for it meant that smaller firms (such as the fledgling MCI) could begin to compete in this emerging market. These new startup companies were not obligated to subsidize local telephone service, as was AT&T, and could therefore undercut Bell prices and still reap especially high rates of profit. For this reason, capital flowed rapidly into the long distance market, and new rivals began to demand the right to encroach on the Bell system's lines (see Kohl 1982; Faulhaber 1987).

Bell sought desperately to shore up its monopoly privileges, at times claiming that the financial and technical "integrity of the system" was at stake and engaging in predatory actions against its rivals. Such behavior only confirmed the perception that Bell had abused its public trust. Ruling after ruling by the FCC went against AT&T, until the pressure to break up the Bell system became all but insurmountable. The breakup was therefore the logical culmination of developments that had been incubating for nearly thirty years.

With divestiture, competitive pressures have increased even more rapidly, most notably within national markets for long distance and information services (as judicial rulings and legislative action have begun to open up the latter market even to the Baby Bells). Markets for communications and customer premise equipment have also grown sharply competitive, with giant multinational firms such as General Electric, Siemens, NEC, and Northern Telecom struggling to capture AT&T's market share. Increasingly, the computer and telecommunications industries have converged into a single 'information industry' (see Borrus and Zysman, 1984:10–12), blurring the industrial boundaries which the 1956 Consent Decree sought to maintain. AT&T's recent acquisition of NCR is the perfect symbol of this process. As Kohl puts it, "Companies which once dominated their respective sectors [in communications or computers] now compete with one another, as their once distinct products collapse into one new market" (1982:59).

The market for local telephone service has been insulated from at least some of these processes, as judicial rulings have enabled the Baby Bells to retain their relatively monopolistic position. Yet even the operating companies have experienced unprecedented economic pressures. Inasmuch as local telephone service is no longer subsidized by long distance revenues, the management of each operating company faces cost pressures as never before. Increasingly, the Bell holding companies have invested large amounts of their capital in unregulated markets and thus look at their telephone holdings with new and more demanding eyes.

Moreover, the provision of networks, special services, and even access to long distance services are increasingly available from numerous suppliers. Hence, many of the assumptions that previously informed the operations of the local Bell firms have rapidly dissolved.

Under these conditions, have workers tended to align their interests with those of their employer? Have economic restructuring and the uncertainties that accompany rising competition induced these unionized workers (most of whom are long-term employees) to redefine their position within the firm and to view the company in a benign light? These questions lead into the character of working-class consciousness within the monopoly corporation.

Culture, Conflict, and Consent   It is not difficult to locate workers who have uncritically embraced the existing structure of authority. At least three distinct but overlapping forms of such consent seem to exist. The first, a vestige from the old regime, is rooted in the worker's *deference* to his or her presumed superiors. This view is well-illustrated in the remarks of a retired craftworker who started at New York Telephone by mopping floors:

> The people who didn't want to cooperate with management were always the lazy ones, the ones who couldn't do their jobs. Always, in the entire twenty-eight years I've worked for the company, I've always been *grateful* to the company for providing me with a living, even with my limited education.

Since this worker views his inferior standing in the labor market as legitimate, he regards his job as a benevolent gift. He therefore feels obligated to reciprocate, demonstrating his unswerving loyalty to the firm.

A second, more *pragmatic* form of consent occurs when workers focus on the economic returns they stand to gain by forming an attachment to the firm. When asked whether it was more important for workers to cooperate with management or to stand up for their rights, a cable splicer explained his outlook by saying: "You do your job, don't make any problems, and everything should be okay. I mean, the stronger the company, the better the chance that there won't be any layoffs, right?" Likewise, a clerical worker replied: "I think you have to cooperate with management. I mean, as goes the company, so go you. I feel the way it is today, you *have* to make the company work. Otherwise, you have nothing."

Still another form of consent seems inspired by an almost *entrepreneurial* orientation and fits quite well with Burawoy's concept of market despotism. Here is an excerpt from the transcript:

TONY. I've said this at a lot of meetings, but people better start waking up! I mean, today it's like *your own business*. You gotta go out and you gotta talk New York Tel, because there are a lot of areas where people can go to the competition...

AUTHOR. So the breakup has made you, in effect, a spokesman for the company?

TONY. Absolutely! Sometimes I even look to make sales for the company [although this is not his job]. I'll give you an example. My wife has a job at an insurance firm in Manhattan, and her boss was considering an inferior company for their telephone service. I mean, it was going to be a hundred and sixty thousand dollar contract. And what I did was, I made *sure* that New York Telephone got some people down there to make that sale, and they did. I would never have done that before. It's a whole new ballgame now.

Such consensual views are often well-developed, and workers who hold them can mobilize strong arguments in their defense. Not surprisingly, one hears in them echoes of certain Reaganist themes, suggesting that the wider political and ideological context has seeped into the politics of the firm. Nonetheless, whatever their form or their origin, such consensual views are clearly the exception rather than the rule. Far more common is an oppositional consciousness, fueled by workers' resentment at being treated like commodities or like rungs on the corporate ladder their managers are eager to climb.

Evidence of an oppositional consciousness seems especially common among operators, who often speak bitterly of management's obsession with the measurement of their productivity. One operator was asked the standard 'football' question about relations between management and workers—whether the two are on 'the same team' or really on two different and opposing sides. A polite and well dressed woman in her forties, the operator said calmly and with precision:

> To some extent we get along, but we really oppose one another. Management will use you for what they can get from you. If they can get blood out of you, they'll get blood out of you. And they don't care how.

Her co-workers underscored their agreement. One recalled that when the air conditioning broke down in their office, her managers brought in large electric fans. "But they aimed them *at the computers*. They just wanted to keep the *machines* cool. They didn't care about *us* overheating." Similar patterns of resentment were expressed by a male operator in his late twenties. When asked an open-ended question involving the things he likes least about his job, he said:

> What I dislike the most is that they think I'm a machine. They say they try to improve the technology, to make it easy for us. [Laughs.] They're not trying to make it easier for us. They're trying *to make us go faster*. Because the faster we go, the more *money* they can make.

Such views are hardly limited to operators: An even more conflictual view of the company exists among the different craft groups. For example, when I asked workers whether top management really cared about the needs of workers such as themselves, one craftsworker replied:

> I don't think top management has *any respect at all* for the workers, to be truthful. Middle management, lower management, yes. But top management, no.

Another craftworker stopped me in mid-sentence as I prepared to ask the same question of him:

> Top management? You mean Ferguson? Salerno? [Chief officers of NYNEX.] *These are the guys that force us to go out on strike!* They don't even care about *lower* management!

Recent sociological analysis has too often used the concept of 'management' in an undifferentiated way, but these workers often make fine distinctions between the nature of authority figures at different levels in the company hierarchy. With important exceptions, workers often view first-line supervisors as occupying situations akin to their own. Several workers expressed sympathy for the situations of their supervisors. One man said:

> They have no authority now. They have to pay for their benefits and we don't. They can't even suspend a worker for cause without going to second- and third-line supervision.

Workers sometimes recount stories of first- and second-line managers who have stood up to defend their subordinates, at great risk to themselves. Beginning roughly at the third level of supervision, however, workers detect the presence of a boundary, demarcating groups with whom their own interests collide. As we ascend the corporate ladder, workers grow skeptical of their managerial superiors, whom many regard as "a bunch of politicians and bullshit artists."

Workers sometimes speak derisively of an older style of manager they term "Bell Heads." These are managers whose long-term attachment to the old Bell system and habitual conformity to its procedures has left them unable to think for themselves. Workers are especially critical of the newer style of manager, however, whom they call "Jet Jobs." Typically recruited from elite business schools, these managers lack even the faintest idea about how telephone work is done. Stories abound about the irrationality of a system that grants managers such power and authority despite their manifest ignorance of the industry's most basic operations. Skilled workers regard it as a particular affront when "someone who doesn't know the job is telling you as a craftsperson what to do!" They are equally suspicious of engineers and other technical experts, whose formal training and penchant for abstract systems approaches blinds them to the most obvious of practical requirements: "Some of these guys [engineers] can't go to the bathroom without asking for help."[8]

Remarks such as these are sometimes surrounded by a web of qualifications, as if workers felt at least some normative constraints on the expression of such views. Thus, one craftworker voiced sharp but wavering resentment at management's use of new technologies:

> That's where the control is now, in the technology. That's what you should look at. *It's like they have a collar on you at all times now.* [Pauses, reflects.] Of course, you're working for them, and they're paying you. [Shakes his head.] But for them to

use, to abuse these technologies...to have to hear their snide remarks, *it's just not right.*

Interestingly, this worker shifted between two distinct moral codes—one based on defiance and indignation, the other on a more deferential, acquiescent set of expectations. Even in such cases as this, intimating a contradictory consciousness, the more defiant and oppositional ideological element prevails.[9]

To gauge the prevalence of this conflictual outlook, we can explore workers' responses to a battery of survey items designed to measure levels of class consciousness.[10] Two-thirds (64.2 percent) believed that management "only cares about profits, regardless of what workers want or need." Roughly the same proportion (67.5 percent) felt that "the people who run large corporations will try to take advantage of the workers if you give them the chance." Moreover, when workers were asked to describe relations between themselves and management using the previously mentioned football metaphor, their responses again indicate the predominance of an oppositional perspective, with nearly three-quarters (73.5 percent) reporting that management and workers belong to "two different and opposing sides." Finally, the largest proportion seemed willing to engage in militant behavior should events so require. Asked what they would do if management demanded worker concessions, 45.4 percent reported a willingness to strike, while only 10.2 percent hesitated to even speak of a work stoppage. (The remainder, an additional 44.2 percent, voiced their opposition to concessions without advocating a strike).

We can penetrate further into the nature of workers' consciousness by considering their views of the process of technological change. This aspect of their perspective is especially relevant for both practical and theoretical reasons. In practical terms, technological change is a constant feature of these workers' lives and is therefore a matter of great concern to most. In more theoretical terms, observers have often argued that managerial ideology portrays technological change as "progress," thus inviting workers to view automation as a socially neutral process that transcends human choice. Have workers succumbed to such ideologies of technological change? To address this issue I applied the classical question—*cui bono?* (who benefits?)—to the issue of technological change. Their responses again indicated that, while some workers have embraced the dominant ideology, most have retained a more conflictual point of view.

A consensual view of advanced technology as an especially useful tool emerged in the view of one worker, a former Deskman named Fuzzy:

> I didn't come to work in a horse and buggy. It's the same thing here. We have to adjust to the new technologies or we'll be left behind.

Likewise, when I asked one clerical worker what management hoped to achieve by introducing the information systems she used, she said:

> It's simply more efficient than wading through papers and line records and yards and yards of index cards. It's just a more efficient way to do things.

Still other workers believed that the underlying factor guiding technological change was simply service improvement. Again, however, workers who hold so benign a view of new technology were clearly in the minority.

This fact emerged in a 1987 survey of workers in one suburban local who were given a forced-choice item which asked whether workers or management "benefited *the most* from the use of computers and other advanced technologies." (Specifically, the item asked whether *workers* benefited the most, management and workers benefited about *equally*, or whether *management* derived the most benefit).[11] The results are instructive. The great majority (72.3 percent) of respondents felt that management, not workers, benefited from new technologies, while a quarter (26.5 percent) felt that new technologies benefited both sides equally. Virtually no one felt that workers benefited most of all. When asked to explain how they felt management had benefited, workers' responses fell into one of two categories.

The first centered on the *economic* consequences of new technology. Although some workers mentioned the intensification of their work in this vein (recall the worker who said "they try to make us go faster"), most focused on management's use of technology to eliminate their jobs. Said one worker: "They just want to do away with everybody. They either automate you or else contract the work out, do away with you that way." Another worker replied: "Top management benefits. They're the ones who are reaping the rewards, by getting rid of bodies."

The second, equally common focus centered on the *political* consequences of new technology, as in the worker who observed that with automation "they can keep track of you better and know where you are at all times." Especially common here were Orwellian comments about electronic surveillance. One worker explained management's motives for introducing new technologies by noting that "Big Brother can watch us all that way." Said another, "Big Brother is here.... They use the computers to watch us all the time."[12]

Some might object that the survey items tap abstract perceptions that may or may not be linked to concrete events. However, the course of labor relations in this industry corresponds to the thrust of the survey results, further indicating the depth of workers' oppositional consciousness. Shortly after these data were collected, management demanded real concessions from workers (mainly involving reductions in health care benefits), much in keeping with the hypothetical demands included in the survey questionnaire. A bitter four-month strike ensued in 1989, in which several workers were seriously injured (one fatally), and the strike ended only when management retracted its demands for concessions.

SOURCES OF VARIATION IN
WORKING-CLASS CONSCIOUSNESS

Thus far it would seem that hegemony theory offers little basis for depicting the attitudes of the sample as a whole. Yet further study suggests that workers in some occupational categories *do* tend to align their interests with management, while other groups manifest a more conflictual or proletarian attitude. The task then becomes one of identifying those social factors that help explain the emergence of working-class consciousness among some groups of workers and managerial inclinations among others. To address this task, the following discussion draws first on quantitative measures of class consciousness and various aspects of workers' jobs. It then draws on field work to capture aspects of work relations the survey data cannot tap.

To unravel the sources of variation in worker consciousness I constructed a set of indices to measure levels of working-class consciousness. In keeping with prior research, my analysis began by distinguishing four conceptually distinct dimensions of the classically 'proletarian' outlook:

1. identification with the working class
2. adherence to a conflictual image of the firm (a 'them' versus 'us' outlook)
3. support for workers' control over the production process
4. a willingness to take militant action (to strike) in defense of one's needs

Table 5.1 presents the results of a factor analysis using indicators of these dimensions.[13]

TABLE 5.1
FACTOR ANALYSIS OF ITEMS MEASURING WORKING-CLASS
CONSCIOUSNESS (VARIMAX ROTATION)

	Rotated Factor Loadings			
Variable	*1*	*2*	*3*	*Communality*
Class identification[a]	-.209	.032	.418	.219
Managers and workers are on same/different teams	.106	-.033	.694	.494
Corporations take advantage of their workers	.267	.380	.694	.698
All management cares about is profits	.336	.247	.726	.702
If workers could make decisions, products would improve	.887	.038	.040	.790
Workers would make better decisions than supervisors	.852	.068	.153	.755
Would strike to defend benefits	.127	.784	.078	.637
Would strike to defend income protection plan	-.075	.827	-.007	.689
Would strike in sympathy with aggrieved workers elsewhere in the Bell System	-.053	.489	.185	.276
Eigenvalue	2.778	1.434	1.050	
% of total variance	30.9	15.9	11.7	

Note: [a]Middle class = 0, working class = 1.

TABLE 5.2
DIMENSIONS OF CLASS CONSCIOUSNESS REGRESSED ON OCCUPATIONAL CATEGORY[a] AND SELECTED OCCUPATIONAL CONDITIONS
(UNSTANDARDIZED COEFFICIENTS, WITH STANDARD ERRORS IN PARENTHESES)

	A			B		
Dependent Variable: Predictor	Image of the Firm	Support for Worker control	Militancy	Image of the Firm	Support for Worker Control	Militancy
Age	-.03*	-.02**	-.02*	-.01*	-.01**	-.01*
	(.01)	(.00)	(.01)	(.01)	(.00)	(.01)
Operators	-.24	-.34	-.41*	-1.30***	-.23	-.74***
	(.35)	(.24)	(.20)	(.37)	(.26)	(.24)
Inside Crafts	-.05	-.42	.15	-.32	-.26	.32
	(.33)	(.23)	(.19)	(.33)	(.23)	(.20)
Clerical Workers	-1.16***	-.04	-.52**	-1.24***	-.09**	-.50**
	(.29)	(.20)	(.17)	(.27)	(.19)	(.17)
Reps	-1.43***	-.71***	-1.15***	-1.37***	-.65**	-1.13***
	(.37)	(.26)	(.22)	(.34)	(.24)	(.22)
Autonomy				-.08**	.03	-.03
				(.03)	(.02)	(.01)
Perceived Opportunity				-.39***	-.15	-.02
				(.12)	(.09)	(.10)
Experience of Promotion				.13	.13	.10
				(.20)	(.14)	(.13)

Job Security (log)				-3.22***	-2.00***	-.34
				(.62)	(.45)	(.40)
Supervisory				-.20***	-.11***	-.07**
				(.04)	(.03)	(.02)
Treatment	-.056***	-.052***	-.076***			
Constant	11.11	7.73	7.73	5.96	4.65	6.22
R²				.238***	.166***	.110***
N	(518)	(518)	(518)	(518)	(518)	(518)

Note: ᵃOutside crafts defined as referent category.

*P < .05
**P < .01
***P < .001

Rather than four factors, the loadings indicate the presence of only three: (1) support for workers' control, (2) militancy, and (3) a conflictual image of the firm. Contrary to expectations, class identification does not emerge as a distinct factor in its own right, but instead loads highly on the third factor (though somewhat less clearly than its other components). This makes intuitive sense: Identification with the working class very likely presupposes an oppositional view of the class structure writ large. Recognizing these three dimensions of class consciousness, I have constructed indices for use as dependent variables. A high score on all three dimensions shows a relatively strong oppositional consciousness, and a low score indicates a managerial or middle-class ideology that betokens acceptance of the existing relations of production.

The left-hand panel of Table 5.2 presents the results of three equations that estimate occupational differences on each dimension of consciousness while controlling for age. A number of preliminary points emerge in these three equations. First, the data indicate that workers in the inside crafts are not significantly different from their outside craft counterparts on any of the three dimensions of class consciousness: As we shall see, skilled manual workers manifest an especially pronounced form of oppositional consciousness. Second, operators are only somewhat less class conscious than the craftworkers. They hold much the same conflictual image of the firm as the outside craft group and are equally supportive of demands for workers' control. However, they are somewhat less willing to strike than the outside craft group.

Third, office employees—the clerks and especially the customer service reps—seem to manifest the most managerially inclined perspective in the sample. Thus, clerical workers express a significantly less conflictual image of the firm than outside craftworkers and appear less militant as well. Clerks do not balk at demands for worker control, however, perhaps reflecting their openness to notions of worker participation. Most notable, however, are the differences between the outside craftworkers and the customer service reps, for the reps emerge as the most managerially inclined workers in the industry. Reps view the firm in significantly more consensual terms than do workers in the outside crafts, are less supportive of demands for worker control, and are less inclined to strike as well.[14]

To illustrate the meaning of these differences, we can inspect each group's responses to particular class consciousness indicators. Whereas two-thirds of the outside craftworkers (67.7 percent) view themselves as belonging to the working class, only half that fraction of the service reps (34.6 percent) share this self identification.[15] Likewise, fully one-half of the workers in the outside crafts (50.5 percent) would walk out in sympathy with striking telephone workers elsewhere in the state, "even if it meant breaking the law," but only one in nine (11.9 percent) reps would reportedly show such labor solidarity. Thus, if the managerial hegemony thesis provides only a poor description of these workers generally, it does seem to fit the service reps and clerical employees: these groups *do* seem to equate the company's interests with their own.

One possible explanation for these ideological variations focuses on differences in the degree of autonomy or control that workers enjoy in their jobs. As we have seen, in his earlier study Burawoy (1979) viewed workplace autonomy as a decisive factor in the reproduction of managerial hegemony. Likewise, Friedman (1977) has argued that workers who enjoy "responsible autonomy" will be more likely to identify with the firm. Arguably, the managerial inclinations of the reps and clerks may stem from their relative freedom from direct managerial control.

A second explanation of these occupational variations holds that the attitudes of the reps and clerks flows from their exposure to privileged conditions of employment that are often reserved for white-collar employees. This view has frequently been developed in Weberian research on office workers, such as the classic studies by Mills (1951), Lockwood (1958), and Crozier (1971), who stressed the persistence of status considerations in the determination of workers' allegiances. Conceivably, the attitudes of the clerks and reps stem from their greater enjoyment of such privileges as more collegial patterns of supervision, or greater job security, than manual workers have traditionally enjoyed.

A third explanation focuses on workers' exposure to internal labor markets. The argument here is that organizational provisions for mobility within the firm, as embodied in the company's Upgrade and Transfer Program, encourage workers to embrace an individualistic, career-oriented outlook that leaves little room for collective solidarity. Located within a more fully developed internal labor market, the reps and clerks would quite naturally tend to identify with the firm.

The equations shown in Table 5.2 (B) allow us to explore the validity of these three predictions.[16] The first hypothesis, concerning workplace autonomy, suggests that the more consensual outlook of the reps and clerks may flow from their greater autonomy at work. The data provide little or no support, however, for this claim. It is true that work autonomy significantly affects worker consciousness: When we include the occupational groups in the equation, we find that greater levels of autonomy leave workers less likely to view the firm in conflictual terms, and less willing to strike as well. However, the managerial inclinations of the service reps and clerks remain significant even when the measure of workplace autonomy is included in the equation. Interestingly, the clerical workers and reps actually report substantially *less* autonomy at work than do the skilled crafts. Hence, ideological differences between the occupational groups can hardly be due to variations in work autonomy.[17]

The second hypothesis, which focuses on occupational conditions that commonly accompany white collar employment, also receives mixed support at best. Patterns of supervision and job security are indeed more favorable for the reps than for the skilled manual workers (not shown). Moreover, such favorable conditions of employment do affect class consciousness. As we see in Table 5.2 (B), when job security is high, workers grow less supportive of demands for workers' control and hold a less conflictual image of the firm. Even more pronounced are the effects of collegial supervision, which significantly reduces class consciousness on all three dimensions. As before, however, the managerial inclinations of the white-collar groups remain significant when these two occupational conditions are included in the equations.

The third hypothesis involves the effects of internal labor markets on worker consciousness. The prediction here is that the most managerially inclined groups enjoy greater opportunities within the firm than do other groups and that the attitudinal differences we have found will disappear when we adjust for this fact.

On the basis of job history data, I have mapped out the structure of workers' mobility patterns for both blue-collar and white-collar workers (including operators among the latter group). The resulting pattern is presented in Figure 5.1. Most noteworthy is the near absence of mobility among the manual crafts. For the most part, these workers are hired from external labor markets and remain in their job titles for the duration of their careers. In fact, nearly two-thirds of the outside craftworkers are still employed in the same job they held when they were first hired. The mean tenure for workers in the crafts (just under 13 years) is greater than in any other occupational category.

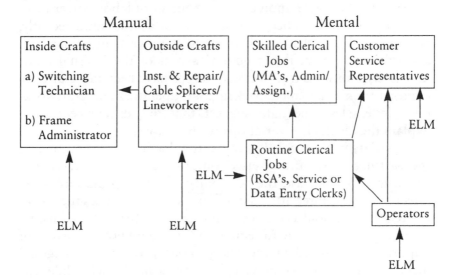

FIGURE 5.1
MOBILITY PATHS AMONG MANUAL AND
MENTAL OCCUPATIONS
Note: ELM = External Labor Market

As Figure 5.1 further shows, operators are somewhat more fully integrated into an internal labor market. Particularly during earlier periods of economic growth, operators were able to move into lower-level clerical jobs (such as Repair Service Attendants), which were viewed as promotions. Yet these job opportunities were rare even before the rise of labor surpluses during the last several years, and the overwhelming majority of operators (80.8 percent) have never gained a promotion. The mean tenure of the operators (12.2 years) is only marginally lower than that among the craftworkers. The difference, of course, is that most craftworkers have chosen to stay in their jobs, while operators have not.

Figure 5.1 indicates that service reps and clerical workers *have* enjoyed significantly greater within-firm mobility than craftworkers and operators. In part, this difference reflects the sharper division of labor among the office occupations, for the finer specialization of office labor (especially in clerical jobs) creates a larger set of positions between which workers can move (Stone 1975). One factor that limits entry into jobs as service reps is the firm's partial reliance upon external sources of labor power (e.g., workers with some college education). But at least until recently, reps enjoyed fair chances of movement upward into first-level supervision. In sum, the structural aspect of the internal labor market hypothesis is true: clerks and reps have been more directly exposed to internal labor markets than operators and craftworkers. Nonetheless, the data suggest that this difference cannot explain the ideological variations we have found.

The data in Table 5.2 (B) suggest that having been promoted in the past has no significant effect on any dimension of class consciousness. By contrast, the possibility of future promotion does affect one of the three attitudinal dimensions: It reduces the worker's tendency to hold a conflictual image of the firm after adjusting for the other variables in the equation. Even with both measures of opportunity included in the analysis, however, the managerial inclinations of the reps remain highly significant. Hence, while reps and clerks have been more fully exposed to internal labor markets, their attitudes do not stem from this fact.[18]

The regression analysis suggests that although several of the job conditions we have considered do have bearing on levels of class consciousness, they cannot account for the attitudinal variations between occupational groups. How, then, can these be explained? Qualitative evidence suggests a number of important points. Some are specific to an occupational group while others bear on the work force as a whole.

As we saw in the previous chapter, clerical workers have increasingly faced the routinization and intensification of their labor, much as de-skilling theory expects. For many routine clerical workers, the result has been an increased level of stress and performance pressure, as well as a growing sense of alienation from work. Marxist sociologists have long predicted that such developments would alter clerical workers' consciousness, extending support for labor struggle and organization into the white-collar ranks. While there have been instances of such struggle—in Suffolk County, Long Island, CWA successfully campaigned for legislation to protect clerical workers against the hazards of VDT use[19]—the transformation of white-collar work has done remarkably little to alter clerical workers' consciousness. Why?

To interview clerical workers is to hear the voices of workers who have been habituated to routinized work and who lack the vocabulary to demand more than this. Said one clerical worker in a highly automated office: "It's just a job like any other. I mean, you have to work, right? And it's really not such a bad job." Asked how closely her manager monitors work performance in her office, another clerical worker said, "I really don't know. I just work hard and make sure I do my own job, and let other people worry about themselves."

As this last worker's remark begins to suggest, one reason for the clerks' inability to challenge the managerial point of view lies in the organization of their work, which gives rise to numerous job classifications and which separates workers into many different functional groups. Although it is hardly unknown for conflict to erupt in clerical work locations, so detailed a division of labor tends to channel such conflict in a lateral direction, as when workers in one section of an office object to the treatment their manager accords to another group. For example, in Loop Assignment Centers, clerical groups are employed around separate 'wheels,' each of which handles work in a different local exchange. When conflict occurs over production standards, it often takes shape as an internecine battle, with workers at one wheel objecting to the standard applied to another. This pattern implicitly encourages parochial patterns of identification that challenge only the specific *application* of managerial authority rather the authority relations themselves. Partly for this reason, clerical workers seem to make up what C. Wright Mills termed an "*in*actionary" force.

The social bases of consent among the service reps are different in certain respects. The rep's job is less subject to functional specialization, yet its historical role as a position meant for relatively well-educated office employees has engendered a middle-class identity among this group. Reps are by no means reluctant to complain about their work situation. Yet the content of their complaints often reflects their discomfort at being treated *like* ordinary workers (an identification they continue to resist). One rep told me, "It's changed from what it used to be, when the company rewarded us for being really professional about our jobs." Another said, "They used to appreciate an excellent job, but now it's like they just expect that from you all the time."

The reps' attachment to a middle-class identity is at least partly bound up with their social backgrounds. For example, most of the reps (59.7 percent) have gone beyond a high-school education, and roughly one in four has completed more than two years of college. By contrast, two-thirds of the operators and craftworkers have only a high-school education, and fewer than 5 percent report having attended college for any length of time (p <.0001). These differences stem from workers' class origins, for the reps are twice as likely as the operators to have had fathers in white-collar occupations (39 percent compared with 18.9 percent, respectively; p < .01). These and other social characteristics are in fact correlated with levels of working-class consciousness, suggesting that the reps' consensual outlook may partly predate their employment at Bell firms, and reflect the process of occupational recruitment rather than occupational conditions alone.

Yet these considerations provide only partial explanations. A more important factor that seems to affect the consciousness of workers across the various occupations centers on *the degree to which the members of each occupational group are able to interact in 'back stage' areas, removed from managerial control* (Scott, 1990). Although clerks enjoy considerable opportunity for interaction with one another, almost all of their contact occurs in contexts that are not conducive to the expression of defiant values. At lunch and during breaks, for example, constraints of time and money invite clerical workers to use the company lounge, eating and talking within close proximity to their managers. Many workers elect to sit at tables that are understood to be reserved "for the girls," informally distinct from the supervisors' tables—in this way gaining at least a modicum of space that they can call their own. But voices carry, and verbal indiscretions easily find their way back to managers. Not surprisingly, lunchtime banter usually follows the path of least resistance, centering on such safe topics as family events, vacation plans, or news about people's movements in the company.

While the situation of the reps is somewhat different, they too lack any back stage area in which they might reflect on their position as workers. Because reps are constantly exposed to the ethos of commercialism that pervades the business offices, any oppositional inclinations they might harbor find little or no soil in which to take root. Not surprisingly, then, the values of the marketplace reach into the reps' informal behaviors at work. It remains the case (as Elinore Langer noted two decades ago) that reps manifest a special fondness for consumer goods (eyeware, clothing, jewelry) that denote refined taste.[20] Their work situation only reinforces these workers' tendency to take exchange relations for granted.

The importance of having 'backstage' areas removed from managerial influence is clearest among the craftworkers, but in ways that are overlaid with two further influences that seem specific to them as a group: the dirty and often dangerous conditions under which they work (which sensitizes them to management's preference for profits over safety), and an ethos of masculinity that defines the worker's manhood in terms of his ability to maintain a measure of freedom and independence from managerial control.

Outside craftworkers in particular encounter a wide array of dangerous and harsh working conditions, including exposure to extreme weather, lead, asbestos, chemical substances, natural gas, insects, and rats. Workers sometimes engage in a gallows humor about these problems; a worker known as Boom Boom earned the nickname when his acetylene torch ignited sewer gas, causing it to explode. There is a serious theme that underlies these experiences, for much as in Halle's (1984) study, workers commonly feel that management shows little or no regard for their health and safety and repeatedly places productivity above workers' well-being.[21] Examples of this are legion. One splicer informed his boss of flaking asbestos at a repair location only to hear the supervisor dismiss the problem, alluding to the longevity of a relative who had worked with asbestos for thirty-five years. Likewise, many workers reported suffering from itching and rashes when the company began using a substance called FlexGel (used to form watertight seals inside cables). The company eventually banned the use of FlexGel, but (as one chief steward recalled) "not before we made a federal case out of it. They always think we're bullshitting them whenever we tell them there's a problem." This ongoing tension between workers' health and management's profit orientation provides workers with palpable evidence of a collision between their interests and those of their employers, imparting a lesson that few office workers need learn.

At the same time that they upbraid management for its failure to protect their health and safety, craftworkers commonly exalt their ability to withstand harsh working conditions, implicitly wearing their physical toughness as a badge of masculinity. This view sometimes fuels a rivalry among craftworkers, as when splicers and linemen challenge the manliness of service technicians, who work with customer equipment and thus avoid many workplace hazards which other workers confront. (Splicers routinely insist that they can tell a service tech just by looking at him. Asked to describe what service techs are like, one splicer said in jest: "Well, a lot of them are women, but *all* of them are pussies.") This conception of physical toughness at times introduces divisions into workers' ranks, but it also impels craftworkers in various categories to maintain a defiant stance toward the company, measuring their manliness in terms of their ability to transcend managerial controls. This equation of manliness with the defiance of company rules finds expression in the very language workers use to criticize their supervisors. When asked how the company selects first-line supervisors, craftworkers often give such responses as: "Supervisors? They're the ones that kiss ass. They plow right up behind their bosses." Added another worker: "The guy that *gets on his knees* is the guy that gets a foreman's job at New York Telephone." Implicit in these comments is the workers' shared assertion that many supervisors lack the technical prowess to make it on the basis of their skills and have to compromise their manhood in order to get ahead. In effect, these working men have turned gender ideology into an ideological weapon with which to challenge the authority of their superiors.[22]

Thus craftworkers' consciousness reflects their employment in dangerous jobs as well as their adherence to a masculine work culture that encourages them to maintain a 'manly bearing' toward the boss. The third condition that explains their relatively strong degree of class consciousness is the freedom they enjoy over when, where, and how to interact with their peers.

Craftworkers commonly work on an individual basis that, formally at least, tends to isolate them from one another. In an effort to cope with their isolation, however, craftworkers often stray from their assigned tasks and congregate with their fellows. Especially among those in the outside crafts, it is not unusual for workers to defy company rules and meet for coffee or beer. Managers are often aware of this practice, but are often powerless to stop it. When I raised this issue with one third-line manager who had come up through the ranks, he said, "You hit on a sore point with me. One of my clerks might be calling this guy, and he's standing around talking about the fish he caught over the weekend!" At times, managers will seek to find and punish workers for such malingering. A supervisor who had only recently been promoted boasted to Cynthia Fuchs Epstein: "I know where they like to hide. I can still think like a splicer." At times, what results is an organizational equivalent of hide-and-seek: a game that allows workers to demonstrate their capacity to defy the company's controls and to revel in their ability to congregate in "back-stage" areas.

As workers well know, the game can be quite risky: workers caught malingering can be suspended without pay or even terminated. Indeed, most outside craftworkers know of people who have been disciplined for such behavior. (One interview with a local union president was interrupted when he had to defend two workers the company had caught: "The dumb fucks kept going back to the same bar all the time!"). Such activities seem to take on a ritual quality, infusing an element of play into a working day that is otherwise all too routine. By their very nature as forbidden activities, they symbolize the workers' ability to control their own working lives and implicitly school workers in the value of defiance.

CONCLUSION

This chapter enables us to draw a number of conclusions about the adequacy of hegemony models of managerial control within the monopoly corporation. First, we find little evidence that workplace reform efforts such as QWL prefigure a new form of labor control. In theory, QWL teams might function like the old company unions, encouraging workers to adopt a stance of cooperation and compromise. In reality, however, their effects seem much more limited. In this case at least, QWL has had very little, if any, effect on workers' consciousness at all.

Nor is it clear that other forms of ideological hegemony have emerged that obscure the antagonistic character of the capitalist firm. There is some evidence that the articulation of internal labor markets tends to hinder the development of working-class solidarity, yet the evidence here is not strong. For one thing, the web of opportunity is far less developed than internal labor market theory would expect: it does not extend very far into the lower ranks of the organization and seems to encompass a limited proportion of the workers in Bell firms. Moreover, sharp occupational variations in consciousness remain even when we control for the structure of opportunity.

It is by no means clear that the economic shocks imposed by growing competition in this industry have invited these workers to align their interests with those of their employer or otherwise consent to managerial authority. To be sure, some workers *have* aligned their interests with those of the firm, partly owing to the economic uncertainty they sense around them. Most notably, clerical workers and especially customer service representatives seem susceptible to the managerial point of view. Yet a majority of workers manifest a set of *oppositional* values quite distinct from these office workers' beliefs. The existence of such variations within a single firm should alert us to the need for a more nuanced, differentiated conception of workers' consciousness than hegemony theory has produced (Storey 1985). Thus, rather than viewing consent as the natural outcome of the advanced capitalist organization, managerial hegemony is better viewed as a problematic occurrence that only obtains under certain specific conditions.

Much as David Halle found in *America's Working Man* (1984), an ethos of masculinity shapes the consciousness of these manual workers, encouraging them to define their manliness at least partly by maintaining their independence from managerial control. Equally important, this chapter begins to suggest that by enacting tacit rituals of defiance (their outlaw congregations), workers can demonstrate their prowess at evading managerial control. Inasmuch as such activities symbolically affirm the value of maintaining one's autonomy at work, they implicitly provide an ideological terrain that is independent of (indeed, arrayed against) managerial influence. Burawoy's view of industrial games, therefore, which views them as adapting workers to the existing structure of authority, may be too narrowly framed. Although much more ethnographic research is needed on this point, the findings presented here imply that workplace games and rituals can easily *reinforce*, rather than merely weaken, the conflictual content of workers' consciousness.

The most important point that emerges from this chapter, finally, is that rank-and-file workers have commonly been able to sustain an oppositional consciousness even in an industry that has often been assumed to provide favorable soil for the growth of managerial hegemony. As we have seen, most workers remain quite aware of enduring conflicts between themselves and their employers; most support demands for increased worker control and are willing to engage in militant actions when the need arises. In short, theories of managerial hegemony seem to have inflated the role ideology plays in the perpetuation of managerial control, for these workers do not lack the ideological resources they need to contest managerial authority. A chief steward put it this way: "It's not that we're fighting any less. It's that *they took the weapons out of our hands*."

CHAPTER 6

Conclusion

In recent years social scientists have engaged in sharp debate over the nature of work, power, and authority within the modern corporation. Three different perspectives have been especially influential in this debate, and this study has examined the capacity of each to shed light on the dynamics of labor control. With an eye toward the increasing centrality of knowledge-intensive industries in the capitalist economy, the present study has explored the transformation of production politics within the communications industry. Doing so has led us to examine the actual significance of scientific management, both historically and in the present conjuncture; the consequences of new technologies for skill requirements and the distribution of control; and finally, the centrality of managerial ideology as a mechanism of labor control. In this final chapter I will draw together the implications of the preceding analysis and briefly sketch the nature of managerial power that has emerged in this branch of production. The chapter concludes by examining the labor strategy that the industry's largest union (the CWA) has pursued in responding to the emerging pattern of managerial power its members increasingly confront.

LABOR CONTROL IN THE MONOPOLY CORE

One especially influential perspective toward the evolution of managerial control under capitalism has been the theory of the degradation or de-skilling of labor. Advocates of this perspective have typically posited a simple historical progression from craft control to scientific management, seeing the latter as "the very bedrock of work design." Among Marxists in particular, the most influential critique of the de-skilling model has centered on three interrelated claims. First, critics have suggested that *multiple* forms of managerial control have emerged in different sectors and

177

branches of capitalism, many of which bear little resemblance to scientific management. Second, they have drawn attention to the limitations involved in purely structural analysis of production, and the need to explore the role of normative or *ideological* influences, which at times "become focal elements in the operation of capitalist control" (Burawoy, 1979:275). Third, critics of the de-skilling model have contended that managerial control does not reside in the technical features of production (the labor process), but is increasingly embedded within the wider political apparatuses of the firm ("systems of control," or "factory regimes").

Using these ideas as their point of departure, critics of the de-skilling paradigm have developed numerous typologies of labor control, the most ambitious of which has been Burawoy's theory of factory regimes. Developing a rich conception of the various forms that authority relations can assume under different economic and political conditions, Burawoy's analysis has been especially useful in making sense of production politics within the Bell system during the first half of this century. Indeed, my analysis of this period lends strong support to many of Burawoy's claims and illustrates the deficiencies of de-skilling theory when applied to this period.

The organization of work in the Bell system made abundant use of scientific management techniques, particularly in the Traffic department, where most of AT&T's work force was employed. Although we tend to project the present characteristics of the operator's job backward in history, imposing its highly structured and relatively unskilled nature onto a previous time, the evidence suggests that operators performed a relatively varied and autonomous set of functions throughout the first generation of the industry's history. Not until the mid-1890s did the rationalization of work lay hold of the operator's tasks, as the company formalized its supervisory practices, codified its work rules and methods, and established an elaborate training regimen that dictated the most minute aspects of the worker's job. On the eve of World War I, the work situation of most operators was as rigid and highly structured as in any factory labor process.

It would therefore be an easy affair to view the transformation of telephone work as simply an exercise in the application of Taylorism. Yet to do so would require that we overlook some of the most decisive aspects of the industry's evolution. For rather than institutionalizing managerial control, the spread of scientific management in this branch of production strained management's relations with its workers to the breaking point, promoting a widening pattern of labor struggle and organization as operators spearheaded a movement to unionize all Bell employees. Although the workers' challenge to management control was exhausted by the mid-1920s (as in the wider society), it served to demonstrate the instablility of a purely Tayloristic regime and underscored management's need for a fuller and more effective means of labor control.

Just as the workers' movement reached its height, Bell companies began to mechanize their work processes, substituting electromechanical switches for the manual switching of calls. Especially inasmuch as this change began to limit workers' capacity to interrupt the labor process during strikes, the question arises as to whether mechanization was part of management's effort to ensure its control over the labor process. The evidence suggests otherwise: the managerial calculus that led to mechanization was less concerned with the need to ensure control over the labor process than with the rising cost of labor power as a commodity. For as World War I tightened the nation's labor markets, driving wages up sharply, the firm found it economical to introduce labor-displacing technologies that had been waiting in the wings. Put differently, mechanization took aim at the economics and not the politics of production. Much as Burawoy contends, the key to worker subordination resided not so much in the labor process (Taylorism or mechanization) as in the political apparatuses of production—specifically, in the paternalistic managerial regime that crystallized throughout the Bell system.

Paternalism was hardly unique to the Bell system. As students of the Southern textile industry have shown, paternalism often succeeded in establishing deferential relations between mill owners and their hands, shaping the employment relation in terms of personal ties of dependence and mutual obligation. But because so much of the research on paternalism has focused on textiles, scholars have generally assumed that this pattern of authority relations can only survive under such conditions—that is, in small firms that are isolated from the larger system of urban-industrial capitalism.

This impression has led scholars to view paternalism as something of an historical curiosity, a remnant of traditional economic structures that cannot persist within advanced capitalism. That paternalism endured for so long in so large a firm as AT&T calls attention to the need for a rethinking of these assumptions.[1]

Comparing Bell paternalism with similar yet less enduring variants in other industries, we have traced the relative persistence of Bell's managerial regime to a set of political and economic conditions that largely accord with Burawoy's schema: Bell's monopoly power, the specific intervention of the state, and workers' dependence on AT&T, the sole buyer of their skills and experience. We have noted some shortcomings in Burawoy's model, however, most notably in its effort to explain the persistence and the transformation of factory regimes such as developed at Bell. In contrast to his view that nonwork influences are derivative attributes that have little effect on production politics, focusing on the social composition of the company's work force helps us explain the tenacity of Bell paternalism. That the company's paternalistic regime endured for so long seems at least partly based on the sharp racial and ethnic distinctions that set Bell workers apart from other layers of the working class, placing workers in a relation of 'exclusive mutuality' toward the firm. This point reminds us that workers are not merely bearers of labor power; they are also embedded within ethnic relations which impinge on their relation to the firm and to other strata of the working class as well (Granovetter 1985).[2]

A second limitation in Burawoy's theory stems from his neglect of endogenous sources of change in the production politics. Burawoy's model is tinged with certain functionalist emphases and therefore views factory regimes as inevitably helping to ensure the reproduction of the wage labor relation. He therefore assumes that the transformation of production politics can only stem from disruptive influences located outside the work organization itself. There is a kernel of truth in this claim. In the case of the Bell system, the shifting pattern of state intervention that accompanied the New Deal had a major effect on managerial authority. Witness the contribution of the Wagner Act to the decay and ultimate collapse of Bell paternalism. Yet the company's regime was not abolished merely because of stresses imposed from outside. As we have seen, it developed certain unanticipated consequences of its own, leading its apparatuses down paths that management could not control. Eventually, the very structure that once constrained Bell workers—especially its system of company unions—evolved into a vehicle of trade-union consciousness and organization, giving rise to the industrial union that represents most of the industry's workers today.

In spite of these limitations, Burawoy's theory seems to fit the transformation of authority relations fairly well during the first half of the century. The same cannot be said, however, when we apply the theory to the current situation within the monopoly firm. Sociologists of work have often criticized overly deterministic views of work organizations; and indeed, Burawoy and many others have criticized de-skilling theorists for their failure to consider ways in which the workers' respond to management control. Yet once we explore the social relations that succeeded the old regime at Bell, it seems that Burawoy and other hegemony theorists are guilty of much the same sin: they reify the power of the firm, exaggerating its ability to shape the ideas and inclinations of the workers it employs.

As we have seen, Burawoy, Edwards, and other theorists of managerial hegemony have suggested that 'coercive' forms of power have historically given way to more 'consensual' patterns that elicit workers' consent to the existing production relations. Yet in the current setting this study finds only weak evidence of such normative controls or of any overall ideological incorporation of the workers within the social life of the firm. Most of the workers in this study identify with the working class and view the company's interests as contrary to their own. Most support demands for increased worker control and are quite willing to strike when the situation demands. Few attach much importance to efforts that seek to infuse a participatory ethos into their work locations. Finally, most adopt a conflictual view of the factors that led the company to introduce new technologies. Although worker consciousness takes several different forms, this terrain offers little evidence that management enjoys any clear ideological hegemony over its employees. Put differently, the social organization of consent and ideological mechanisms more generally seem much less decisive for the exercise of managerial control than hegemony theorists have claimed.

The implications of this point are twofold. First, rather than viewing managerial hegemony as the natural result of the monopoly corporation, it seems better to view its success as problematic, specifying with greater precision those conditions under which managerial hegemony does in fact succeed. Although much more ethnographic data is needed before the point can be established, the present study suggests that a critical element that affects the character of workers' response to management is the degree to which their routine activities enable them to interact in 'backstage' contexts under their own control. Office workers (especially those in business offices) only rarely enjoy such situations and are therefore that much less likely to develop a culture of defiance. By contrast, craftworkers can choose when, where, and how they interact in groups, sometimes even engaging in games and rituals that symbolize their capacity to control their working lives. In combination with other factors—a masculine ethos that encourages defiance of the company and physical conditions of work that make their subordinate roles palpably clear—this fact enables them to maintain a muted culture of resistance.

Second, when we place the evidence on worker consciousness alongside the historical canvas of Bell paternalism, we begin to suspect that the fundamental assumption that guides hegemony theory—its presumption that working-class consciousness has historically eroded—may be empirically unwarranted. For rather than declining levels of working-class consciousness, what emerges here is an apparent increase in workers' capacity to articulate an oppositional consciousness. Although a number of explanations can be given for such a trend—the expansion of the welfare state, which reduces workers' dependence on their employers, as well as wider cultural shifts in responses to authority—one important condition is surely the greater organizational resources workers now command. For despite its inadequacies (a matter discussed further following), trade union organization has apparently enabled workers to shed their ideological dependence on the firm and to collectively define their work situations in their own terms. This part of the study thus contributes to a number of other recent studies whose substance challenges the 'consensual' image of American workers.[3]

If normative or ideological controls do not explain the continuing subordination of labor in the present period, then what factors *do* serve to perpetuate managerial control? The question quite naturally leads us look for the sources of labor control within the structure of the labor process. One key foray in this direction has centered on the changing distribution of skill and technical expertise as formulated by de-skilling theory. As we have seen, its claims are directly contravened by advocates of an 'enskilling' or upgrading perspective, generating a continuing controversy over temporal shifts in skill requirements. My analysis of the links between new technology, skill requirements, and the exercise of control bears directly on this debate and prompts a number of important conclusions.

We have just noted one major factor that begins to cast doubt on the validity of the upgrading thesis. Advocates of this perspective often contend that the transformation of work processes acts to dissolve the traditional sources of worker alienation and discontent. Yet there is no evidence here of any tendency toward the integration of the worker into the firm. Organizational efforts to achieve a stronger sense of unity or shared purpose between managers and workers, which some theorists expect to thrive in technologically advanced contexts, have apparently had little effect. Moreover, where shifts in alienation from work *have* occurred, these have run counter to the upgrading thesis. Especially among routine office employees, the introduction of information technologies has led to substantial *in*creases in levels of alienation. Finally, we find little or no indication that information technologies promote an egalitarian shift in the nature of workplace authority.

On occasion we do find evidence of an enskilling tendency. Historically, the mechanization of Bell operations did tend to increase skill requirements: the most routinized occupations at the switchboard have steadily declined, and skilled craft jobs have absorbed an increasing share of the industry work force. In fact, machines displaced the *least* skilled workers and swelled the ranks of workers holding skilled maintenence jobs.[4] Likewise, more recent waves of technological change involving programmable automation have occasionally tended to reintegrate workers' tasks, redistributing skills in ways that have at times entailed an upgrading trend. This has been the experience of the outside craft group, whose use of CATs and other microelectronic systems has elevated the conceptual content of their jobs. To some extent it has been true of craftworkers in the Switching Control Centers, who have had to acquire a newer and more 'mental' set of intellective skills, using VDTs to peer into the circuits of remote switching and frame installations.

Yet on balance, the evidence provides limited support for the enskilling thesis. To begin with, the clearest evidence of an upgrading trend has stemmed from the *mechanization* of labor, not the introduction of *automated* systems. Hence the historical expansion of skilled occupations reflects the growth of traditional manual occupations rather than the spread of innovative patterns of organizational design. And while the use of automated systems *has* at times increased skill requirements, its overall effects on levels of worker autonomy or responsibility have been far less beneficial than the theory would claim. In fact, when we compare the labor process of the 1950s with that which evolved by the late 1980s, one of the most appreciable changes is the sharp *decline* in levels of flexibility in the latter period. Before the coming of automation, the work process was characterized by informal customs and traditions that left craftworkers considerable residues of discretion in the conduct of their jobs. The wave of automation that has swept over the labor process has drained away much of this discretion, enabling management to regulate the conduct of work much more fully than before.

To say this is by no means to embrace the de-skilling thesis, for the analysis identifies serious limitations in this perspective as well. By focusing on the Plant department at New York Telephone in the post-1971 years, I have explored in some detail a case that should be especially favorable to de-skilling theory. As we have seen, the rise of competitive forces led management to embark on a rationalization campaign that disrupted customary work arrangements in the Plant department, engendering a pattern of conflict that culminated in a decisive defeat for labor in 1971. Hence when information technologies were introduced in the ensuing decade and a half, management was well-positioned to take full advantage of them. Even so, the outcome of automation has run counter to the theory in several important respects.

First, the elimination of skill has proved far more difficult for management to achieve than the theory allows. There have of course been important and occasionally quite dramatic instances of skill dilution. As noted, the experience of the Deskmen epitomizes the destruction of an elite craft, whose skills were encoded into software that could be run by lower-paid office employees with little substantive knowledge or experience. Yet when we shift our focus beyond this specific case to the changes it implied in the labor process writ large, we find that craft skills were not simply destroyed or diluted. Often they were redistributed among claimants at other points in the labor process. Thus, after the de-skilling of the Deskmen, outside craftworkers gained greater access to the testing system via hand-held terminals, shifting much of the conceptual content of the troubleshooting process into their own hands. In other cases, craft skills changed their character, but without any apparent loss in substantive complexity. This has occurred with the establishment of automated Switching Control Centers, where mechanically based forms of knowledge have given way to more cognitive-analytic ones. Either way, the qualitative evidence reveals the reproduction (rather than simply the dissolution) of skilled manual labor as an element within production. The quantitative analysis lends further support to this conclusion, for levels of alienation have not appreciably grown among the various craft groups. To focus only on the fate of the Deskmen, then, and to view the transformation of work through their experience alone, is to introduce serious elements of distortion into the analysis.

A second point at which de-skilling theory fails us is that there has been no apparent trend toward the homogenization of work processes among the various occupational categories in this industry. Recall that during the manual era of the industry's operations, craftworkers in Bell's Plant departments occupied the most autonomous and rewarding jobs, while their female co-workers performed the most routine tasks, filing and retrieving data needed by their more privileged male co-workers. The coming of the automated era, it seems, has left this schism largely intact. The content of craft jobs remains relatively complex and free from direct control, but clerical workers have encountered an increasingly "Traffic"-like environment at work. Indeed, the jobs of many clerical workers have come to resemble those of the operators, with their work performance measured to within a tenth of a second. The data therefore indicate that the automation of work has reproduced pre-existing patterns of inequality, perpetuating a dualistic job structure rather than imparting a growing homogeneity (Crompton and Jones, 1984; Epstein, 1989). Much as Duncan Gallie found in his cross-national study of petro-chemical refineries in Western Europe (1978), workplace technologies have been assimilated into the prevailing institutional pattern, conforming to a structure that was already in place.

The third and surely most important failing of de-skilling theory involves changes that have affected workers in all occupations, regardless of their skill category. De-skilling theory has commonly assumed that management's thrust for control forces it to remove virtually all elements of skill from the workers' tasks. In this respect it has posited the existence of an invariant link between workers' possession of skill and their ability to control the production process. This tie has often been observed in older manufacturing industries such as printing, metalworking, and machine-tools, where much of the existing support for the de-skilling thesis has been found.[5] Yet the developments uncovered in this study suggest that information technologies have severed the historical tie between workers' skills and their ability to control the work process, for management has been able to extend its control over the production process with little abiding need to uproot workers' skills.

This "disconnection" of skill and power has stemmed at least partly from the translation of the Bell System Practices (the technical manuals that define work methods procedures) into the algorithms of computer code, a process that has reduced the room for informal negotiation and placed material constraints on the work methods that workers can employ.[6] Workers must still master the command syntax of their computer systems and grasp the logic of each system's operations, but the new information systems tie their hands in ways that did not exist before. Hence even when their jobs remain highly complex, their skills no longer confer the same power or control over the work process as was previously the case.

Yet the more important reason for this uncoupling of skill and power stems from the fact that new technologies have assumed a *more central and relatively autonomous role* in the labor process than before. During the manual era, the processing of service orders or requests for repairs depended largely on the ability of supervisors to elicit cooperation from their workers and to coordinate their actions in accordance with company procedures. With the coming of automation, however, the work process is increasingly governed by programmable machines. For example, when service orders flow into an automated Business Office, a system called COSMOS conducts the handling of the work. COSMOS scans its electronic database, finds available telephone numbers and wiring, and dedicates them to each line. It electronically forwards relevant information to the computerized Electronic Switching System in a remote Central Office, and assigns the final installation order to a craftworker's log, together with a due date. All of these operations are now performed automatically, without need for human intervention. The increasing centrality of information technologies is also apparent in the industry's Installation and Maintenance Centers (where the Deskmen had been employed). The great bulk of reported troubles are now diagnosed automatically, with work screened, tested and assigned to workers by programmable machines. In the Switching Control Centers, information systems such as CIMAP constantly monitor the functioning of remote installations and detect faults as they occur—in some cases, even before the trouble is apparent to workers or subscribers. And as separate departments become more interwoven, information systems can increasingly share information among themselves, directing the flow of work between offices and making decisions independent of the workers involved.

These and other developments suggest that while management has indeed extended its control over production, it has done so not by uprooting workers' skills but by placing information systems at the directive nodes of the productive circuitry and progressively removing workers to more peripheral locations in the labor process. It was precisely this goal which a Bell technical planner had in mind when he spoke of achieving a system in which *"there are no decisions to be made"* [by workers]. *That's how we want the work to be."* What seems to be emerging, then, closely conforms to what Appelbaum and Albin (1989) have called an "algorithmic" system of control, whose effect is to "reduce decision-making as much as possible to a set of self-contained rules...implementable by a computer."[7]

This development has several implications for the study of work. First, it begins to call for a reorientation of the labor process debate, away from a single-minded focus on the issue of skill requirements and toward the relative capacity of the new machines to regulate, direct, and constrain the overall process of production, regardless of the complexity of workers' tasks. Moreover, it invites us to ask how viable such forms of control are likely to be in the foreseeable future.

Some authors who have begun to address these issues have suggested that technologies which use programmable systems to minimize workers' discretion in production often invite failure, whether owing to technical or economic factors. Thus Zuboff (1988) points to the irrationality of automating work organizations that cling to the principle of 'rule by command', while Noble (1984) finds that the management's very preference for machine-controlled processes betrays a technological conceit that is inherently self-defeating. There is at least some evidence of such tendencies in this industry, most notably in the well-publicized examples of network failures in long-distance communications. Yet what is most remarkable about the algorithmic regime in the communications industry is the very stability it has achieved even as it has grown more dependent on programmed means of controlling the labor process. The questions naturally arise: Is this outcome characteristic of knowledge-based industries, where the objects of production—data in various forms—are more compliant than in manufacturing? Or is it likely to prove equally successful in industries where the objects of production are material commodities? The answer is as yet unclear.

Yet if algorighmic control has achieved a pattern of stability in the communications industry, that fact rests partly on external supports that are decidedly non-technological in their nature. Two seem especially worthy of comment. One concerns the juridical rules that surround production relations in the United States. The other centers on the nature of collective bargaining as it has unfolded in this industry and beyond.

In his influential book, *Classes*, Erik Olin Wright has shown that a much higher proportion of American employees hold formal positions as supervisors than in nations such as Sweden. The reason, he suggests, is that

managerial employees in the United States are generally excluded by law from the union bargaining unit. This means that it is
in the interests of American capitalists to integrate into the
lower levels of management at least some jobs which otherwise
would remain working class (1985:224).

This point is of special relevance in so automated an industry as
this, which employs an inordinately large proportion of its work
force in lower-level supervisory and technical occupations. While
some of these employees are professional engineers, a large proportion lack formal credentials and hold staff positions as technical workers or first-line supervisors, performing some programming and maintenance in support of management's algorithmic
regime. Especially during labor disputes, management needs to
secure the allegiances of these workers if it is to establish and
maintain its new form of control. The state's exclusion of these
workers from coverage under federal labor legislation indirectly
aids the companies' effort to maintain their algorithmic regime.

One can hardly assume that changes in federal labor legislation would prompt technical and supervisory employees to join
labor organizations or even to shift their allegiances. In nations
where scientific and technical personnel are unionized, these
workers have sometimes adopted trade union organization as a
means with which to maintain their advantages over other, less-
privileged workers.[8] Nonetheless, exclusion of these employees
from the state-sanctioned system of industrial governance limits
the alliances and coalitions that are possible among the industry's
employees, ensuring that management's technologies remain
wholly under company control.[9]

Even more important is a second structural support that
underpins management's algorithmic controls—the institutional
pattern of collective bargaining that has emerged in the wake of
the Wagner Act and the collapse of Bell paternalism. For the first
half of this century, Bell workers struggled, however erratically, to
establish a system of industrial unionism that could challenge
managerial control. More than four decades after their union
signed its first contract, however, it seems clear that the establishment of trade union representation has not only failed to prevent
the restoration of managerial control over labor; it has become a

condition of existence for management's nascent regime.[10] As information technologies have reduced workers' capacity to informally negotiate with their supervisors, workers have grown increasingly dependent on the formal levers of union power. Yet the industry's collective bargaining agreements explicitly grant the company full control over work methods, equipment, and job classifications, while at the same time denying workers the right to strike for the duration of the agreement. Workers therefore find themselves caught in a web of legal obligations that shifts the initiative away from the shop floor and seems only to institutionalize managerial control over production (Brody 1980). The combined effect has been to reduce the resources with which workers can challenge the company, leaving workers little choice in their everyday working lives but to submit to management control.

BEYOND THE NEW REGIME

What possibilities exist for a breach in capital's defenses? Can we discern any contradictions within capital's nascent regime, or suggest paths leading beyond the subordination of labor in this industry and beyond? Answers to these questions are necessarily speculative, especially given the relative youth of this new regime. Nonetheless, some important lessons of wider import can be drawn by considering the nature of trade union strategy more closely than we have done thus far.

Like most American unions during the postwar period, the CWA adopted a strategy of accomodation in its relations with management, trading control over the labor process in return for regular improvements in wages and benefits.[11] Implied in this arrangement was the union's "willing acceptance"[12] of management's right to unilaterally determine work methods (including technology). During the 1950s and 1960s, this strategy seemed to bear fruit, as communications workers enjoyed strong improvements in wages and benefits. Referring to this period of material gains, one former union official recalled, "We almost ran out of things to ask for. I mean, what'd we want, our pants cleaned and pressed for us?" Like many others in his position, this man viewed management prerogatives as unalterable facts of economic life.

While communications workers' wages increased rapidly after 1945, wage gains were outpaced by even more rapid gains in productivity, signaling an increasing rate of exploitation of workers' labor power.[13] Equally important, this period witnessed a steady erosion of the strike weapon, leading a former president of the CWA to lament that "striking was like throwing rocks at the Queen Mary as she sailed down the river" (Brooks 1977:58). Finally, the increasing application of machines to the labor process eliminated tens of thousands of operators' jobs during the 1950s, especially in Traffic departments and AT&T Long Lines. Inasmuch as these were women workers who had little power or representation on the union's executive board, threats to their livelihood generated little concern among union leaders.[14]

By the 1970s, technological change began to exert an even more adverse effect on workers' situations, placing the viability of the union's strategy in doubt. When Bell firms introduced MLT systems that destroyed the industry's most strategic craft, the change caught national officers of the CWA completely unprepared. Immersed in an institutional system of bargaining that focused mainly on the negotiation of monetary packages, union leaders lacked any vocabulary with which to address the issue of workplace power. At the same time that AT&T launched a nationally coordinated plan to automate its testing bureaus, CWA's officers were unable to respond. Hence local union officers were left to fend for themselves.

The major effort to respond came from CWA's largest local union, New York City's Local 1101. Under pressure from its core constituents, local and district-level union leaders invoked the grievance machinery, hoping to forestall or even reverse the diluting effect of new technology. The local union claimed that the reassigment of testing functions to clerical workers had violated the collective bargaining agreement. Ruling in favor of the company, however, the arbitrator quoted chapter and verse from the contract, citing passages that gave management unlimited authority (in his words, an "absolute right") to design and redesign its work methods and occupational categories (e.g., Howard 1985:48; Newman 1982). The union could do nothing more than bargain over the pay and job classification of the workers who replaced the skilled craftsmen.[15]

These developments had a sobering effect on CWA leaders, who were forced to acknowledge the need for new approaches toward technology. Yet (in terms of the Slichter-McLaughlin typology), union leaders merely gravitated toward the "adjustment" of technological change. That is, they now sought to cushion workers against the adverse effects of new technology, but still declined to claim any right to shape the process of technological change itself.

One means of adjusting technological change centered on the establishment of joint (labor/management) committees designed to foster an exchange of information about company plans for changes in work methods. The most revealing effort in this direction was the establishment of Technology Change Committees in 1980, which initially seemed to provide a mechanism for union participation in management's decisions about technology. In their public statements, union leaders portrayed the Technology Change Committees as signaling a new, more egalitarian approach toward the process of technological change. In testimony before the U.S. Congress, one high-ranking CWA staff member even suggested that mechanisms like the Technology Change Committees would eventually provide CWA members with "complete and effective union involvement in all aspects of technological change, including veto power over the introduction of new equipment."[16] Although these efforts seemed to suggest a new departure for American labor, they ultimately came to naught. Within a few years the Technology Change Committee structure became little more than an early warning system, giving the union advance notification of actions (and layoffs) the company had unilaterally planned. Union participation has been limited to suggesting ways of minimizing the number of jobs that will be cut.

A second means of adjustment has involved efforts to protect workers against the economic dislocations caused by changes in technology. Under contract provisions introduced in 1977, any worker who suffers a downgrade because of automation no longer faces an immediate cut in his or her wage. Instead, the worker is paid at the previous (higher) wage for a period of time that depends on his or her seniority. In much the same financial vein, in 1980 CWA announced the Supplementary Income Protection Plan (SIPP), which allows workers faced with technology-related downgrades to opt for early retirement, receiving cash inducements to leave the company payroll.

These efforts at adjustment have indeed provided some cushion against the adverse effects of changes in technology and job classifications. Notification of such changes six months in advance is, after all, not a meaningless provision, and few of the workers who have received monetary settlements would have preferred a system that granted them no compensation at all. Yet these recent union efforts have dealt only with the *consequences* of technological change, leaving the decision-making process itself completely untouched. Union leaders have merely assumed the function of damage control, responding to events after they occur but never shaping the course of events themselves. Even more important, by defining job incumbency as a form of property, the union has encouraged workers to *sell* their rights rather than to *exercise* them—that is, to 'exit' from the firm rather than stand and use their collective 'voice'. In a sense, the union's efforts at adjustment have made it that much more palatable for workers to swallow the pill management has prescribed, in effect anesthetizing workers whose jobs are slated for surgery.

Will the patient survive, and with what capacities? The workers in this industry are in a highly vulnerable position. Wider political and economic conditions are scarcely favorable to the workers' movement. Moreover, divestiture has led the regional Bell holding companies to invest in high-tech, non-union branches of the economy, exerting tremendous pressure on the unionized side of their operations. The specter of layoffs has thrown workers on the defensive, often enabling operating company managements to demand concessions from labor. Moreover, the need for high-speed transmission of integrated services (voice and data), combined with the expansion of Bell companies into broadcast transmission, will prompt the installation of fiber cables that will cause major cuts in craft personnel, at least in the long term. Under these conditions, the strengthening of management's new regime would seem almost a foregone conclusion.

Yet workers retain important resources that might well be deployed. As we have seen, most workers harbor an oppositional consciousness and remain responsive to trade unionism. In most cities, workers' unions have established networks of rank-and-file activists whose members can be mobilized when the situation demands. For the most part, communications workers are relatively well-educated and have formed a long-term attachment to their jobs that encourages them to dig in their heels when their well-being is threatened. This was recently made clear in New York when, following a succession in district-level leadership in 1986, the union led a successful campaign for legislation to regulate the working conditions of VDT operators. It was equally clear in the 1989 strike at NYNEX, in which a relatively senior work force fended off concessions in health-care benefits, fearing the loss of insurance at the very stage in their lives when they needed it most.

Conceivably, the inclusion of new groups within the trade union structure—especially women and minorities, who have yet to be fully integrated into the union leadership and who occupy the most subordinate positions in Bell firms—might lend support to a new strategy for labor. Moreover, the union might also build relationships with sympathetic members in the engineering profession at large, who could regularly apprise workers and their local union leaders of the new technologies in store for them and the alternatives that exist. The union has yet to establish the members' right to participate in the design or the selection of new technologies. When changes are made, rank-and-file workers are usually given directives without even any consultation. (Said one worker: "They brought in the computers and told us, 'You *will use* these machines.' Then they accused *us* of creating a 'hostile user environment' in our office!'").

As the occupational structure of the industry continues to change and union-eligible positions decline, union leaders may need to explore the formation of voluntary associations that speak on behalf of 'exempt' employees such as supervisors and technicians. Such associations might provide vehicles for the development of new organizational coalitions and alliances, opening up new possibilities for communications workers. Ultimately, it may be that the prospects for greater workers' control in the most advanced sectors of industrial capitalism can no longer be advanced via neo-syndicalist efforts to directly challenge management's regime, and that state policy must figure prominently into any contemporary labor strategy. Thus, in a context marked by increasing recognition of the need for an "industrial policy," it seems likely that any public effort to develop a macro-economic program will stress telecommunications and kindred industries, such as this study has discussed. These are, after all, among the most internationally competitive of all branches of the American economy (Cohen and Zysman, 1987, ch. 5), and may represent a key element within future economic planning. If so, then the task for workers and their organizations will be to struggle to define a more nearly co-equal role *for labor* within an increasingly corporatist "partnership." How (or, indeed, whether) this can be done is far from certain. Amidst this welter of uncertainty, one thing does seem clear: If trade union leaders cling to the old apparatus of collective bargaining despite the rise of a new and more potent managerial regime, in the end it will be organized labor (not capital) that contributes to its own demise.

APPENDIX
RESEARCH METHODS AND
SAMPLE DESIGN

This study began when union officials of CWA District I agreed to support a survey of telephone workers in the industry's major occupations. The union was particularly interested in exploring two practical concerns—the health risks associated with VDT usage and the ideological effects of the QWL process—but soon agreed to expand the breadth of the survey to include the full range of issues developed here—the link between new technology and the labor process, patterns of informal work relations, levels of alienation, and forms of worker consciousness. At no time did union staff seek to exert influence over the survey instruments or design; I was therefore free to collect data in a fashion that was representative of the population of telephone work sites.

Staff representatives from CWA District I provided access to local union presidents and board members. The latter participants in the study introduced me to rank-and-file workers, arranged for field visits and observations at company sites, and compiled lists of respondents that were instrumental in the conduct of the surveys. Seeking to have the study encompass as representative a set of local unions as possible, I secured the participation of eight local unions in various parts of New Jersey and New York State. These locals were chosen largely because of their occupational composition, enabling me to include the full range of jobs in the sample design. They ranged in size from a few hundred to more than ten thousand workers, and are located in towns and cities of widely varying character. I should note that two local unions declined to participate—in one case because Labor Department litigation put the leadership in an awkward position, and in the other because of a procedural misstep on my part. Before I approached the union leadership, I briefly met with a reform candidate for union office, raising suspicions in the leadership's eyes that I was unable to allay. Hence to the extent that any bias occurred in the selection of local unions, it would have tended to produce an overrepresentation of stronger, better-functioning locals. Such bias would in any case be small and unlikely to affect the substance of the results. I am confident that the eight locals fairly represent the nature of local union organizations in the region under study.

Upon request, local union officials provided lists of discrete work locations—physically or organizationally distinct work sites within their jurisdictions—that were then used as the sampling frame. A random sample of work locations was drawn, stratified by organizational division (the Plant, Traffic, and Commercial departments), local union and workplace size. Note that the primary sampling unit was the workplace, not the worker—a procedure that enabled me to conduct analysis at both the individual and contextual levels (as discussed in Chapter 4). The final sample of the survey included twenty-nine work locations employing 1,585 workers. During the summer of 1985, questionnaires were distributed to all workers employed at each sampled site, with the survey presented as an independent study being conducted with permission of the local union. By September, 802 valid responses were collected, yielding a response rate of 50.6 percent. This response rate is somewhat low, prompting some concern of bias— for example, that supporters of the union structure were over-represented in the final sample of respondents. Two considerations held to address this concern. First, there was no correlation between response to the survey and attitudinal inclinations in a second, similar study done two years later. When respondents were classified according to the promptness of their participation (immediate, after one followup, and only after several repeated followups), the groups were not significantly different in any attitudinal or demographic respect. Second, the occupational composition of the respondents conforms (with minor deviations) to the population paramaters. The relatively low response rate seems mainly to reflect my inability (owing to resource limitations) to establish personal contact with workers at each of the sampled sites. Where contact was established, response rates tended to be higher.

The survey instrument for the first survey was designed to support the construction of multi-item indices bearing on technology, work content, alienation, relations toward supervisors, working conditions, alienation, class consciousness, and other facets of the work experience. The items comprising each index and the methods used to contruct each are given in the text.

The second survey, fielded in the summer of 1987, was conducted in much the same manner, now with respect to a single suburban local. A stratified random sample of individual craft and clerical workers was drawn, yielding a usable sample of 175 cases, representing a response rate of 61.1 percent.

Interview and observational data were gathered not only prior to the survey research (in order to guide the design of the survey instrument), but throughout the duration of the study as well. The process emerged in a classic inductive/deductive iterative loop: prior data would spawn a certain line of analysis, giving rise to new questions requiring further data collection. These data would address the themes that prompted them, but then give rise to new issues that prompted a new round of exploration. Nonetheless, important questions remain that the data cannot address.

Roughly seventy-five workers and twenty-five managers were interviewed—the managers singly but the workers both singly and in groups. Most were semi-structured interviews whose interview schedules were devoted to open-ended questions. Roughly half of the interviews with workers were taped and transcribed; for most of the remainder, verbatim notes were taken. Some of the interviews related to the character of the work situation; others were directed at reconstructing the changes in work relations at New York Telephone from the 1950s to the present. A particularly useful source of information (especially on company policies) proved to be interviews with former managers (many of whom were newly retired) who felt few constraints in their responses.

Top management's reluctance to participate directly in the study resulted in obvious constraints on the use of ethnographic methods. Nonetheless, I was able to conduct field visits throughout work locations of varying types, under auspices of the union. I used these occasions to develop relations with managers as best I could, often asking for further visitation and interview rights at the behest of the manager. Managers often came to trust me enough to 'place' me at a given work station with an employee, enabling me to sit through ordinary work routines, eat lunch in the cafeteria, and sit in on QWL meetings. In most cases, workers saw me not as 'someone with the union,' but as an academic who was simply writing about their working lives, telling their side of the story to a public that depends on their work but which has almost no knowledge of its nature.

A final source of data has been the use of historical evidence in the collection of the AT&T Archives—mainly correspondence, internal memoranda, company reports and publications, and formal papers and presentations. While not an historian, I have tried to be circumspect in the use of company documents, looking for latent organizational functions that may lie hidden in the expression of certain ideas. It does seem that formal presentations at AT&T conferences invited speakers to adopt (or genuflect in the direction of) the official values of the company. This has limited the use of AT&T conference papers for the purposes herein, especially after 1920, when the papers were formally bound and published. Generally more revealing and authentic have been private correspondence and memoranda generated by the mechanisms of organizational functioning, on which I have relied.

NOTES

PREFACE

1. See Bluestone and Harrison (1988); Aronowitz (1974, 1986); Katznelson (1981); Goldfield (1987); Form (1986); and Rieder (1985).

2. See Edwards (1979), Zuboff (1987), Cornfield (1987), which are discussed further below.

CHAPTER 1. INTRODUCTION

1. The outlines of the debate and its major participants will be discussed more fully in Chapter 2 below.

2. See Spenner's seminal analyses of the DOT data (1979, 1983), as well as his more recent discussion (1990) of the state of the art of skill research.

3. For a discussion of these issues, see the contributions to the special issue on "The Concept of Skill" in *Work and Occupations* (November 1990).

4. For a discussion of this strategies as they bear on the study of skill, see Vallas (1990).

5. Thus, in *The Affluent Worker* studies, Goldthorpe and his colleagues (1969) selected industrial settings that were especially likely to favor the *embourgeoisement* thesis, thus affording the researcher a strong test of its claims. Efforts to grasp the implications of technological change commonly select a few high technology worksites or occupations (Kraft 1977; Halle 1984) for similar reasons.

6. Some studies in this vein are Blauner (1964); Wedderburn and Crompton (1972); Nichols and Beynon (1977); Hull, Friedman, and Rogers (1982); and Halle (1984).

7. As discussed below, AT&T's officers were leading members of the National Civic Federation, a national association of enlightened cap-

italists who sought to articulate civilized methods with which to dominate the working classes. See Weinstein (1968).

8. On the implicit role of syndicalism among skilled workers in the U.S., see Montgomery (1979, 1987). On the auto workers, see Glaberman (1980) and, on the CIO movement more broadly, Lichtenstein (1982) and Brody (1980).

9. Useful accounts of labor struggle within the Bell system are the works by Barbash (1952), Schacht (1985), and especially Norwood (1989).

10. Toward the end of my research, the workers in my study had occasion to act on these verbal expressions and conducted a strike against NYNEX for nearly four months.

CHAPTER 2. WORK, POWER, AND THE MONOPOLY CORPORATION

1. Karl Marx, *Capital*, volume III. New York: International, 1967/1894, p. 791.

2. One effort to develop a multi-dimensional conception of work structures is Kalleberg and Berg, *Work and Industry: Structures, Markets and Processes* (New York: Plenum), 1987.

3. Major exceptions to this point can be found in the work of Gouldner (1954a, 1954b) and the late Reinhard Bendix (1960; rev. 1976). Bendix in particular anticipated many trends that later developed in the field, such as the effort to understand how managerial and entrepreneurial classes seek to justify their dominant position within capitalist society. Yet Bendix also foreshadows one major weakness in the recent literature in that he pays almost no attention to the actions of the subordinate classes in responding to managerial ideology.

4. Thus David Noble (1978, 1984) and Barry Wilkinson (1983) find evidence of a managerial imperative within the architecture of machine tools and factory design, while Cynthia Cockburn (1983) has shown how gender politics conditioned the adoption of the linotype keyboard. See also Wacjman (1991) Webster (1985) and Winner (1987).

5. See Sabel's (1982) critique of convergence theory. On variations in labor control within advanced capitalist societies, see Burawoy (1985), Edwards (1979), Friedman (1977, 1990), and P. Thompson (1989, 1990).

6. The literature on de-skilling is now vast. Case studies have focused on printers (see Wallace and Kalleberg 1982; Zimbalist 1979; and Cockburn 1983), machinists (Noble 1978, 1984; Wilkinson 1982; Shaiken 1984), clerical workers (Glenn and Feldberg 1979; Crompton and Jones 1984; Vallas 1987), and other occupational groups. For more general commentary, see especially Braverman (1974), Carchedi (1977), Zimbalist, ed., (1979), Noble (1977, Stark (1980), Littler and Salaman (1982), Child (1985), and Form (1987).

7. The position of white-collar workers is discussed in Chapter 4. See also Przeworski (1977), Przeworski and Sprague (1986), and Vallas (1987).

8. See Friedman (1977, 1990), Edwards (1975, 1979), Burawoy (1979, 1985). For commentary, see P. Thompson (1989, 1990).

9. There is some overlap between theories of managerial hegemony and analysis of technology. For example, many scholars have argued that ideologies of technological determinism serve to disarm workers by robbing them of a critical perspective toward the process of technological change. See, for example, Noble (1978) and Webster (1985). This point is discussed more fully in Chapter 4.

10. For critical studies of the *embourgeoisement* theory, see Hamilton (1967), and Goldthorpe, et al. (1969). More recent studies are Halle (1984), Vanneman and Cannon (1987), and Jackman and Jackman (1987).

11. See the HEW Task Force (1973). Other useful discussions were Zernan (1974), Andrisani, et al. (1979), Hyman (1975) and Pizzorno and Crouch (1975).

12. Related works were Marglin (1975), Stone (1974), Palmer (1975), Noble (1977, 1978), and Montgomery (1979).

13. The standard analysis of this process remains Maurice Dobb, *Studies in the Development of Capitalism* (New York: International), 1947. For criticism see Sweezy et al., *The Transition from Feudalism to Capitalism* (London: Verso), 1978.

14. See Etienne Balibar's effort to systematize this point, in Althusser and Balibar (1971).

15. Much of this argument was adumbrated in the first volume of Marx's *Capital*. In place of Marx's concepts of the formal and real subordination of labor, Braverman inserts Taylorism and mechanization. What Braverman contributes, however, is an elaboration on a theme

only implied in Marx's writings: the increasing separation of conceptual tasks from the labor of execution. Moreover, Braverman applies this theme to growing sectors of the capitalist economy (not only white collar occupations, but also the service sector) that Marx had failed to anticipate.

16. Evidence of management's thrust for control is found in Shaiken (1984). Note that Shaiken's research, as well as studies by Noble (1978 (1984), Wilkinson (1983), Adler (1989), and Kelley (1990) suggest that the effects of NC technology are much less straightforward than Braverman assumed.

17. On the significance of Taylorism for craft labor, see Montgomery (1974), Palmer (1975), Stark (1980), and Meiksins (1984). On power and the division of labor, see Marglin (1975), and Rueschemeyer (1986). For studies of new technology and workers' skills, see the literature discussed in Vallas (1990).

18. For a controversial development of this theme, see the work of Charles Sabel and his colleagues, who see the dominance of mass production methods over craft labor as an arbitrary historical outcome rather than the necessary working-out of economic laws. See Sabel and Zeitlin, "Historical Alternatives to Mass Production," *Past and Present* (1986); and Piore and Sabel, *The Second Industrial Divide* (New York: Basic), 1984.

19. These studies seem concentrated in manufacturing industries, where craft occupations have apparently been uprooted. See Wallace and Kalleberg (1982), Noble (1984), Shaiken (1984), Wilkinson (1983), Cockburn (1983). On white collar occupations see Crompton and Jones (1984).

20. See M. Burawoy (1978), Littler and Salaman (1982), and Salaman (1986).

21. On managerial orientations and values, see Noble (1984), Shaiken (1984), and Shostak (1987). On the informal web of shopfloor relations, see Sabel (1982), and Wilkinson (1983). On gender differences and the outcome of job redesign, see Cockburn (1983), Feldberg and Glenn (1983), McMillen and Form (1983), Crompton and Jones (1984), Hartmann, et al. (1987).

22. See especially Baron and Bielby (1980), C. M. Tolbert (1982), and Hodson and Kaufman (1982). For recent discussion, see Kalleberg and Berg (1987), and Cornfield (1987).

23. See Littler and Salaman (1982), Edwards (1978, 1979), Storey (1985), and especially Burawoy (1979, 1985).

24. Jeffrey Leiter aptly describes paternalism (1986:950) as appealing "to the image of father and child, evoking both the naturalness of inequality and the need of the subordinate for protection."

25. This tragic view of shop-floor culture is also developed in Paul Willis, *Learning to Labour: How Working Class Kids Get Working Class Jobs* (New York: Columbia, 1977); and Sallie Westwood, *All Day, Every Day: Factory and Family in the Making of Women's Lives.* (Urbana: University of Illinois, 1982).

26. Edwards' conception of bureaucratic control, while similar to Burawoy's notion of hegemonic regimes, offers a different perspective on the effects of economic retrenchment. Edwards suggests that the promise of permanent employment has been a lynchpin in the system that sustains workers' commitment to the firm, and that when this promise is violated, the consensual basis of managerial control rapidly falls away. See Edwards (1979), especially Chapter 6.

27. The most important study in this vein is Halle's (1984) analysis of a petrochemical plant owned by a multinational corporation, which provides little or no evidence of managerial hegemony. For similar results elsewhere, see Costello (1985), Lamphere (1985), Hodson and Sullivan (1984), Vanneman and Cannon (1987).

28. Burawoy himself defines the labor process as those social activities involved in "the transformation of raw materials into useful products" (1985:87), ignoring the socio-political content of work itself. His distinction between the labor process and the factory regimes seems uncritically to emulate the Human Relations distinction between the technical and the social system of production.

29. The assumption that affluence necessarily moderates the political attitudes of workers has been subject to sharp critique. See, for example, Hamilton (1968), Goldthrope, et al. (1969), Evansohn (1977).

30. Note that I have made no effort to discuss the burgeoning literature on "flexible specialization" in the United States and Western Europe (see Piore and Sabel 1984; Kern and Schuman 1984). This emerging perspective does expect skill requirements and worker autonomy to increase, much as does upgrading theory. But it rejects any emphasis on technological determinism, and bases its argument largely on the changing structure of consumer markets and the rise of competi-

tion, which erode the prevalence of mass production processes and their single-purpose machinery. For discussion, see the papers in Wood (1989) and Colclough and Tolbert (1992).

31. Note that Zuboff studied the switching department of one Bell operating company, albeit with little effort to place the process of automation in its historical context. Moreover, the developments she found in her study of the switching department were not easily squared with her theoretical model. The contrast between her analysis and my own will become clear below. For a fuller commentary on Zuboff's formulation, see my essay "Computers, Managers and Control at Work," *Sociological Forum* 4 (June), 1989.

32. For a rich case study that demonstrates management's attachment to power and hierarchy, even when these threaten the firm's profitability, see David Noble's (1984) study of technological change at a General Electric plant in Lynn, Massachusetts.

CHAPTER 3. THE OLD REGIME AT AT&T: TAYLORISM, PATERNALISM, AND LABOR STRUGGLE, 1890–1947

1. Employment, equipment, and revenue data are from the Historical Statistics of the United States 1975:785–87. See Noble (1977) for an account of the institutionalization of scientific research in the Bell system and kindred firms.

2. Bell System Statistical Manual, 1946. AT&T Archives.

3. R. T. Barrett, "The Changing Years as Seen From the Switchboard." Box 750-81, AT&T Archives.

4. Memorandum to Joseph Archer, Chief Operator, Pennsylvania Telephone Company, 2 June 1882. Box 1029, AT&T Archives.

5. Quoted in Barrett, "Changing Years," 1936, p. 11.

6. The total number of Bell employees is taken from the U.S. Department of Commerce, *Historical Statistics of the United States*, Part II, 1975:785. The number of women operators is given in a memorandum by John Hudson, President of American Bell, in 1894. Box 1146, AT&T Archives.

7. Lockwood to John Hudson, 9 October 1891. Box 1146, AT&T Archives. Note that although Lockwood expresses confidence in the abilities of women workers, he retains the traditional paternal belief in

their need for male protection. New England's winter storms, he writes, "are apt to disconcert women, and a man ought therefore to be on hand."

8. Barrett, "Changing Years," Box 750-81-36.

9. Data from Bell records estimate that in as late as 1920, "the cost of labor is three-fouths of the total operating expenses (exclusive of depreciation) of the [Bell] System." Hathaway, "Wages and Working Conditions of Employees," Bell Plant and Engineering Conference, New York City, December 1920. Box 187-07-02, AT&T Archives.

10. Quotes from Katherine Schmitt's recollections (1930:18–19).

11. Lockwood to Hudson, 9 October 1891. Box 1146, AT&T Archives.

12. R. T. Barrett, "Changing Years," p. 5. AT&T Archives, Box 1059.

13. In R. T. Barrett, "Changing Years," p. 5.

14. Katherine Schmitt, 1930:18.

15. Switching work at the trunk table was the most complex aspect of the operation; it was here that the last male operators were employed.

16. See Mueller (1989), Chapuis (1982), esp. pp. 55–57, and R. T. Barrett, "Changing Years." On the WWI era, see Currie (1915).

17. Box 1021, AT&T Archives.

18. Op. cit., p. 27. Note that according to a later report by AT&T, the company itself noted that the "employment of supervisors did not become general throughout the Bell system until the late 1890s or the beginning of the present century." R. T. Barrett, "Changing Years," p. 18.

19. The first training school in the Bell system was established in New York in 1902, and was soon followed by identical programs in Chicago, Philadelphia, Boston, Denver, and elsewhere in the Bell system.

20. The quotes are from Currie (1915:35) and throughout.

21. For discussions of craft union struggles in this industry, see Norwood (1990), Barbash (1952), and Schact (1985).

22. For discussion of living expenses and telephone workers'

wages, see the report of a government investigation cited above (Currie 1915). On other issues, see T. Brooks (1977), Barbash (1955), and especially Norwood (1990), Chapters 3 and 4.

23. On the 1919 strike, see Norwood (1990), Ch. 5, Schacht (1985), Barbash (1952), Ch. 1, and Brooks (1977):14–17. The impact of the strike was well described in *The New York Times* (16 April 1919, p. 6.): "Substitute operators in some of the suburban and rural exchanges were able to do no more than care for a few local emergency calls. No connections could be made through the exchanges in Boston, and the toll lines were tied up."

24. See Norwood (1990), Ch. 4; Schatz (1985), Ch. 1–3. For similar events in the printing industry, see Cockburn (1983). On gender and class dynamics in auto and electrical industries, see Ruth Milkman (1987).

25. Later, in 1919 and 1923, craftsmen refused to support key strikes, crossing operators' picket lines. The enduring division between male and female occupations is discussed in Chapter 4.

26. Thayer to C. F. Sise and others, 14 June 1912. Box 47, AT&T Archives.

27. Thayer to J. H. Keller, 2 August 1912. Box 47, AT&T Archives.

28. See Noble (1978). See also his full-length study of a G.E. plant in Lynn, Massachusetts (1984), which found that managers followed policies that enabled them to maintain their power even at the expense of the company's profits. Other studies that support the 'power' thesis of workplace technology are Wilkinson (1983), Shaiken (1984), Shostak (1987), Garson (1988), and to some extent Zuboff (1987). An older study that shows the social and political content of machine systems is that of Ozanne (1967).

29. Interestingly, one operator recalled the manual era of call switching by saying that "we were so young and naiive then.... You see, with only a manual board there, if we had been militant and had known what we were doing we could have driven Ma Bell nuts." This operator was Selina Burch, who later rose to a leadership position within the CWA. The quote is on p. 273 of Devereaux (1980).

30. Purves letter to Gherardi (Chief Engineer of AT&T), 3 March 1919. Box 1, AT&T Archives.

31. By 1940, the ratio of operators per 1,000 telephones had fallen to less than half the figure for 1925, even as the traffic grew by more than 40 percent (Greenwald 1980:231).

32. Many members of the public had strong reservations and anxieties about the changes that mechanization had wrought. For example, *The New York Times* doubted whether direct dialing of telephone numbers would in fact prove workable. Thus in its editorial of 7 April 1920, the *Times* openly wondered "What is going to happen when the *amateur telephonist* has to manipulate dials and get a lot of letters and numbers into an exactly predetermined relation with each other?" (My emphasis.)

33. Katherine Schmitt (1930:123).

34. Norwood, *Labor's Flaming Youth*, p. 264.

35. Norwood, op. cit., 264–65.

36. Thayer to Cise, 14 May 1912. AT&T Archives, Box 47. Emphasis added.

37. Thayer to Cise, 14 May 1912. AT&T Archives, Box 47. Norwood's interpretation of this letter notwithstanding, Thayer's outlook viewed the automatic in terms of profits, not power.

38. Thus in 1919 a company report on technology recalled that "about two years ago we became satisfied that there would be increased economy and efficiency in some use of machine switching. Having determined in a general way what we would probably desire to use, we applied ourselves to an examination of the patent situation..." The report then reviews the results of such an examination. See materials on Automatic Switching Equipment, Box 47, AT&T Archives.

39. The data on wage levels are from "Wages and Working Conditions of Employees in the Plant Department," AT&T Plant and Engineering Conference, 1922, Section III, p. 71. Box 185-05-03 AT&T Archives. On the factors that led to rising wages, see Gentry letter to Bethell (AT&T Vice President), 6 September 1918. Box 11, AT&T Archives.

40. Box 6, AT&T Archives. Emphasis added.

41. Obviously labor organization had a great deal to do with the company's rising labor costs. But many other factors besides union power forced wages up, including the wartime economy (which increased demand for labor and forced employers to bid up the price of labor power even in unorganized situations).

42. Jewitt, Gherardi, and Carty to Thayer, 1921. Box 8, AT&T Archives. See also Thayer to DuBois, Carty, and Gherardi, 5 August 1921. Box 6, AT&T Archives. When management selected a union conscious city such as Lawrence for full mechanization, as Norwood observes, its decision may have been either aberrant or else spurious.

43. New York Telephone apparently began holding Family Night events in Rochester in 1917 and then January 1919 in Buffalo. See *The Telephone Review* (company magazine) January 1917, p. 13 and March 1919, p. 85

44. Box 55-09-01, p. 24.

45. Quoted in Norwood (1990:50).

46. General Traffic Conference, 12–21 April 1923, vol. II, esp. p. 436. Box 185-09-02, AT&T Archives.

47. On paternalism in other industrial contexts, see Joyce's study of textile workers in the English midlands (1980), Hall et al.'s history of Southern textile workers (1987; cf. Leiter 1982, 1986), Hareven's analysis of mill villages in the Northern U.S. (1987), Staples's analysis of an English metal working firm (1987), and Meyer's study of paternalism at Ford Motor Company (1985). Some of this literature is discussed later in this chapter.

48. H. J. Berndt, "History of Employee Benefits," Box 75, AT&T Archives.

49. H. J. Berndt, "History of Employee Benefits," loc. cit, p. 1.

50. H. J. Berndt, "History of Employee Benefits," loc. cit, p. 10.

51. Brandt, "History," p. 3.

52. Standard Oil's system of employee representation had been spawned in 1914, following the company's massacre of striking miners in Ludlow, Colorado. Standard Oil hoped that the plan would demonstrate its commitment to pursue a more enlightened labor policy, while at the same time providing a means of fending off further efforts at union organization.

53. Vail to W. B. Jones, President, New England Telphone and Telegraph, Box 15, AT&T Archives.

54. T. Vail, President's statement, Annual Report of AT&T to its Stockholders, 1919, p. 28–29.

55. T. N. Vail, "Policy of the Bell System," 27 June 1919. Box 49, AT&T Archives. Emphasis added.

56. J. L. R. Van Meter, Comments at AT&T Personnel Conference, White Plains N.Y., April 1922, p. 7. Box 185-07-01-03, AT&T Archives.

57. For example, the General Traffic Manager of AT&T Long Lines asked his employees to "draw up their own constitutions and submit them to the management for consideration and acceptance, *if satisfactory.*" Thus management had to approve the final product. Company domination over this process was so complete that when his workers submitted their constitution, this manager observed that "I don't see how the management could have done better if it had tackled the job itself." See comments by J. L. R. Van Meter at AT&T Personnel Conference, April 1922, p. 7. Box 185-07-01-03, AT&T Archives.

58. Both Schacht (1985:40–45) and Brooks (1977:12–26) cite cases in which management responded to "immoderate behavior" on the part of workers—remarks judged as too critical, for example—by disciplining or dismissing the workers involved.

59. J. L. R. Van Meter, op. cit., p. 10.

60. On work and power in the textile industry, see Hall, et al. (1987), and Leiter (1986); and the articles in Leiter, Schulman and Zingraff, eds. (1991).

61. The Five Dollar Day gave eligible workers the chance to participate in a profit-sharing plan that would double their ordinary wage (in 1913, $2.46 per day). Yet to qualify for the profit component of the wage, workers had to submit their moral character to the firm's scrutiny. Ford's Sociological Department inspected workers' private lives to determine that candidates for the profit-sharing plan regularly attended church, frugally saved their earnings, shouldered their family obligations, and avoided unsavory activities such as drinking, trade unionism, or the Socialist movement. Much as at Bell, Ford's system of labor control presumed that workers needed the directive hand of management to prevent them from being led astray. See Meyer (1985, 1989).

62. While Ford Motor Company did not rely on Taylor's own methods, it did make sufficient use of the principles of scientific management as to earn praise from Frederick Taylor himself. After visiting the Highland Park plant in 1913, Taylor was quoted in the press as saying that "here is the first instance in which a group of manufacturers had

undertaken to install the principles of scientific management without the aid of experts" (in Meyer, 1985:20).

63. According to the recent analysis of Southern textile mills by Hall, et al. (1987), the rise of sharp economic competition during the 1920s strained mill paternalism to the breaking point.

64. Calculations based on U.S. Dept. of Commerce (1975), Tables R17–30, R31–45.

65. See Danielian (1939), J. Brooks (1976), and following.

66. In his book *An Autoworker's Journal,* Frank Marquart observes that autoworkers sometimes moved between different employers in the space of a single working day. See Marquart (1975).

67. Statistics of the Bell System, p. 706, AT&T Archives.

68. See Norwood (1990), throughout. Interestingly, Samuel Cohn's study of postal workers in Great Britain also found no gender difference in industrial militance: "There seems to have been no tendency for women to be less strike prone than men." See Cohn (1985:232).

69. In the Southern New England area, local unions of Bell workers "actively supported the Irish nationalist movement and devoted coverage to it" in union publications. Julia O'Connor, who led the Operators' movement, "even travelled to Ireland to meet with nationalist leaders." See Norwood (1990:18, 261–262).

70. On these wider developments, see especially Preis (1964), Bernstein (1964), Aronowitz (1974), Brody (1980), and Lichtenstein (1982).

71. This narrative draws on accounts found in Schacht (1985), Barbash (1952), and Brooks (1977).

72. In several cases the courts ruled that Bell operating companies illegally sought to dominate the new unions by providing them with company time, space, and telephone resources free of charge—activities the Wagner Act clearly defined as unfair labor practices. See especially Schacht (1985:48–52).

73. Memorandum to non-supervisory employees, April 1937. Buckley folder, Box 78-10-01, AT&T Archives.

74. See correspondence between Julius Emspak (General Secretary of the United Electrical Workers) and Frank Jewett (President of Bell Laboratories), April and June 1937, as well as minutes of an NLRB hearing of 2 June 1937. Box 78-10-01, AT&T Archives.

75. The Board represented only unionized workers who were affiliated with the AFL or CIO.

76. Bell System Statistical Manual, 1946, p. 709, AT&T Archives.

77. For an excellent discussion of the unanticipated consequences of company unionism at AT&T see Schacht (1985:35–45).

78. Brody (1960) observed a similar process in the steel industry, though in much less pronounced a form.

79. This point lends credence to the "resource" theory of corporate structure, which contends that systems of corporate control themselves provide workers with opportunities for resisting managerial initiatives. See Hodson and Kauffman 1982.

CHAPTER 4. CAPITAL, LABOR, AND NEW TECHNOLOGY

1. Figures are from Batten and Schoonmaker (1987:322).

2. One high-ranking officer of AT&T recalled this period by saying, "That's the wonderful thing about economic growth. It lets you transfer people, distribute promotions, do whatever you want. Those are the easy times for management."

3. The phrase is Hirschhorn's (1984).

4. Sophisticated quantitative studies have appeared that claim to refute the de-skilling thesis. Yet almost all of these have fastened on job complexity as their dependent variable, with little or no attention to levels of autonomy or control at work. For critical discussion of positivistic studies in this vein, see Vallas (1990) and Attewell (1990). A more sympathetic view is that of Spenner (1990).

5. It can hardly be denied that professional and managerial women in Bell firms have benefited enormously from the Consent Decree, as opportunities have expanded for women in these ranks. Yet nearly twenty years after the Consent Decree, the survey data reveal that women remain substantially overrepresented in the poorest paid, traditionally female jobs. Operators remain homogeneously female, and skilled manual jobs remain between 91.5 and 96.1 percent male. Not surprisingly, the strongest predictor of pay is sex, even when other relevant variables (such as skill requirements, autonomy, seniority, education, and working conditions) are held constant.

6. See volume one of Marx's *Capital* (1967/1865), especially Chapter 15, "Machinery and Modern Industry."

7. It should become apparent from the following discussion that the appellation 'skilled' was far from an arbitrary label and that craftworkers have continued to perform complex work demanding substantial elements of discretion. The survey data provide ample support for this conclusion, indicating extremely sharp differences in the autonomy and conceptual content of the jobs held by operators and skilled craftworkers (see Vallas 1988). In view of these enduring differences it seems beyond all reasonable doubt that before the late 1970s changes in the occupational structure generated a compositional shift toward increasing skill requirements.

8. Usually, Deskmen acquired their knowledge through long experience in Plant work, but transferred to inside jobs to escape its physical hardships in the later stages of their working lives. On the working conditions to which outside repair workers are exposed, see Chapter 5.

9. Note how the architecture of mechanized switching systems still resembled the old systems which contained a case and trunk table (as described in Chapter 3).

10. Thus AML-2 equipment, which enabled a single pair of wires to carry the equivalent of two telephone lines (a physical and a virtual line), was introduced into New York Telephone with no formal training in its use at all. "We were flying by the seat of our pants. It was all hit or miss until we figured it out." Likewise, workers' schooling is often based on one supplier's equipment, while workers encounter completely different technologies out in the field.

11. Ironically, strikes gave the company a chance to reinvigorate its knowledge of the labor process. By vacating the field, craftworkers enabled their bosses to grow more familiar with work methods, work loads, and other elements of the job.

12. In Bell parlance, a "loop" is the wire that connects a customer's premise to the cable. Hence "loop assignment" involves the dedication of specific places in the cabling and switching system to each customer's number.

13. On the rise of competition in the industry, see Chapter 5.

14. This whole era closely resembles Gouldner's (1956) classic account of industrial conflict and bureaucracy in a Midwestern gypsum processing plant. On the role of informal custom in the achievement of organizational goals, see also Gresham Sykes, *Society of Captives* (1958).

15. Strikes over holiday work schedules were reported several times in *The New York Times* during the early 1960s. Disputes over craft jurisdictions were reported on 18–20 November 1964 and later, from 30 October to 12 November 1969. Safety strikes occurred in May and August 1967, while conflict over subcontracting broke out in July 1969 and reached its peak in January 1971.

16. It seems likely that operators would have sided with the Plant workers, but lacked organizational autonomy for this to occur: traffic workers were still represented by an employees' association that was notorious for its friendly relations to management. Few workers in the Commerical Department (the business offices) would have supported the strike, however. As one former local union official recalled, "when we walked on the picket line, some of these people (customer service representatives) tried to run us over! They didn't want to hear about any union."

17. See especially Willis (1977, 1979) and Cockburn (1983). The role of gender in the culture of telephone work is explored in Cynthia Epstein's research (e.g., 1988).

18. The company has taken a step in this direction by organizing a sort of cultural exchange program between MAs and the repair crafts. This has entailed having MAs ride with craftsmen out in the field to understand what the outside job is like, as well as the reverse—bringing outside workers into the testing offices to understand the work situation of the MA. Few craftworkers I spoke with expressed any positive feelings about this program. "One day riding in a truck? That's not gonna show them what we go through."

19. For technical discussions, see Almquist and Fessler (1979), Amin, et al. (1981). For a more sociological discussion from a de-skilling perspective, see Newman (1982).

20. The standard work here remains that of Spenner (1979, 1983, 1990).

21. For other efforts in this direction, see Archibald (1978), Torrance (1981), Archibald, et al. (1981), and Erikson (1990).

22. Using a 4-point frequency coding, the items asked workers how often they experienced each of the feelings articulated in Table 4.4. (An additional statement not shown in the table was "the time really drags for me while I'm at work.") The resulting index has an alpha of .84. The index ranges from 5 through 20, with high scores indicating greater alienation from work.

23. To measure work autonomy, I designed six items that asked respondents how often each of the following characteristics described their jobs: "My job requires that I do things just the way I am told. If I leave my work area for a moment, my supervisor starts wondering where I am. The amount of work I do is carefully measured by the people above me. My job requires that I complete a certain amount of work per minute or hour. My job requires that I keep working every minute of the day. My job requires that I work very fast." Cronbach's alpha for the index is .85. The index ranges from 0 to 18, with high scores denoting greater autonomy.

To measure the conceptual content of workers' jobs, I adapted four items crudely based on the *Dictionary of Occupational Titles* index of occupational complexity (for discussion, see Spenner 1979, 1990; Kohn 1969; and Kohn and Schooler 1983). Each of these items presented respondents with roughly opposed ends of a continuum, and asked them to indicate where their job tasks typically fall. Items were designed to bear on the use of data, people and things, with one item bearing on overall levels of routinization. Although the Cronbach's alpha for the resulting index is low (.59), the index is a significant predictor of wages (r =.50). The index also correlates with the DOT scores from 1977 (Spearman's rho =.60). The index ranges from 0 through 16, with high scores denoting greater conceptual content.

24. Clerical workers' scores were based on the frequency with which they used VDTs in their work. Those using VDTs very little or not at all were assigned scores of 1; occasional VDT users (between 25% and 75% of the day) were given scores of 2; while constant VDT users (those who use terminals more than 75% of the day) were assigned values of 3.

Automation scores for switching craftworkers were based on the generation of switching technology they mainly use. Those who work with electromechanical equipment (mainly Cross-Bar switches) were coded as 2, while users of electronic or other programmable systems were assigned the highest score (3).

Scores of outside craftworkers, finally, were based on the number of advanced technologies (among them, SLC–96 equipment, Dimension systems, and fiber optic cables) the worker commonly uses in his or her job. Those using none of the technologies were given manual scores of 1; those using one type were scored at the intermediate level, while those using two or more of the new technologies were assigned the highest automation score (3).

For more discussion, see Vallas (1988:158).

25. Note that these data were collected immediately before the CATs were introduced. If anything, they underestimate the upgrading trend apparent among the outside crafts.

26. This pattern fits Roger Penn's "compensatory" theory of skill, as mentioned in Chapter 2. Although some skilled occupations may be de-skilled, automation compensates for this change by shifting skills into other occupational groups.

27. The meaning of these findings can be explained in more concrete terms. If the degree of automation at an office increases by one standard deviation (as would occur when an office is cut over to a new system), workers who become constant users of VDTs can expect to find their autonomy reduced by more than half a standard deviation (.54 units).

28. This finding may reflect the preponderance of central office switching workers in the sample. As was suggested, these workers enjoy more of a sense of "owning your own switch" than do workers in the Control Centers, and apparently do not experience automation in the same way as do workers in the latter worksites.

29. Recall the ordeal of solidarity which the craftworkers experienced earlier in this century. Note that as late as the 1950s, the president of the CWA made a widely quoted statement that evaluated the loss of women's jobs as less important than the loss of male employment. See Hacker (1979), Schacht (1985). On class and gender interests among unionized workers, see Milkman (1987).

CHAPTER 5. THE LIMITS OF MANAGERIAL HEGEMONY

1. An exception here is Burawoy, who has conducted ethnographic research on the ideological substance of shop-floor culture. Nonetheless, Burawoy seems to exaggerate the consensual substance of workers' consciousness, which he too hastily projects onto the American working class writ large. See Halle (1984) and following.

2. For studies that challenge hegemonic or consensual portrayals of the American political culture, see Hamilton (1968), Huber and Form (1973), Jackman and Jackman (1983), and Vanneman and Cannon (1987). Especially important are studies by Hodson and Sullivan (1984) and Halle (1984), both of which find precious little commitment to the firm within monopoly core firms. For further discussion, see Vallas (1990).

3. See unpublished report, "The Quality of Work Life Process of AT&T and the CWA: A Research Study after Three Years," January 1984.

4. Preface to "The Quality of Work Life Process of AT&T and the CWA," op. cit., 1984.

5. Note that the usefulness of the Labor Department study for the present purposes is limited. The ten teams on which it focused were selected by officials from both the union and the company, and its measures bear only indirectly on issues of ideology and class consciousness.

6. CWA/NYT Quality of Work Life News Briefs, v. III, no. 2 (November 1984).

7. The latter three measures are described in greater detail later in this chapter.

8. Workers pull no punches when they must deal with an especially arrogant or incompetent engineer. Workers in one garage confronted such a figure, who happened to be Asian-American, and responded by dubbing him "Sum Dum Fuk." I should note that these workers regard racial bigotry as foolish; they do take particular delight, however, in flouting liberal sensitivities.

9. For applications of the Gramscian concept of "contradictory consciousness," see Femia (1975) and Parkin (1971), esp. p. 91–94.

10. For varying approaches to the measurement of class consciousness, see Leggett (1968), Mann (1970), MacKenzie (1973), Blackburn and Mann (1975), Zingraff and Schulman (1984), Leiter (1986), and Vallas (1987).

11. Some workers resisted the choices provided, and noted *no one* benefited. They deemed the new systems less effective than the older, manual ones and the change largely counterproductive. These responses were relatively rare, however.

12. These workers would apparently disagree with Attewell's skeptical view of Orwellian imagery as applied to the labor process. See Paul Attewell, "Big Brother and the Sweatshop: Computer Surveillance in the Automated Office," *Sociological Theory* 1987, 5 (Spring: 87–99).

13. In retrospect, this conceptualization seems insufficiently precise. A number of different forms of worker consciousness exist, including trade union, craft or contradictory consciousness. Yet my schema classifies them all as *class* consciousness. Clearly, greater conceptual and

operational clarity is needed. The schema suffices for the task at hand, however, inasmuch as the hegemony thesis expects little evidence of *any* such forms of oppositional consciousness.

14. One union local's past president reported: "When we were on strike, the customer service people would drive right through our picket line. I mean, they'd try to run you over. You couldn't even mention union to them." Ironically, one striker was in fact run over and killed while picketing in 1989 (though not by a service rep).

15. This finding reinforces Elinore Langer's observations regarding service reps: "The women (reps) do not see themselves as 'workers' in anything like the classical sense." See Langer (1970).

16. The measure of work autonomy is comprised of the same multi-item index described in Chapter 4. To measure exposure to internal labor markets, I have used two distinct indicators of the firm's provisions for worker mobility. The first bears upon the *past* experience of mobility—whether workers have been promoted since being hired. The second involves *future* prospects for promotion—the amount of opportunity workers perceive in their own departments.

The measure of job security is an index formed using three survey items that asked workers "how worried are you that you may be laid off and have to look for another job," "will have to accept a job in a lower classification, with a cut in pay," and "will have to accept a transfer to a distant job location." Cronbach's alpha for this index is .76.

The measure of supervision is conceived as a continuum between collegial and coercive forms of supervision. The variable is assessed using items which asked workers how often their immediate supervisors are "considerate of the worker's feelings," "able to understand things from the worker's point of view," and "easy to talk to when things get tough on your job." Cronbach's alpha for this index is .83. For more detail see Vallas (1991).

17. Note that in Table 5.2 (B), an ideological difference emerges between operators and outside craftworkers not apparent in (A). Further analysis suggests that this is mainly due to the inclusion of work autonomy in the equations. In short, the low autonomy operators experience explains their relatively high class consciousness, when autonomy is held constant, their class consciousness plummets.

18. Indeed, since the breakup of the Bell system, these workers have experienced sharp declines in their prospects for upward mobility. Yet this change in their levels of opportunity has not reconfigured their atti-

tudes toward management. Hence contrary to Edwards, who expects to find the spread of disillusionment in this context, we find little evidence of any ideological shifts among these workers. In this respect, Burawoy is right to suggest that managerial hegemony endures despite (and perhaps even draws strength from) the emergence of adversity.

19. Thus CWA activists were instrumental in supporting the first law to regulate the working conditions of VDT operators in the United States, in Suffolk County (N.Y.) in June 1988. San Francisco has since passed similar legislation.

20. See Langer, "The Women of the Telephone Company," 1970.

21. Many workers fear that they won't live long enough to enjoy the good pensions they have secured. Workers sometimes tell stories of friends who have retired but died before collecting their first pension check.

22. For a historical discussion of the importance of maintaining a "manly bearing" toward the boss, see Montgomery (1979, Ch. 2). For more contemporary analysis of gender and class consciousness, see Willis (1977), Cockburn (1983), Halle (1984), and Yarrow (1987).

CHAPTER 6. CONCLUSION

1. Frederic Deyo (1989) introduces a useful distinction between "communal" and "corporate" types of paternalism. Although his concern is with East Asian forms of labor subordination, this distinction nicely fits the contrast between the Piedmont mill villages and AT&T's paternalistic regime, respectively.

2. The literature on the labor aristocracy (partly informed by Weberian themes) has often been sensitive to the role of racial and ethnic influences, but labor control theory has not.

3. See especially Halle (1984), DiFazio (1985), Vanneman and Cannon (1987), Costello (1985), Lamphere (1985), and Fantasia (1988).

4. On similar processes in other industries, see Crozier (1960), and Penn (1986).

5. On printing, see Wallace and Kalleberg (1982) and Cockburn (1983). For metalworking, see Brody (1960), Stone (1974), and Montgomery (1979). On the machine-tool industry, see Wilkinson (1983), Noble (1984) and Shaiken (1984).

6. Charles Perrow (1986:21) has noted the tendency for organizational rules to be inscribed within new technologies, and for this reason muses that the "thoroughly automated factory...would be one with few or no written rules of regulations." Binding expectations would be embedded in the design of the machines.

7. See Appelbaum and Albin (1989:252). Interestingly, these authors' study of the insurance industry found that large firms are especially prone to favor algorithmic controls.

8. This seems to be true of the Association of Scientific, Technical and Managerial Staffs (ASTMS) in Great Britain. See R. Carter (1979). See also Prandy (1965), Roberts, et al. (1972), Gorz (1976), and Meiksins (1991).

9. In the past, management has maintained these workers' allegiances through the granting of rewards (opportunities, bonuses, prestige of rank) that reinforced their membership within the managerial class. Yet with the company's rationalization campaign, lower-level managers in particular find these rewards rapidly disappearing: In fact, union-eligible employees now have a substantially better benefit package than do lower-level managers. It is less and less clear to many first-liners in particular that they are members of the management team.

10. The following remarks center solely on the Communications Workers of America, which represents an overwhelming majority of the unionized workers in the industry. The other major union organizations are the IBEW and the Telecommunications International Union.

11. On the limits of industrial unionism in the United States, see Aronowitz (1974), Brody (1980), Lichtenstein (1982), and Form (1990).

12. The concept is from Slichter's typology of union responses toward technology. See Slichter, J. Healy and E. R. Livernash, *The Impact of Collective Bargaining on Management* (Brookings Institute (1960) and D. McLaughlin *The Impact of Labor Unions on the Rate and Direction of Technological Innovation* (Washington, D.C.: National Technical Information Service (1979). For discussion, see Cornfield (1987:8–13), and David Newman, "New Technology and the Changing Labor Process in the Telephone Industry: The Union Response" (unpublished manuscript, 1982).

13. "Technology and Labor in Five Industries," Bulletin 2033, Bureau of Labor Statistics, U.S. Department of Labor, September 1979.

14. Joseph Beirne, CWA President was widely quoted as seeing little cause for alarm in the loss of his members' jobs, because "frankly,

technological innovation affected telephone operators and clerical operatives" (quoted in Hacker 1979:538).

15. This account is based on interviews with leaders of CWA District One. For discussion of these events see Newman (1982:24–26) and Howard (1985:47–52).

16. See the testimony of Ronnie Straw before the House Subcommittee on Science, Research and Technology of the Committee on Science and Technology, 19 September 1981. (Reprinted in Kohl 1984:72–76).

REFERENCES

Adler, Paul. 1988. "Automation, Skill and the Future of Capitalism." *Berkeley Journal of Sociology* 33:1–36.

———. 1989. "Automation and Skill: Three Generations of Research on the N. C. Case." *Politics and Society* 17, 3:377–402.

———. 1990. "Marx, Machines and Skill." *Technology and Culture* 31, 4:780–812.

Almquist, Milton L., and George E. Fessler. 1979. "Switching Control Centers: Switching System Maintenance—and More." Bell Laboratories Report (June).

Althauser, Robert P., and Arne Kalleberg. 1981. "Firms, Occupations and the Structure of Labor Markets: A Conceptual Analysis." In I. Berg, ed., *Sociological Perspectives on Labor Markets*. New York: Academic Press.

Althusser, Louis, and Balibar, Etienne. 1971. *Reading Capital*. London: New Left Books.

Alwin, Duane F. 1976. "Assessing School Effects: Some Identities." *Sociology of Education* 49 (October):249–303.

Amber, G. S., and P. S. Amber. 1962. *Anatomy of Automation*. Englewood Cliffs, N.J.: Prentice-Hall.

Amin, Ashok T., Walter Haun, and Donald Mulder. 1981. "Sleuthing for Troubles in ESS Networks." Bell Laboratories Report (October).

Anderson, Perry. 1976. *Considerations on Western Marxism*. London: Verso.

Andrews, Stewart, K. Prandy, and R. M. Blackburn. 1980. *Social Stratification and Occupations*. New York: Holmes and Meier.

Andrisani, Paul, et al. 1979. *Work Attitudes and Labor Market Experience: Evidence from the National Longitudinal Survey*. New York: Praeger.

Appelbaum, Eileen, and P. Albin. 1989. "Computer Rationalization and the Transformation of Work: Lessons from the Insurance Industry." In S. Wood, ed., *The Transformation of Work?* London: Unwin and Hyman.

Archibald, W. Peter. 1978. "Using Marx's Theory of Alienation Empirically." *Theory and Society* 6:119–132.

Archibald, W. Peter, Owen Adams, and John Gartrell. 1981. "Propertylessness and Alienation: Re-Opening a 'Shut' Case." In R. F. Geyer and D. Schweitzer, eds. *Alienation: Problems of Meaning, Theory and Method.* London: Routledge and Kegan Paul.

Aronowitz, Stanley. 1974. *False Promises: The Shaping of American Working Class Consciousness.* New York: McGraw-Hill.

———. 1985. "Why Work?" *Social Text* (Fall).

Attewell, Paul. 1987. "The De-skilling Controversy." *Work and Occupations* 14:323–346.

———. 1987b. "Big Brother and the Sweatshop: Computer Surveillance and the Automated Office." *Sociological Theory* 5:87–99.

———. 1990. "What is Skill?" *Work and Occupations* 17, 4 (November):422–449.

Barbash, Jack. 1952. *Unions and Telephones.* New York: Harper and Row.

Baron, Ava. 1987. "Masculinity and the Woman Question: The Transformation of Gender and Work in the Printing Industry, 1850–1920." Paper presented at the Berkshire Conference on the History of Women, Wellesley College.

Baron, James, and William T. Bielby. 1980. "Bringing the Firm Back In: Stratification and the Organization of Work." *American Sociological Review* 45:737–765.

Baron, James N., and William T. Bielby. 1982. "Workers and Machines: Dimensions and Determinants of Technical Relations in the Workplace." *American Sociological Review* 47 (April):175–188.

———, Frank Dobbin, and P. D. Jennings, 1986. "War and Peace: The Evolution of Public Administration in the United States." *American Journal of Sociology* 92:2.

Batten, Dick, and Sara Schoonmaker. 1987. "Deregulation, Technological Change and Labor Relations in Telecommunications." In D. Cornfield, ed., *Workers, Managers and Technological Change.* New York: Plenum.

Baudrillard, Jean. 1976. *The Mirror of Production.* St. Louis: Telos.

Baxandall, Rosalind, E. Ewen, and L. Gordon. 1976. "The Working Class Has Two Sexes." In Baxandall, et al., eds., *Technology, the Labor Process and the Working Class.* New York: Monthly Review.

Bell, Daniel. 1960. "Work and Its Discontents." In *The End of Ideology*. Glencoe, Ill.: Free Press.

———. 1973. *The Coming of Post-Industrial Society*. New York: Basic Books.

Bendix, Reinhard. 1976. *Work and Authority: Managerial Ideologies in the Course of Industrialization*. Berkeley: University of California Press.

Berger, Bennett. 1960. *Working-Class Suburb: A Study of Auto Workers in Suburbia*. Berkeley: University of California Press.

Bernstein, Irving. 1969. *Turbulent Years: A History of the American Worker, 1933–1941*. Boston: Houghton Mifflin.

Best, Ethel. 1933. "The Change from Manual to Dial Operation in the Telephone Industry." U.S. Department of Labor, Women's Bureau. Bulletin no. 110. Washington, D.C.: GPO.

Blackburn, Robin, and Michael Mann. 1975. "Ideology in the Non-Skilled Working Class." In *Working Class Images of Society*, ed. Martin Bulmer. London: Routledge and Kegan Paul.

Blauner, Robert. 1964. *Alienation and Freedom: The Factory Worker and His Industry*. Chicago: University of Chicago Press.

Bluestone, Barry, and Harrison, Bennett. 1982. *The De-Industrialization of America*. New York: BasicBooks.

Borrus and Zysman, 1984. Cited in Cohen and Zysman, 1988. *Manufacturing Matters*. New York: Basic Books.

Brandes, Stuart. 1976. *American Welfare Capitalism, 1880–1940*. Chicago: University of Chicago Press.

Braverman, Harry. 1974. *Labor and Monopoly Capital: The Degradation of Work in the Twentieth Century*. New York: Monthly Review.

Bright, James. 1958. Automation and Management. Boston: Harvard Business School.

Brody, David. 1960. *Steelworkers in America: The Non-Union Era*. New York: Harper and Row.

———. 1980. *Workers in Industrial America: Essays on The Twentieth Century Struggle*. New York: Oxford.

Brooks, John. 1976. *Telephone: The First Hundred Years*. New York: Harper and Row.

Brooks, Thomas R. 1977. *The Communications Workers of America: Story of a Union*. New York: Mason-Charter.

Burawoy, Michael. "Braverman and Beyond: The Labor Process under Monopoly Capitalism." *Politics and Society* 3–4:247–312.

————. 1979. *Manufacturing Consent: Changes in the Labor Process Under Monopoly Capitalism*. Chicago: University of Chicago Press.

————. 1985. *The Politics of Production: Factory Regimes under Capitalism and Socialism*. London: Verso.

Carchedi, G. 1977. *The Economic Identification of Social Classes*. London: Routledge and Kegan Paul.

Carter, Reginald. 1979. "Class, Militancy and Union Character: A Study of the Association of Scientific, Technical and Managerial Staffs." *Sociological Review* 27 (2).

Centers, Richard. 1949. *The Psychology of Social Classes*. Princeton: Princeton University Press.

Charles, Tony. 1986. "New Technology and the Future of Work: The State of Current Research." Paper presented at the World Congress of Sociology XI, New Delhi.

Child, John, R. Loveridge, J. Harvey, and A. Spencer. 1984. Microelectronics and the Quality of Employment in Services. In P. Marstrand, ed., *New Technology and the Future of Work and Skills*. London: Pinter.

Child, John. 1986. "Technology and Work: An Outline of Theory and Research in the Western Social Sciences." In Peter Grootings, ed., *Technology and Work: East-West Comparisons*. London: Croom-Helm.

Clawson, Dan. 1980. *Bureaucracy and the Labor Process*. New York: Monthly Review.

Cockburn, Cynthia. 1983. *Brothers: Male Dominance and Technological Change*. London: Pluto.

Cohen, Stephen, and J. Zysman. 1987. *Manufacturing Matters: The Myth of a Post-Industrial Economy*. New York: Basic.

Cohn, Samuel. 1985. *The Process of Occupational Sex-Typing*. Philadelphia: Temple University Press.

Colclough, Glenna, and Charles M. Tolbert II. 1992. *Work in the Fast Lane: Flexibility, Divisions of Labor and Inequality in High-Tech Industries*. Albany, N.Y.: SUNY Press.

Coleman, James R. 1969. "Relational Analysis: The Study of Social Organizations with Survey Methods." In A. Etzioni, ed., *A Sociological Reader on Complex Organizations*. New York: Holt, Rinehart and Winston.

Cornfield, Daniel. *Workers, Managers and Technological Change: Emerging Patterns of Labor Relations*. New York: Plenum.

Costello, Cynthia. 1985. "WEA're Worth It: Work Culture and Conflict at the Wisconsin Education Association Insurance Trust." *Feminist Studies* 11 (3).

Cotgrove, Stephen, and Clive Vamplew. 1972. "Technology, Class and Politics: The Case of the Process Workers." *Sociology* 6:169–85.

Crompton, Rosemary, and Gareth Stedman Jones. 1984. *White Collar Proletarians: Deskilling and Gender in Clerical Work*. Philadelphia: Temple University Press.

Crozier, Michel. 1964. *The Bureaucratic Phenomenon*. Chicago: University of Chicago Press.

———. 1971. *The World of the White Collar Worker*. Chicago: University of Chicago Press.

Currie, Nelle B. 1915. "Report: Investigation of the Wages and Conditions of Telephone Operating." U.S. Commission on Industrial Relations. Washington, D.C.: GPO.

Danielian, N. R. 1939. *AT&T: The Story of Industrial Conquest*. New York: Vanguard Press.

Davies, Marge. 1982. *Woman's Place is At the Typewriter*. Philadelphia: Temple University Press.

Devereux, Sean. 1980. "The Rebel in Me." In Marc S. Miller, ed., *Working Lives: The Southern Exposure History of Labor in the South*. New York: Random.

Deyo, Frederic. 1989. *Beneath the Miracle: Labor Subordination in the New Asian Industrialization*. Berkelely: University of California Press.

DiFazio, William. 1985. *Longshoring: Community and Resistance on the Brooklyn Waterfront*. South Hadley, Mass.: Bergin and Garvey.

Doeringer, P., and M. Piore. 1971. *Internal Labor Markets and Manpower Analysis*. Lexington, Mass.: D. C. Heath.

Dunlop, J., et al. 1975. *Industrialization and Industrial Man Reconsidered*. Princeton: Inter-University Study of Human Resources in Economic Development.

Dymmel, Michael D. 1979. "Technology in Telecommunications: Its Effect on Labor and Skills." *Monthly Labor Review* (January).

Edwards, Richard C. 1975. "Social Relations of Production at the Point of Production." In R. Edwards, M. Reich, and D. Gordon, eds., *Labor Market Segmentation*. Lexington, Mass.: D. C. Heath.

———. 1979. *Contested Terrain: The Transformation of the Workplace in the Twentieth Century*. New York: Basic Books.

Epstein, Cynthia Fuchs. 1990. "The Culture of the Workplace." In K. Erikson, and S. P. Vallas, eds., *The Nature of Work*. New Haven: Yale University Press.

———. 1989. "Workplace Boundaries: Conceptions and Constraints." *Social Research* 56 (3):571–590.

Erikson, Kai. 1990. "On Work and Alienation." In Erikson and Vallas, eds., *The Nature of Work*. New Haven: Yale University Press.

Etzioni, Amitai. 1964. *Modern Organizations*. Englewood Cliffs, N.J.: Prentice Hall.

———. 1975. *A Comparative Analysis of Complex Organizations*. 2nd ed. New York: Free Press.

Evansohn, John. 1977. "Imperialism and the Working Class: Where Is the Aristocracy of Labor?" *Insurgent Sociologist* 7 (2).

Fantasia, Rick, Dan Clawson, and G. Graham. 1988. "A Critical View of Worker Participation in American Industry." *Work and Occupations* 15 (4).

Faulhaber, Gerald. 1987. *Telecommunications in Turmoil: Technology and Public Policy*. Cambridge, Mass.: Ballinger.

Faunce, William. 1965. "Automation and the Division of Labor." *Social Problems* 13 (Fall).

Federal Communications Commission. 1939. *Investigation of the Telephone Industry in the U.S.* Washington, D.C.: GPO.

———. 1950–1980. *Statistics of the Communications Industry*. Washington, D.C.: G.P.O.

Feldberg, Roslyn, and Evelyn Glenn. 1979. "Male and Female: Job vs. Gender Models in the Sociology of Work." *Social Problems* 26 (5).

———. 1983. "Technology and Work Degradation: Effects of Office Automation on Clerical Workers." In Joan Rothschild, ed., *Machina Ex Dea*. New York: Pergamon.

Femia, Joseph. 1975. "Hegemony and Consciousness in the Thought of Antonio Gramsci." *Political Studies* 23 (1):29–48.

Fenwick, Rudy, and Jon Olson. 1986. "Support for Worker Participation: Attitudes Among Union and Non-Union Workers." *American Sociological Review* 51 (4).

Fischer, Frank, and Carmen Sirianni, eds. 1984. *Critical Studies in Organization and Bureaucracy*. Philadelphia: Temple University Press.

Form, William, and D. B. McMillen. 1983. "Men, Women and Machines."

Work and Occupations: An International Journal 10 (2):147–78.

Form, William. 1980. "Resolving Ideological Issues on the Division of Labor." In Hubert Blalock, ed., *Sociological Theory and Research: A Critical Appraisal*. Glencoe, Ill.: Free Press.

―――. 1986. *Divided We Stand*. Urbana, Illinois: University of Illinois Press.

―――. 1987. On the Degradation of Skills. *Annual Review of Sociology* 13:29–47.

―――. 1990. "Organized Labor and the Welfare State." In Kai Erikson and Steven P. Vallas, eds., *The Nature of Work*. New Haven: Yale University Press.

Fox, Mary F., and Sharlene Hesse-Biber. 1984. *Women at Work*. Palo Alto, Calif.: Mayfield Publishing Company.

Friedlander, Peter. 1975. *The Emergence of a UAW Local, 1936–1939*. Pittsburgh: University of Pittsburgh. *

Friedman, Andrew. 1977. *Industry and Labor: Class Struggle at Work and Monopoly Capital*. London: MacMillan.

―――. 1990. "Managerial Strategies, Activities, Techniques and Technology: Toward a Complex Theory of the Labour Process." In Knights and Wilmott, eds., *Labour Process Theory*. London: MacMillan.

Gallie, Duncan. 1978. *In Search of the New Working Class*. Cambridge: Cambridge University Press.

Garson, Barbara. 1988. *The Electronic Sweatshop: How Computers are Transforming the Office of the Future into the Factory of the Past*. New York: Simon and Schuster.

Geyer, R. Felix, and David Schweitzer, eds. 1981. *Alienation: Problems of Meaning, Theory and Method*. London: Routledge and Kegan Paul.

Giddens, Anthony. 1973. *The Class Structure of the Advanced Societies*. New York: Harper and Row.

Glaberman, Martin. 1980. *War-time Strikes: The UAW and the No-Strike Pledge*. Detroit: Bewick.

Glenn, Evelyn, and Rosalyn Feldberg. 1979. "Proletarianizing Clerical Work: Technology and Organizational Control in the Office." In *Case Studies on the Labor Process*, edited by A. Zimbalist. New York: Monthly Review.

Goldfield, Michael. 1987. *The Decline of Organized Labor in the United States*. Chicago: University of Chicago Press.

Goldthorpe, John. 1966. "Attitudes and Behaviour of Car Assembly Workers: A Deviant Case and A Theoretical Critique." *British Journal of Sociology* 17 (September).

Goldthorpe, John, et al. 1969. *The Affluent Worker in the Class Structure*. London: Cambridge University Press.

Gorz, Andre. 1982. *Farewell to the Working Class: An Essay in Postindustrial Socialism*. Boston: South End Press.

Gouldner, Alvin. 1954a. *Patterns of Industrial Bureaucracy*. Glencoe, Ill.: Free Press.

———. 1954b. *Wildcat Strike*. Glencoe, Ill.: Free Press.

Gramsci, Antonio. 1971. *Selections from the Prison Notebooks*. Edited by Quentin Hoare. New York: International Publishers.

Granovetter, Mark. 1985 "Economic Action and Social Structure: The Problem of Embeddedness." *American Journal of Sociology* 91:481–510.

Greenwald, Maurine W. 1980. *Women, War and Work: The Impact of World War I on Women Workers in the United States*. Westport, Connecticutt: Greenwood Press.

Grenier, Guillermo. 1988. *Inhuman Relations: Quality Circles and Anti-Unionism in American Business*. Philadelphia: Temple University Press.

Habermas, J. *Toward a Rational Society*. Boston: Beacon.

Hacker, Sally. 1979. "Sex Segregation, Technology and Organizational Change: A Longitudinal Study of AT&T" *Social Problems* 26, 5.

Hall, Jacqueline. 1987. *Like a Family: The Making of a Southern Cotton Mill World*. Chapel Hill: University of North Carolina Press.

Halle, David. 1984. *America's Working Man: Work, Home and Politics Among Blue-Collar Property Owners*. Chicago: University of Chicago Press.

Hamilton, Richard. 1967. *Affluence and the French Worker in the Fourth Republic*. Princeton, New Jersey: Princeton University Press.

———. 1968. *Class and Politics in the United States*. New York: Wiley.

Hareven, Tamara. 1982. *Family Time and Industrial Time: The Relationship between the Family and Work in a New England Industrial Community*. Cambridge, Mass.: Cambridge University Press.

Hartmann, Heidi, R. Kraut, and L. Tilly, eds. *Computer Chips and Paper Clips: Technology and Women's Employment*. 2 vols. Washington, D.C.: National Research Council.

Heckscher, Charles. 1989. *The New Unionism: Quality Circles and Employee Involvement in the United States*. New York: Twentieth Century Fund/Basic.

Heinz, W. 1981. "Notes on the Normative Acceptance of Alienated Labor." In Geyer and Schwartz, eds., *Alienation: Meaning, Theory and Method.* London: Routledge and Kegan Paul.

Hill, Stephen. 1981. *Competition and Control at Work: The New Industrial Sociology.* Cambridge, Mass.: MIT Press.

Hirschhorn, Larry. 1984. *Beyond Mechanization.* Cambridge, Mass.: MIT Press.

Hodson, Randy. 1985. "Working in 'High-Tech': Issues and Opportunities for the Industrial Sociologist." *The Sociological Quarterly* 26, 3:351–364.

Hodson, Randy, and R. L. Kaufman. 1982. "Economic Dualism: A Critical Review." *American Sociological Review* 47:727–739.

Hodson, Randy, and Teresa Sullivan. 1984. "Totem or Tyrant? Monopoly, Regional and Local Sector Effects on Worker Commitment." *Social Forces* (March):716–31.

Horton, John. 1964. "The Dehumanization of Alienation and Anomie." *British Journal of Sociology* 15:283–300.

Howard, Robert. 1985. *Brave New Workplace.* New York: Penguin.

Huber, Joan, and William Form. 1973. *Income and Ideology: An Analysis of the American Political Formula.* Glencoe Ill.: Free Press.

Hull, Frank, N. S. Friedman, and T. Rogers. 1982. "The Effect of Technology on Alienation from Work: Testing Blauner's Inverted U-Curve Hypothesis." *Work and Occupations* 9, 1 (February).

Hunt, Timothy L., and H. Allan Hunt. 1984. *An Assessment of Data Sources to Study the Employment Effects of Technological Change.* Washington, D.C.: National Academy of Sciences, Committee on Women's Employment and Related Social Issues.

Hyman, Richard. 1978. "Occupational Structure, Collective Organization and Industrial Militancy." In A. Pizzorno and C. Crouch, eds., *The Resurgence of Class Conflict in Western Europe Since 1968.* New York: Holmes and Meier.

International Association of Machinists. 1983. "Workers' Technology Bill of Rights." *democracy* 3, 2 (Spring):25–28.

Israel, Joachim. 1971. *Alienation: From Marx to Modern Sociology.* Boston: Allyn and Bacon.

Jackman, Mary R., and Robert W. Jackman. 1983. *Class Awareness in the United States.* Los Angeles: University of California Press.

Joyce, Patrick. 1980. *Work, Society and Politics: The Culture of the Fac-*

tory in Later Victorian England. New Brunswick: Rutgers University Press.

Kalleberg, Arne. 1977. "Work Values and Job Rewards: A Theory of Job Satisfaction." *American Sociological Review* 42, 1 (September):124–44.

Kalleberg, Arne, and Ivar Berg. 1987. *Work and Industry: Structures, Markets and Processes*. New York: Plenum.

Kalleberg, Arne, and Aage Sorensen. 1979. "The Sociology of Labor Markets." *Annual Review of Sociology* 5:351–379.

Kalleberg, A., and K. Leicht. 1986. "Jobs and Skills: A Multivariate Structural Approach." *Social Science Journal* 15:269–296.

Kanungo, R. N. 1982. *Work Alienation: An Integrative Approach*. New York: Praeger.

Katznelson, Ira. 1981. *City Trenches: Urban Politics and the Patterning of Class in the United States*. New York: Pantheon.

Kelley, Maryellen. 1990. "New Process Technology, Job Design and Work Organization: A Contingency Model." *American Sociological Review* 55, 2 (April):191–208.

Kendall, Patricia, and Paul Lazarsfeld. 1955. "The Relation Between Individual and Group Characteristics in The American Soldier." In *The Language of Social Research*, edited by Lazarsfeld and Morris Rosenberg. Glencoe, Ill.: Free Press.

Kern, H., and Schumann, M. 1987. "Limits of the Division of Labour." *Economic and Industrial Democracy* 8, 2:151–70.

Kerr, Clark, et al. 1960. *Industrialism and Industrial Man*. Cambridge, Mass.: Harvard University Press.

Kerr, Clark, and Lloyd Fisher. 1957. "Plant Sociology: The Elite and the Aborigines." In M. Komaronsky, ed., *Common Frontiers of the Social Sciences*. Glencoe, Ill.: Free Press.

Kocka, Jurgen. 1980. *White Collar Workers in America, 1890–1940: A Socio-Political History in International Perspective*. Beverly Hills, Calif.: Sage.

Kohl, George. 1982. "Changing Competitive and Technology Environments in Telecommunications." In *Labor and Technology: Union Response to a Changing Environment*, edited by Donald Kennedy, Charles Craypo and Mary Lehman. University Park: Department of Labor Studies, Pennsylvania State University.

———. n.d. "Divestiture: The Framework." Internal memorandum.

Washington, D.C.: Development and Research Department, Communications Workers of America.

Kohn, Melvin. 1969. *Class and Conformity: A Study of Values*. Homewood, Ill.: Dorsey Press.

———, Carmi Schooler, et al., 1983. *Work and Personality: An Inquiry into the Impact of Social Stratification*. Norwood, New Jersey: Ablex.

Kraft, Philip. 1977. *Programmers and Managers: The Routinization of Computer Programming in the United States*. New York: Springer-Verlag.

Kraft, Philip. 1979. "The Industrialization of Computer Programming: From Programming to 'Software Production'." In *Case Studies on the Labor Process*, edited by A. Zimbalist. New York: Monthly Review.

Lamphere, Louise. 1985. "Bringing the Family to Work: Women's Culture on the Shop Floor." *Feminist Studies* 11, 3 (Fall):519–540.

Langer, Elinor. 1970. "The Women of the Telephone Company." *New York Review of Books* (March 26):14–22.

Lee, D. J. 1981. "Skill, Craft and Class: A Theoretical Critique and a Critical Case." *Sociology* 15, 1 (February).

Leiter, J. 1982. "Continuity and Change in the Legitimation of Authority in Southern Mill Towns." *Social Problems* 29, 5 (June):540–50.

———. 1986. "Reactions to Subordination: Attitudes of Southern Textile Workers." *Social Forces* 64, 4.

Leiter, Jeffrey, Michael Schulman, and Rhonda Zingraff, eds. 1991. *Hanging by a Thread: Social Change in Southern Textiles*. Ithaca, New York: ILR Press.

Lichtenstein, Nelson. 1982. *Labor's War at Home: The CIO in World War II*. Cambridge, Mass.: Cambridge University Press.

Lincoln, James, and Gerald Zeitz. 1980. "Organizational Properties from Aggregate Data: Separating Individual from Structural Effects." *American Sociological Review* 45 (June):391–408.

Lipset, S. M., and R. Bendix. 1959. *Social Mobility in Industrial Society*. Berkeley: University of California Press.

Littler, Craig. 1982. *The Development of the Labour Process in Capitalist Societies: A Comparative Analysis of Work Organization in Britain, the USA and Japan*. London: Heinemann.

Littler, Craig, and Graehm Salaman. 1982. "Bravermania and Beyond: Recent Theories of the Labor Process." *Sociology* 16, 2 (May).

Lockwood, David. 1958. *The Blackcoated Worker: A Study in Class Consciousness*. London: Allen and Unwin.

———. 1966. "Sources of Variation in Working Class Images of Society." *Sociological Review* 14:249–67.

Lopreato, Joseph, and L. E. Hazelrigg, eds. 1972. *Class, Conflict and Mobility: Theories and Studies of Class Structure*. San Francisco: Chandler.

Low-Beer, John R. 1978. *Protest and Participation: The New Working Class in Italy*. London: Cambridge University Press.

MacKenzie, Gavin. 1973. *The Aristocracy of Labor: Skilled Craftsmen in the Class Structure*. London: Cambridge University Press.

Maddox, Brenda. 1978. "Women and the Switchboard." In I. de Sola Pool, ed. *The Social Impact of the Telephone*. Cambridge Mass.: MIT Press.

Mann, Michael. 1970. "The Social Cohesion of Liberal Democracy." *American Sociological Review* 35.

———. 1973. *Consciousness and Action among the Western Working Class*. London: MacMillan.

Marcuse, Herbert. 1968. *Negations: Essays in Critical Theory*. Boston: Beacon.

Marglin, Stephen. 1974. "What do Bosses Do? The Origins and Functions of Hierarchy in Capitalist Production." *Review of Radical Political Economy* VI (Summer):60–112.

Marquart, Frank. 1975. *An Autoworker's Journal: The UAW from Crusade to One-Party Union*. University Park, Pa.: University of Pennsylvania Press.

Marshall, Gordon. 1983. "Some Remarks on the Study of Working Class Consciousness." *Politics and Society* 12, 3:263–301.

Marx, Karl. 1961. *Economic and Philosophic Manuscripts of 1844*. Moscow: Foreign Languages Press.

———. 1967. *Capital*, volume I. *A Critical Analysis of Capitalist Production*. New York: International Publishers.

———. 1973. *Grundrisse*. Translated with an introduction by Martin Nicolaus. New York: Viking.

———, and F. Engels. 1976. *The German Ideology*. New York: International.

Meiksins, Peter. 1984. "Scientific Management and Class Relations: A Dissenting View." *Theory and Society* 13, 2:177–209.

————, and Chris Smith. 1991. "The Organization of Professional Technical Workers: A Comparative Analysis." Paper presented at the American Sociological Association meetings, Cincinnati, Ohio.

Melman, Seymour. 1951. "The Rise of Administrative Overhead in the Manufacturing Industries of the United States, 1899–1947." *Oxford Economic Papers*, new series, 3.

Meyer, Stephen. 1985. *The Five Dollar Day: Labor Management and Social Control in the Ford Motor Company*. Albany, N.Y.: SUNY Press.

Milkman, Ruth. 1987. *Gender at Work: The Dynamics of Job Segregation by Sex During World War II*. Chicago: University of Illinois Press.

Miller, Ann R., Donald J. Treiman, Pamela S. Cain, and Patricia A. Roos. 1980. *Work, Jobs and Occupations: A Critical Review of the 'Dictionary of Occupational Titles'*. Washington, D.C.: National Academy Press.

Mills, C. Wright. 1951. *White Collar: The American Middle Classes*. New York: Oxford University Press.

Monds, Jean. 1976. "Workers' Control and the Historians: A New Economism." *New Left Review* 97.

Montgomery, David. 1979. *Workers' Control in America: Studies in the History of Work, Technology and Labor Struggles*. New York: Cambridge University Press.

Morris, Richard T., and Raymond J. Murphy. 1974. "A Paradigm for the Study of Class Consciousness." In *Social Stratification: A Reader*, ed. by J. Lopreato and Lionel S. Lewis. New York: Harper and Row.

Mottaz, Clifford J. 1985. "The Relative Importance of Intrinsic and Extrinsic Rewards as Determinants of Work Satisfaction." *The Sociological Quarterly* 26, 3.

Mueller, Eva, et al. 1969. *Technological Advance in an Expanding Economy: Its Impact on a Cross-Section of the Labor Force*. Ann Arbor: Institute for Social Research, University of Michigan.

Mueller, Milton. 1989. "The Switchboard Problem: Scale, Signaling and Organization in Manual Telephone Switching, 1877–1897." *Technology and Culture* 30, 3 (July).

Newman, David. 1982. "New Technology and the Changing Labor Process in the Telephone Industry: The Union's Response." Unpublished manuscript. New Brunswick, N.J.: Rutgers University, Department of Labor Studies.

Nichols, Theo, and H. Beynon. *Living with Capitalism: Class Relations and the Modern Factory*. London: Routledge and Kegan Paul.

Noble, David. 1977. *America By Design: Science, Technology and the Rise of Corporate Capitalism*. Cambridge, Mass.: MIT Press.

———. 1978. "Social Choice in Machine Design: The Case of Automatically Controlled Machine Tools, and a Challenge for Labor." *Politics and Society* 8:3–4.

Noble, David. 1984. *Forces of Production: A Social History of Industrial Automation*. New York: Knopf.

Norris, G. M. 1978. "Industrial-Paternalist Capitalism and Local Labor Markets." *Sociology* 12, 3 (Sept.):469–89.

Norwood, Stephen. 1989. *Labor's Flaming Youth: Telephone Workers and Worker Militancy, 1878–1923*. Urbana, Ill.: University of Illinois Press.

Offe, Claus. 1976. *Industry and Inequality. The Achievement Principle in Work and Social Status*. New York: St. Martin's Press.

Oppenheimer, Martin. 1973. "The Proletarianization of the Professional." *Sociological Review*, monograph 23. Ed. by Peter Halmos.

———. 1985. *White Collar Politics*. New York: Monthly Review.

Ozanne, Robert. 1967. *A Century of Labor-Management Relations at McCormack and International Harvester*. Madison, Wisconsin: University of Wisconsin Press.

Palmer, Bryan. 1975. "Class, Conception and Conflict: The Thrust for Efficiency, Managerial Views of Labor and Working Class Rebellion, 1903–1922." *Review of Radical Political Economics* (Summer).

Parker, Mike. 1985. *Inside the Circle: A Union Guide to QWL*. Boston: South End.

Parkin, Frank. 1971. *Class Inequality and Political Order: Stratification under Capitalism and Communism*. New York: Penguin.

Penn, Roger. 1985. "Skill, Class and Labor: A Compensatory Model." *British Journal of Sociology*.

Perrow, Charles. 1986. *Complex Organizations: A Critical Essay*. New Haven, Conn.: Yale University Press.

Piore, M., and C. Sabel. 1984. *The Second Industrial Divide*. New York: Basic Books.

Pizzorno, A., and C. Crouch, eds. 1978. *The Resurgence of Class Conflict in Western Europe Since 1968*. New York: Holmes and Meier.

Poulantzas, Nicos. 1974. *Classes in Contemporary Capitalism*. London: Verso.

Prandy, Kenneth. 1965. *Professional Employees: A Study of Scientists and Engineers*. London: Faber and Faber.

Preis, Art. 1964. *Labor's Giant Step: Twenty Years of the* CIO. New York: Pioneer Publishers.

Przeworski, Adam. 1977 "Proletariat into a Class: The Process of Class Formation, from Karl Kautsky's *The Class Struggle* to Recent Debates." *Politics and Society* 7, 4.

Przeworski, Adam, and John Sprague. 1986. *Paper Stones: A History of Electoral Socialism.* Chicago: University of Chicago Press.

Rieder, Jonathan. 1985. *Canarsie: The Jews and Italians of Brooklyn Against Liberalism.* Cambridge Mass.: Harvard University Press.

Roberts, B. C., et al. 1972. *Reluctant Militants: A Study of Industrial Technicians.* London: Heinemann.

Roethlisberger, F. J., and William Dickson. 1939. *Management and the Worker.* Cambridge, Mass.: Harvard University Press.

Roy, Donald. 1952. "Quota Restriction and Goldbricking in a Machine Shop." *American Journal of Sociology* 57:427–42.

Rubin, Lillian. 1976. *Worlds of Pain: Life in the Working Class Family.* New York: Basic Books.

Rumberger, Russell W. 1981. "The Changing Skill Requirements of Jobs in the U.S. Economy." *Industrial and Labor Relations Review* 34:578–91.

Sabel, Charles. 1982. *Work and Politics: The Division of Labor in Industry.* Cambridge, Mass.: MIT Press.

Salaman, Graeme. 1975. "Occupations, Community and Consciousness." In *Working Class Images of Society,* ed. by Martin Bulmer. London: Routledge and Kegan Paul.

———. 1986. *Working.* London: Tavistock.

Schacht, John. 1985. *The Making of Telephone Unionism, 1920–1947.* New Brunswick, N.J.: Rutgers University Press.

Schmitt, Katherine. 1930. "I Was Your Old Hello Girl." *Saturday Evening Post,* 12 July.

Scott, James. 1990. *Domination and the Arts of Resistance.* New Haven: Yale University Press.

Seeman, Melvin. 1959. "On the Meaning of Alienation." *American Sociological Review* 24.

———. 1975. "Alienation Studies." *Annual Review of Sociology* 1:91–123.

Seidman, Joel, et al. 1958. *The Worker Views His Union.* Chicago: University of Chicago Press.

Shaiken, Harley. 1984. *Work Transformed: Automation and Labor in the Computer Age*. New York: Holt Rinehart and Winston.

Shepard, Jon. 1971. *Automation and Alienation: A Study of Office and Factory Workers*. Cambridge, Mass.: MIT Press.

———. 1977. "Technology, Alienation and Job Satisfaction." *Annual Review of Sociology*.

Shlakman, Vera, 1951–1952, "Status and Ideology of Office Workers." *Science and Society XVI*, 1 (Winter):1–26.

Shostak, Arthur. 1987. "Technology, Air Traffic Control and Labor Management Relations." In Cornfield, ed., *Workers, Managers and Technological Change*. New York: Plenum.

Silver Marc. 1986. *Under Construction: Work and Alienation in the Building Trades*. Albany, N.Y.: SUNY Press.

Simpson, Richard L. 1981. "Labor Force Integration and Southern US Textile Unionism." *Research in the Sociology of Work* 1:381–401.

Sobel, Rick. 1989. *The White Collar Working Class*. New York: Praeger.

Special Task Force to the Secretary of Health, Education and Welfare. 1973. *Work in America*. Cambridge, Mass.: MIT Press.

Spenner, Kenneth I. 1983. "Deciphering Prometheus: Temporal Changes in the Skill Level of Work." *American Sociological Review* 48:824–37.

———. 1979. "Temporal Changes in Work Content." *American Sociological Review* 44:968–75.

———. 1990. "Skill: Meanings, Methods and Measures." *Work and Occupations* 17, 4 (November).

Staples, William. 1987. "Technology, Control and the Social Organization of Work at a British Hardware Firm, 1791–1891." *American Journal of Sociology* 93, 1 (July):62–88.

Stark, David. 1980. "Class Struggle and the Transformation of the Labor Process: A Relational View." *Theory and Society* 9, 1 (January).

Stewart, Andrew, K. Prandy, and R. Blackburn. 1984. *Social Stratification and Occupations*. New York: Holmes and Meier.

Stone, Katherine. 1975. "The Origins of Job Structures in the Steel Industry." In Edwards, Reich, and Gordon, eds., *Labor Market Segmentation*. Lexington, Mass.: D.C. Heath.

Storey, John. 1985. "The Means of Management Control." *Sociology* 19, 2 (May):193–211.

Sutton, John R. 1980. "Some Determinants of Women's Trade Union Membership." *Pacific Sociological Review* 23, 4 (October).

Sykes, Gresham. 1958. *Society of Captives: A Study of a Maximum Security Prison*. Princeton: Princeton University Press.

Tannenbaum, Arnold, and Gerald Bachman. 1964. "Structural versus Individual Effects." *American Journal of Sociology* 69 (May): 585–95.

Tannenbaum, Arnold, et al. 1974. *Hierarchy in Organizations: An International Comparison*. San Francisco: Jossey-Bass.

Tausky, Curt. 1978. *Work Organizations*. Itasca, Ill.: Peacock.

Thompson, E. P. 1963. *The Making of the English Working Class*. New York: Random House.

Thompson, Paul. 1989. *The Nature of Work: An Introduction to the Labour Process Debate*. Second edition. London: MacMillan.

———. 1990. "Crawling from the Wreckage: The Labour Process and the Politics of Production." In D. Knights and H. Wilmott, eds., *Labour Process Theory*. London: MacMillan.

Tolbert, Charles M. 1982. "Industrial Segmentation and Men's Career Mobility." *American Sociological Review* 47:457–477.

U.S. Department of Commerce. 1975. Historical Abstracts of the U.S.: Colonial Times to 1970. Part II. Bureau of the Census.

U.S. Department of Labor. 1978. *Dictionary of Occupational Titles*. 4th Edition. Washington, D.C.: U.S. Government Printing Office.

U.S. Dept. of H.E.W. 1973. *Work in America*. Cambridge, Mass.: MIT Press.

Vallas, Steven P. 1987. "White Collar Proletarians? The Structure of Clerical Work and Levels of Class Consciousness." *The Sociological Quarterly* 28, 4:523–541.

———. 1988. "New Technology, Job Content and Worker Alienation: A Test of Two Rival Perspectives." *Work and Occupations: An International Journal* (May).

———. 1990. "The Concept of Skill: A Critical Review." *Work and Occupations* 17, 4 (November).

———. 1991. "Workers, Firms and the Dominant Ideology: Hegemony and Consciousness in the Monopoly Core." *The Sociological Quarterly* 32, 1 (February).

Vallas, Steven P., and Cynthia Fuchs Epstein. 1988. "The Workers' Response to the Labor Process: The Limits of Job Centered Analysis."

Paper presented at the American Sociological Association meetings, Atlanta.

Vallas, Steven P., and Michael Yarrow. 1987. "Advanced Technology and Worker Alienation: Comments on the Blauner/Marxism Debate." *Work and Occupations: An International Journal* (February).

Vanneman, Reeve, and Lynn Weber Cannon. 1987. *The American Perception of Class*. Philadelphia: Temple University Press.

Wacjman, Judy. 1991. "Patriarchy, Technology and Conceptions of Skill." *Work and Occupations* 18, 1 (February).

Wallace, Phyllis, ed. 1976. *Equal Employment Opportunity and the AT&T Case*. Cambridge: MIT Press.

Wallace, Michael, and Arne L. Kalleberg. 1982. "Industrial Transformation and the Decline of Craft: The Decomposition of Skill in the Printing Industry, 1931–1978." *American Sociological Review* 47:307–24.

Webster, Frank. 1985. "The Politics of New Technology." *Socialist Register*. London: Merlin.

Wedderburn, Dorothy, and Rosemary Crompton. 1972. *Workers' Attitudes Toward Technological Change*. Cambridge, Mass.: Cambridge University Press.

Weinstein, James. 1968. *The Liberal Ideal in the Corporate State*. Boston: Beacon.

Weir, Stan. 1973. "Rebellion in American Labor's Rank and File." In G. Hunnius, G. Garson and J. Case, eds., *Workers' Control*. New York: Vintage.

Westwood, Sallie. 1982. *All Day, Every Day: Factory and Family in the Making of Women's Lives*. Urbana, Ill.: University of Illinois Press.

Wilentz, Sean. 1984. *Chants Democratic: New York City and the Rise of the American Working Class, 1788–1850*. New York: Oxford.

Wilkinson, Barry. 1983. *The Shop Floor Politics of New Technology*. London: Heinemann.

Willis, Paul. 1977. *Learning to Labour: How Working Class Kids Get Working Class Jobs*. New York: Columbia University Press.

———. 1979. "Shop Floor Culture, Masculinity and the Wage Form." In John Clarke, ed., *Working Class Culture*. London: Hutchinson.

Winner, Langdon. 1982. "Do Artifacts Have Politics?" *Daedalus*. Winter, 1980:121–137.

Wood, Stephen J. 1982. *The De-Skilling of Labour? Skill, De-Skilling and the Labour Process*. London: Hutchinson.

S. Wood, ed., *The Transformation of Work?* London: Unwin and Hyman.

Wright, Erik Olin. 1979. *Class, Crisis and the State.* London: New Left Books.

————. 1985. *Classes.* New York: New Left Books.

Wright, Erik Olin, and Joachim Singelmann. 1982. "Proletarianization and the Changing American Class Structure." In *Marxist Inquiries: Studies of Labor, Class and States,* ed. by Michael Burawoy and Theda Skocpol. Chicago: University of Chicago Press.

Zernan, John. 1974. "Organized Labor Versus the 'Revolt Against Work': The Critical Contest." *Telos* 21 (Fall).

Zimbalist, Andrew. 1979. "Introduction." In *Case Studies on the Labor Process.* New York: Monthly Review.

Zingraff, R., and M. D. Schulman. 1984. "Social Bases of Class Consciousness: A Study of Southern Textile Workers, with a Comparison by Race." *Social Forces* 63 (September):98–116.

Zipp, John F., Paul Luebke, and Richard Landerman. 1984. "The Social Bases of Support for Workplace Democracy." *Sociological Perspectives* 27, 4 (October):395–425.

Zuboff, Shoshana. 1987. *In the Age of the Smart Machine.* New York: Basic Books.

INDEX

06/01/09

It was the hand-in date for a piece of coursework today, and basically I thought this book was going to help with it. I was wrong. I'm wreaking my slightly pathetic revenge in the most tedious way I could think up.

I've been up since about 11pm last night, and it's about quarter to one in the afternoon now, strange sleeping pattern I know.

I'm halfway through my 3rd and final year in Glam now, and to be hugely honest I am a bit anxious about becoming what has been described to me as a 'real person'.

I don't know what year it is that you are reading this in, it's probably a good few after I wrote this, unless I've misjudged how rubbish & obscure this particular text is.

In essence this is a sort of lo-fi time capsule hidden in the back of the worst book, in the worst library in the worst Uni in the grand old land of Wales.

Os ydych chi'n gallu darllen y darn yma dwi'n either hapus, gan ei fod yn meddwl, efallai, fod yr iaith Gymraeg ddim yn erfrys eto.

I suppose I should list a couple of my heroes now, and if you google them, or use whatever means you future people have for searching, and you could see if they are still working well, or alive. If they are dead however, maybe have a sort of crazy bonfire/burlesque funeral for them. Or if you're a student, just get arseholed/bladdered/beuled (drun

I am currently listening to Tim Minchin, who is an Australian comedian/songwriter. He's only just getting famous at the moment, the Joe Bloggs on the street wouldn't know him, so if he's a huge famous monster-star that would be amazing that I was ahead of the trend, yeah? And if you've never heard of him, go look him up! And if you're him then hello Tim!